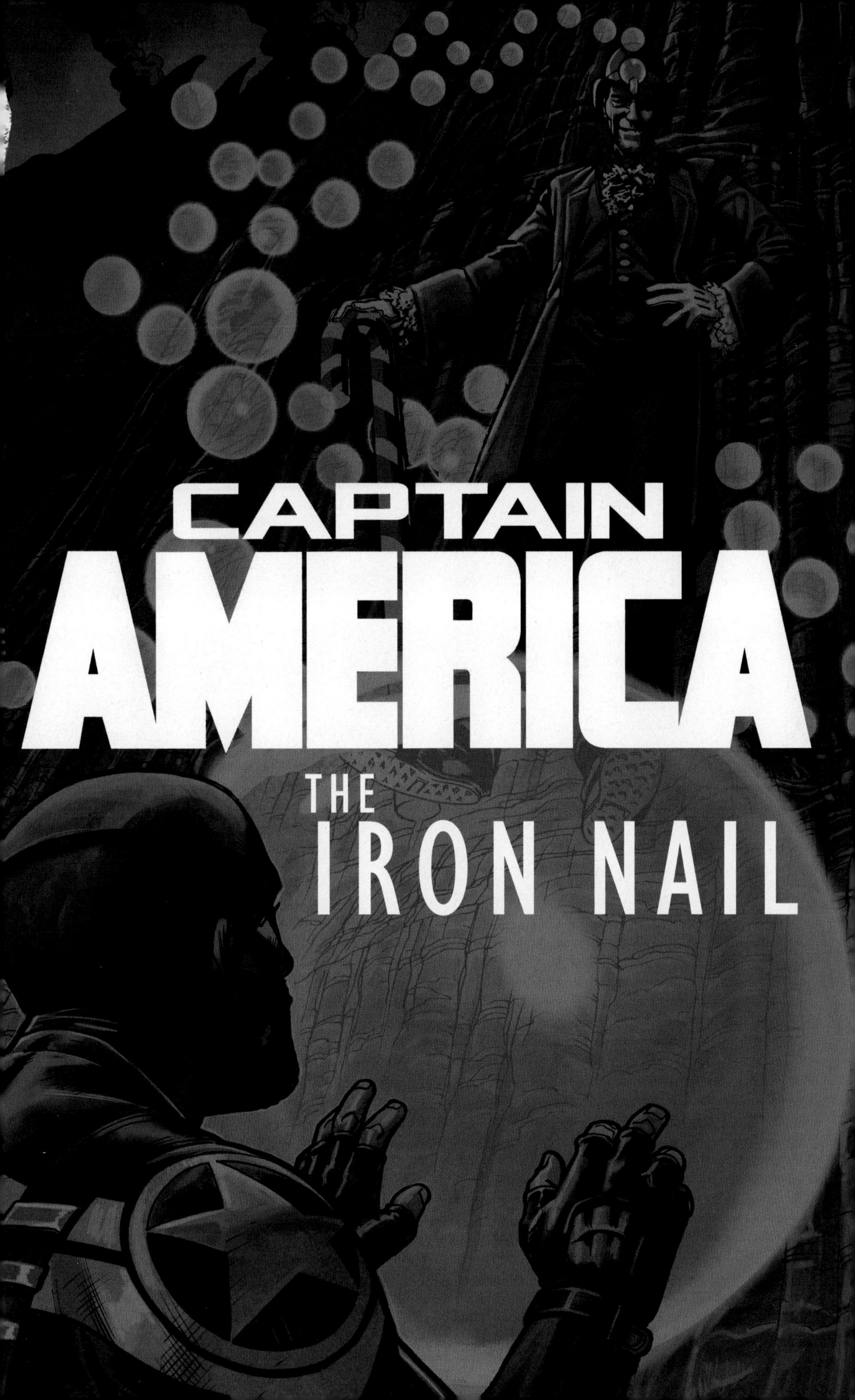
CAPTAIN
AMERICA
THE
IRON NAIL

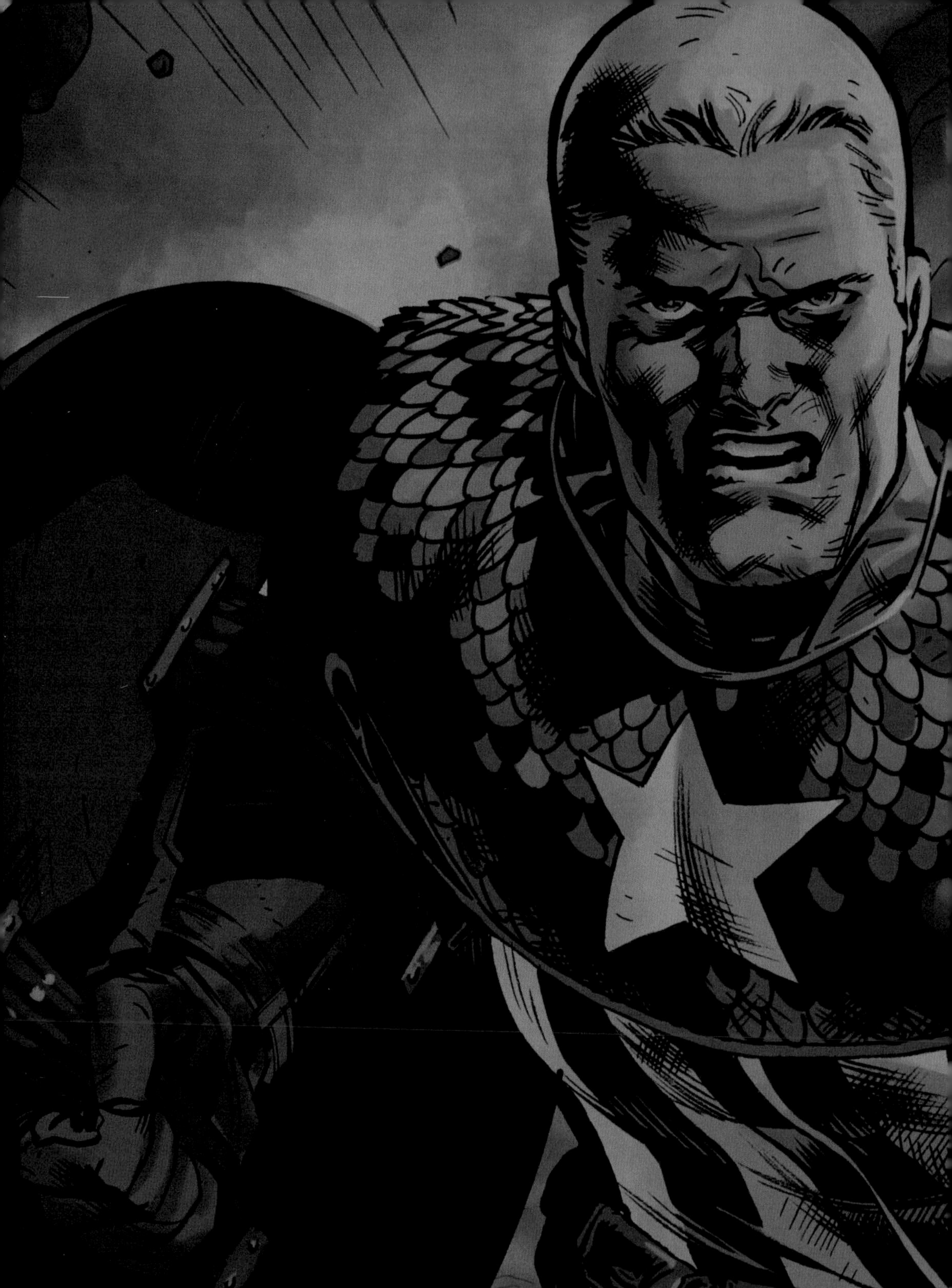

COLLECTION EDITOR
ALEX STARBUCK

ASSISTANT EDITOR
SARAH BRUNSTAD

EDITORS, SPECIAL PROJECTS
JENNIFER GRÜNWALD & MARK D. BEAZLEY

SENIOR EDITOR, SPECIAL PROJECTS
JEFF YOUNGQUIST

SVP PRINT, SALES & MARKETING
DAVID GABRIEL

BOOK DESIGNER
NELSON RIBEIRO

EDITOR IN CHIEF
AXEL ALONSO

CHIEF CREATIVE OFFICER
JOE QUESADA

PUBLISHER
DAN BUCKLEY

EXECUTIVE PRODUCER
ALAN FINE

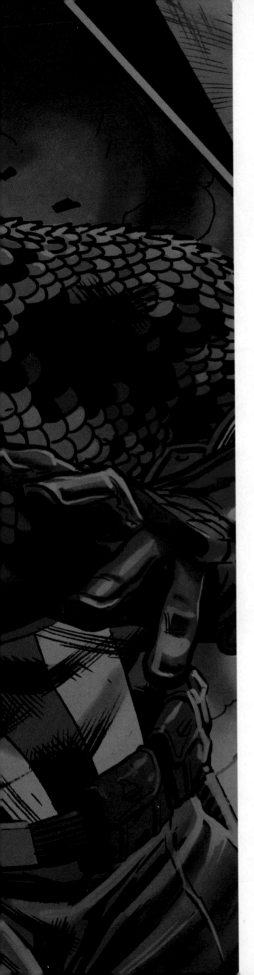

THE
IRON NAIL

WRITER
RICK REMENDER

ISSUE #16
PENCILER
PASCAL ALIXE
COLOR ART
EDGAR DELGADO,
ANTONIO FABELA
& ISRAEL SILVA

ISSUES #17-21
ARTIST
NIC KLEIN
COLOR ARTIST
DEAN WHITE

COVER ART
NIC KLEIN

LETTERER
VC'S JOE CARAMAGNA

ASSISTANT EDITOR
JAKE THOMAS

EDITOR
TOM BREVOORT

CAPTAIN AMERICA CREATED BY JOE SIMON & JACK KIRBY

CAPTAIN AMERICA VOL. 4: THE IRON NAIL. Contains material originally published in magazine form as CAPTAIN AMERICA #16-21. First printing 2014. ISBN# 978-0-7851-8953-4. Published by MARVEL WORLDWIDE, INC., a subsidiary of MARVEL ENTERTAINMENT, LLC. OFFICE OF PUBLICATION: 135 West 50th Street, New York, NY 10020. Copyright © 2014 Marvel Characters, Inc. All rights reserved. All characters featured in this issue and the distinctive names and likenesses thereof, and all related indicia are trademarks of Marvel Characters, Inc. No similarity between any of the names, characters, persons, and/ or institutions in this magazine with those of any living or dead person or institution is intended, and any such similarity which may exist is purely coincidental. **Printed in the U.S.A.** ALAN FINE, EVP - Office of the President, Marvel Worldwide, Inc. and EVP & CMO Marvel Characters B.V.; DAN BUCKLEY, Publisher & President - Print, Animation & Digital Divisions; JOE QUESADA, Chief Creative Officer; TOM BREVOORT, SVP of Publishing; DAVID BOGART, SVP of Operations & Procurement, Publishing; C.B. CEBULSKI, SVP of Creator & Content Development; DAVID GABRIEL, SVP Print, Sales & Marketing; JIM O'KEEFE, VP of Operations & Logistics; DAN CARR, Executive Director of Publishing Technology; SUSAN CRESPI, Editorial Operations Manager; ALEX MORALES, Publishing Operations Manager; STAN LEE, Chairman Emeritus. For information regarding advertising in Marvel Comics or on Marvel.com, please contact Niza Disla, Director of Marvel Partnerships, at ndisla@marvel.com. For Marvel subscription inquiries, please call 800-217-9158. **Manufactured between 6/13/2014 and 7/28/2014 by R.R. DONNELLEY, INC., SALEM, VA, USA.**

10987654321

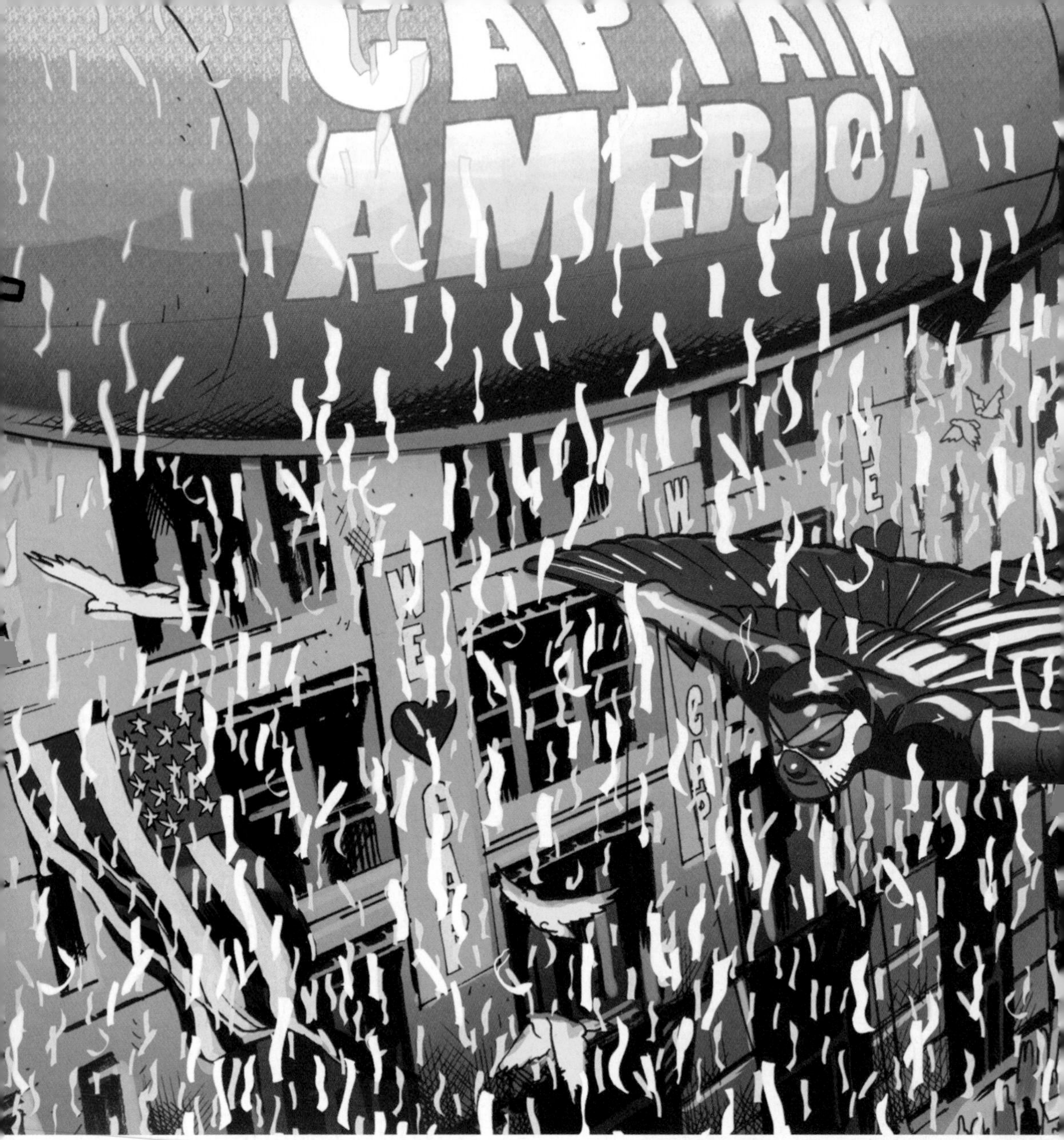
CAPTAIN
AMERICA

During WWII a secret military experiment turned scrawny Steve Rogers into America's first super-soldier, Captain America. Near the end of the war Rogers was presumed dead in an explosion over the English Channel.

Decades later Captain America was found frozen in ice and revived. Steve Rogers awakened to a world he never imagined, a man out of time. He again took up the mantle of Captain America, defending the U.S. and the world from threats of all kinds.

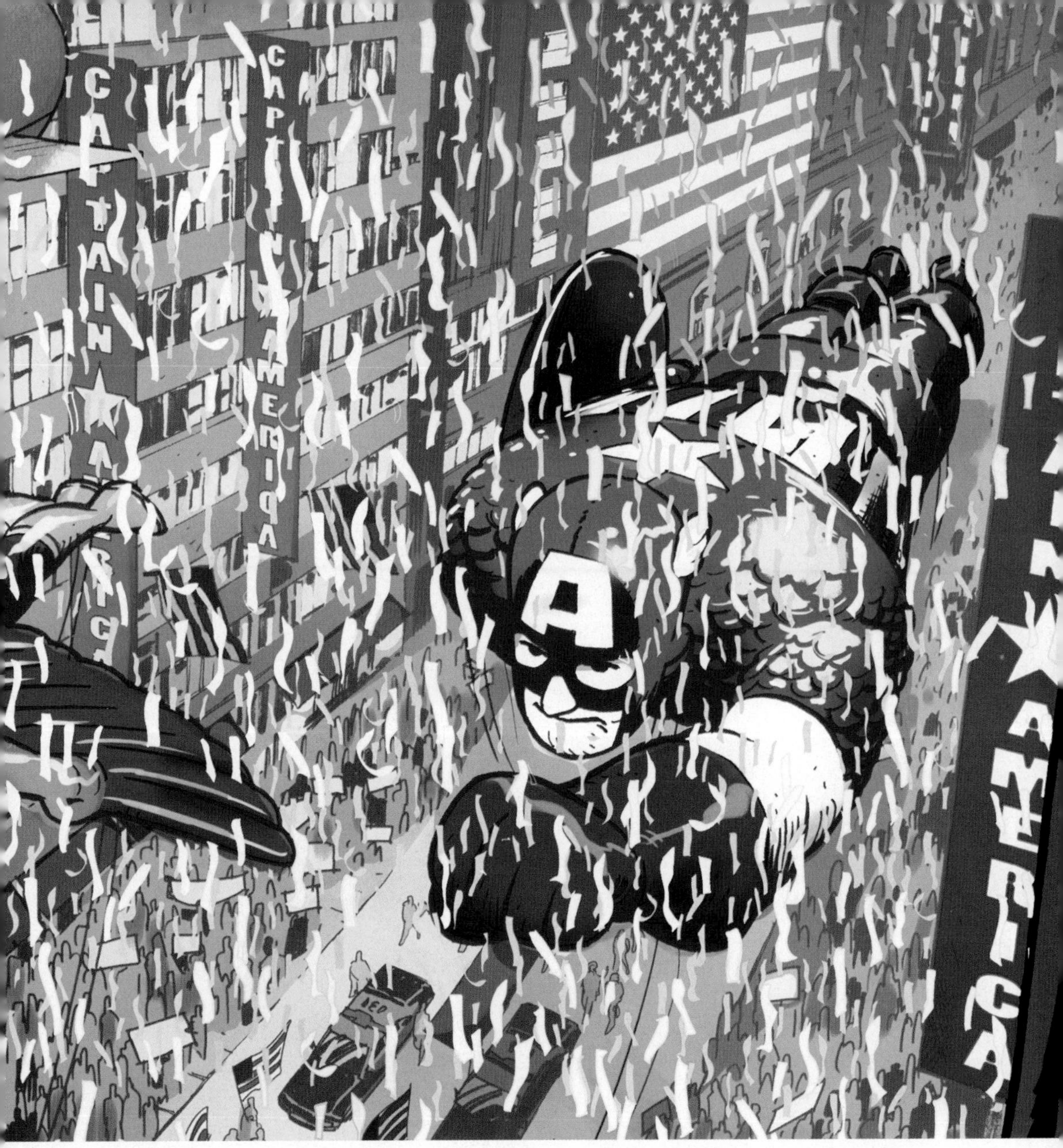
CAPTAIN
AMERICA
AMERICA

PREVIOUSLY...

Captain America escaped from Dimension Z with Jet Black, Arnim Zola's daughter and Cap's unexpected ally. In the final confrontation with Zola and their subsequent escape, Steve lost his lover Sharon Carter and his adopted son Ian, who was also Jet Black's brother. After Zola's defeat, the villain gave his life to save Jet Black, and with his dying words tasked her with continuing his legacy.

Now living in a world she doesn't understand, Jet Black is torn between the compassionate heroism of Captain America and the heritage of her father, Arnim Zola.

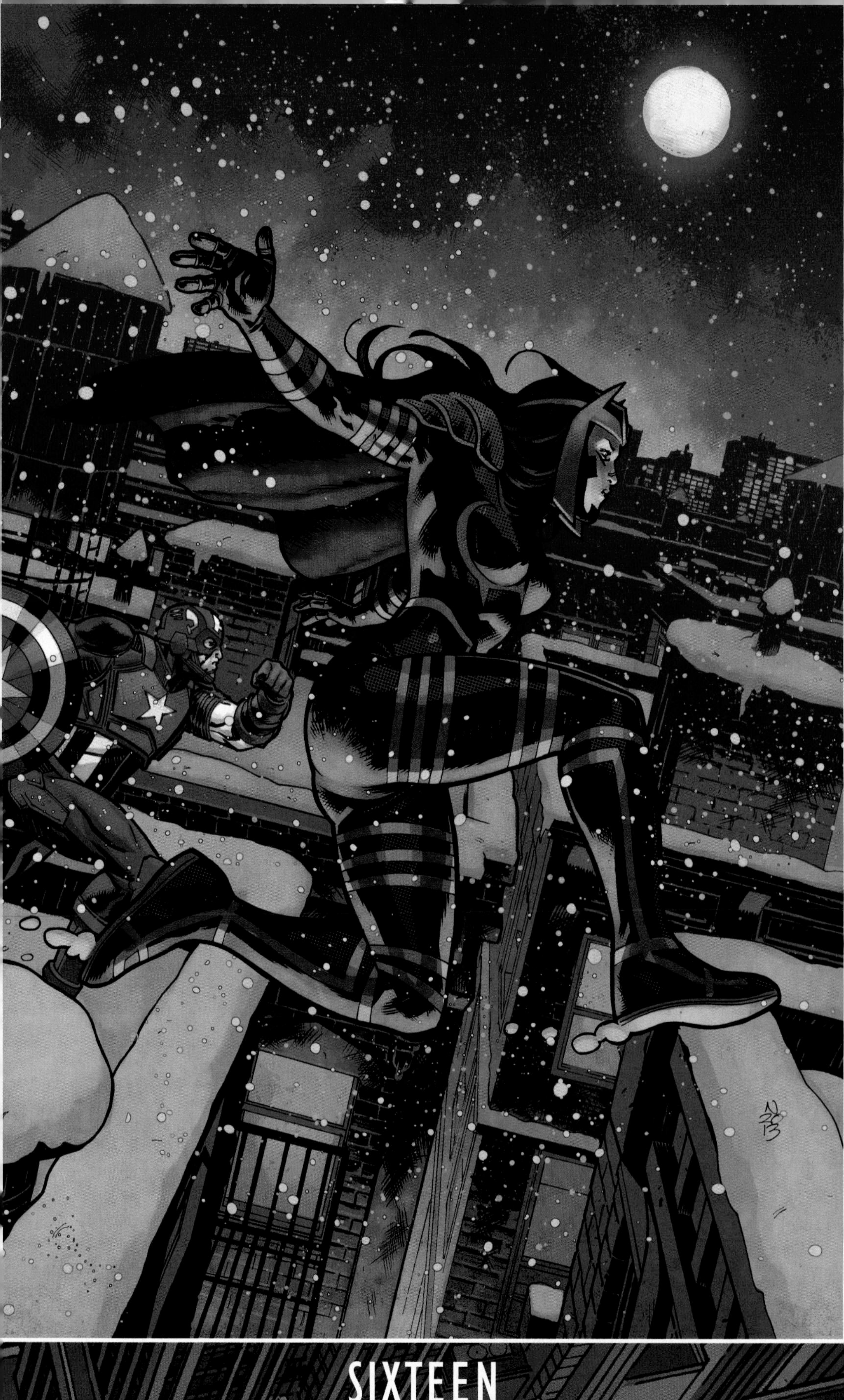

SIXTEEN

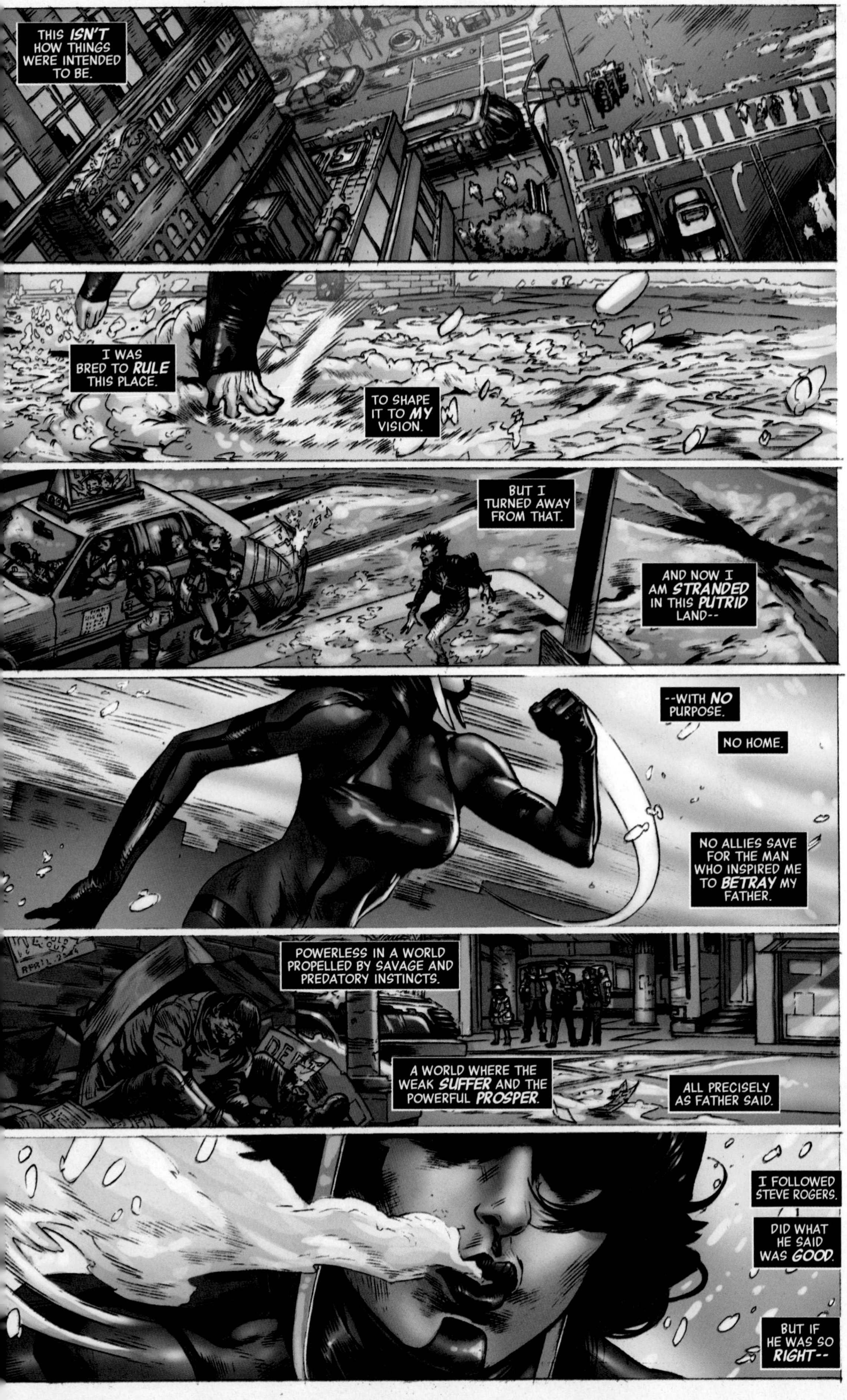
THIS ISN'T HOW THINGS WERE INTENDED TO BE.
I WAS BRED TO RULE THIS PLACE.
TO SHAPE IT TO MY VISION.
BUT I TURNED AWAY FROM THAT.
AND NOW I AM STRANDED IN THIS PUTRID LAND--
--WITH NO PURPOSE.
NO HOME.
NO ALLIES SAVE FOR THE MAN WHO INSPIRED ME TO BETRAY MY FATHER.
POWERLESS IN A WORLD PROPELLED BY SAVAGE AND PREDATORY INSTINCTS.
A WORLD WHERE THE WEAK SUFFER AND THE POWERFUL PROSPER.
ALL PRECISELY AS FATHER SAID.
I FOLLOWED STEVE ROGERS.
DID WHAT HE SAID WAS GOOD.
BUT IF HE WAS SO RIGHT--

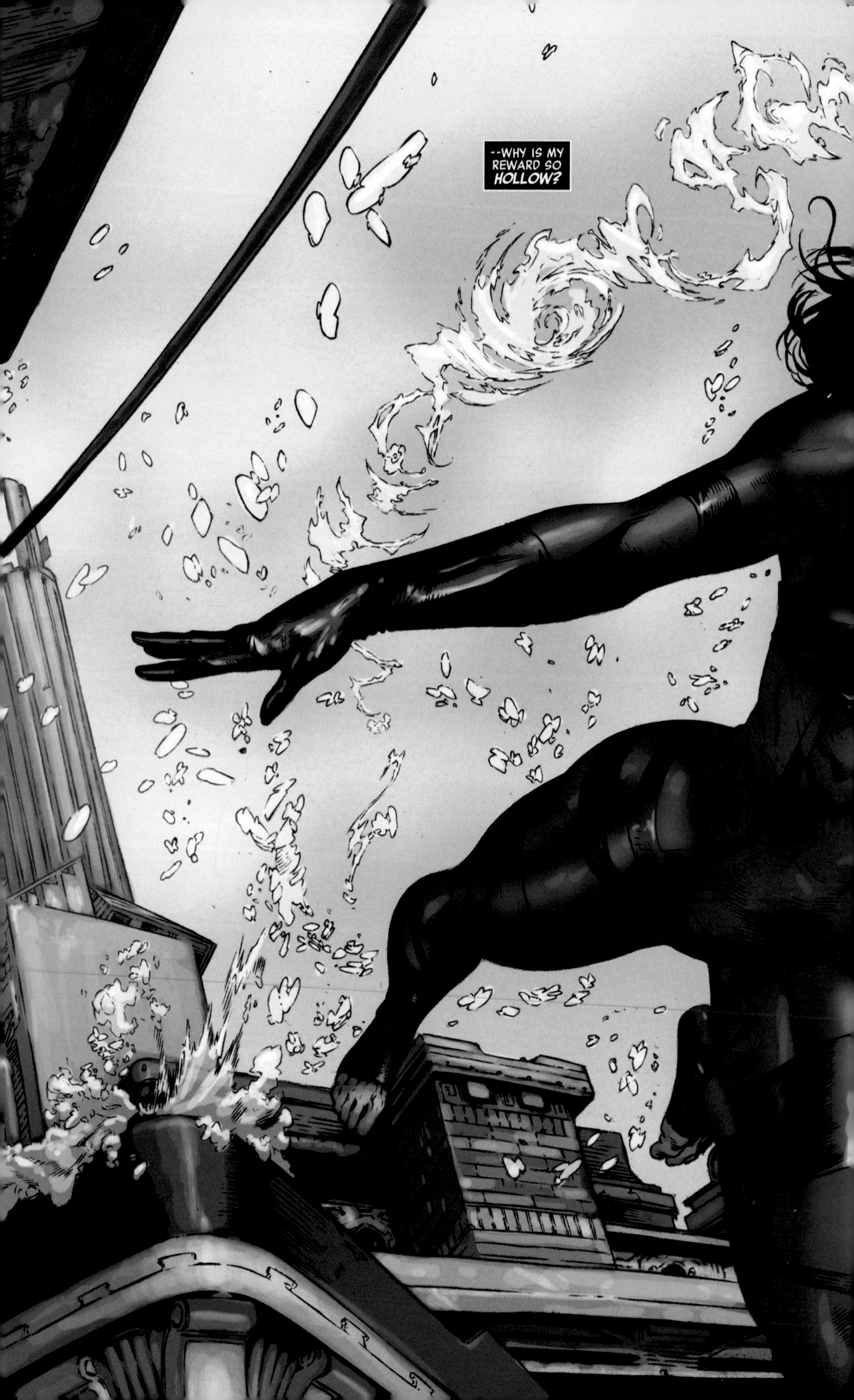
--WHY IS MY REWARD SO HOLLOW?

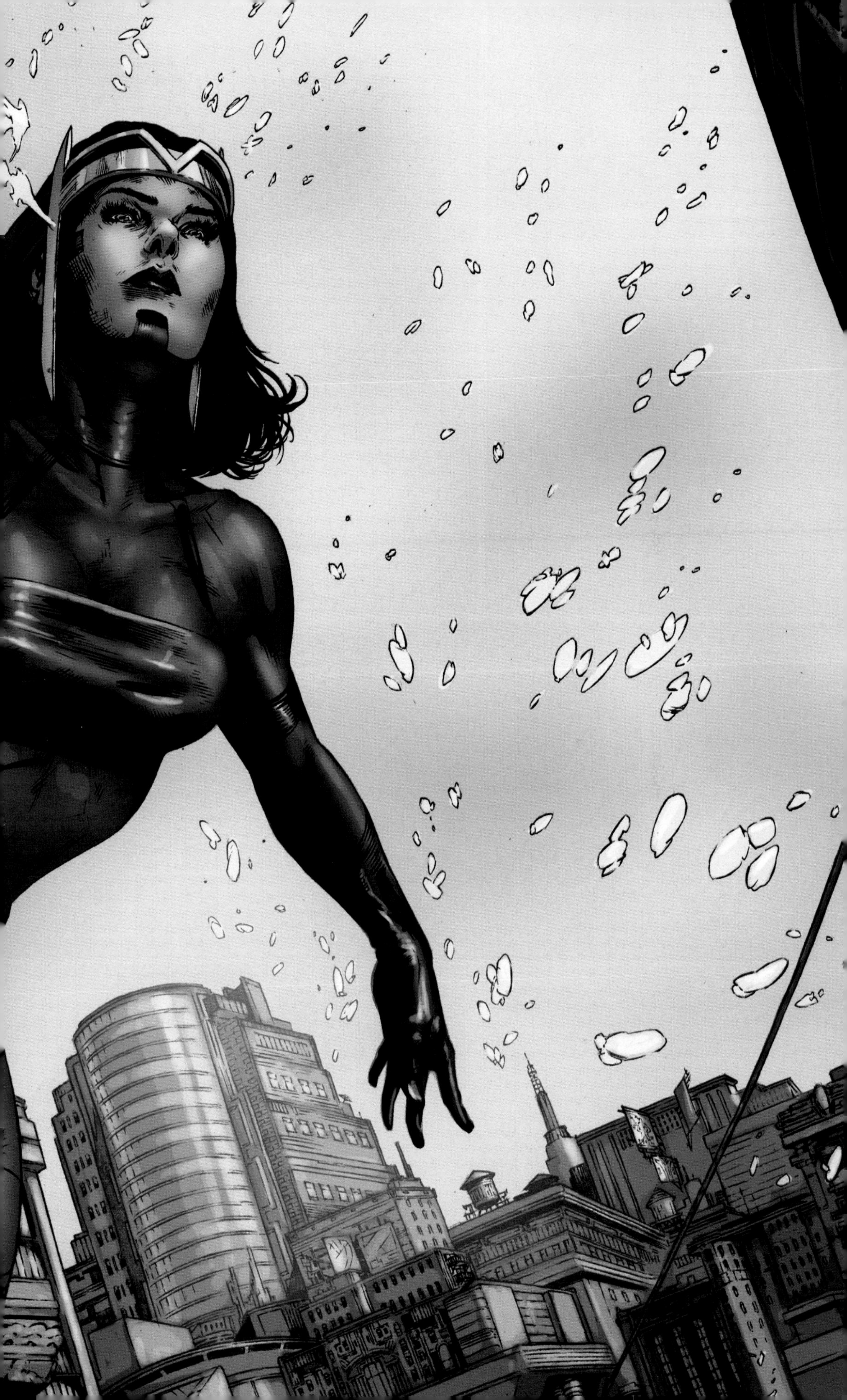

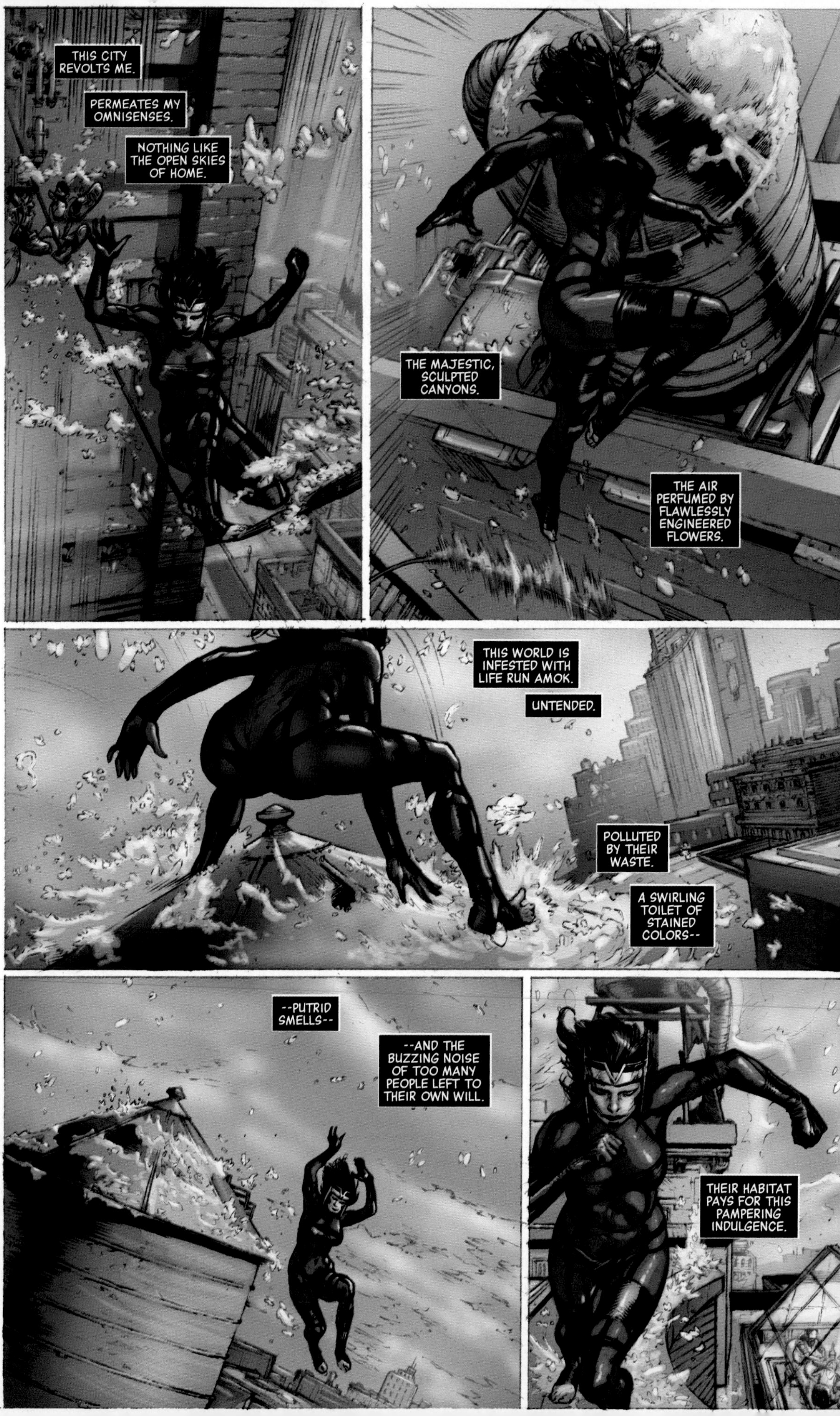
THIS CITY REVOLTS ME.
PERMEATES MY OMNISENSES.
NOTHING LIKE THE OPEN SKIES OF HOME.
THE MAJESTIC, SCULPTED CANYONS.
THE AIR PERFUMED BY FLAWLESSLY ENGINEERED FLOWERS.
THIS WORLD IS INFESTED WITH LIFE RUN AMOK.
UNTENDED.
POLLUTED BY THEIR WASTE.
A SWIRLING TOILET OF STAINED COLORS--
--PUTRID SMELLS--
--AND THE BUZZING NOISE OF TOO MANY PEOPLE LEFT TO THEIR OWN WILL.
THEIR HABITAT PAYS FOR THIS PAMPERING INDULGENCE.

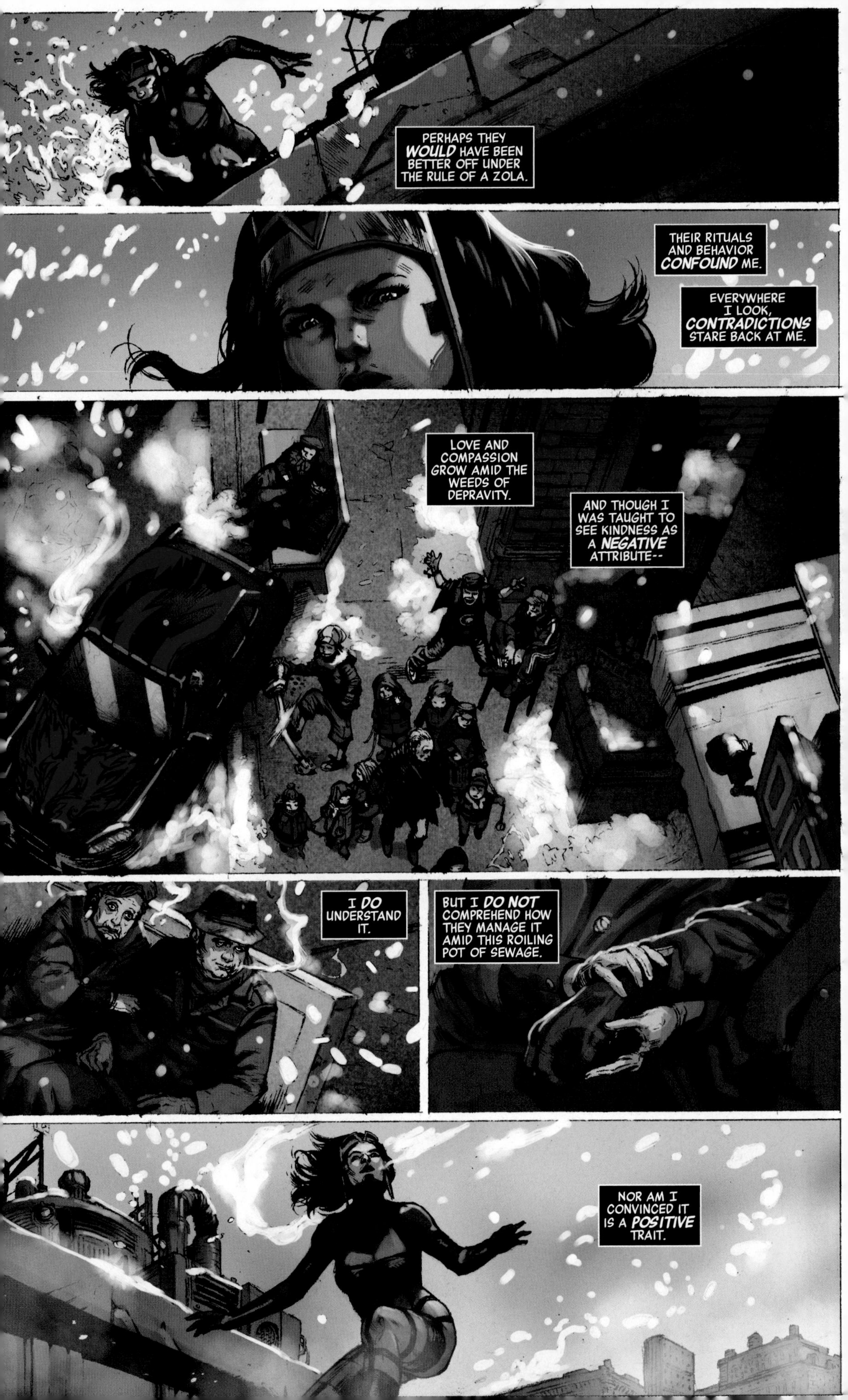
PERHAPS THEY WOULD HAVE BEEN BETTER OFF UNDER THE RULE OF A ZOLA.
THEIR RITUALS AND BEHAVIOR CONFOUND ME.
EVERYWHERE I LOOK, CONTRADICTIONS STARE BACK AT ME.
LOVE AND COMPASSION GROW AMID THE WEEDS OF DEPRAVITY.
AND THOUGH I WAS TAUGHT TO SEE KINDNESS AS A NEGATIVE ATTRIBUTE--
I DO UNDERSTAND IT.
BUT I DO NOT COMPREHEND HOW THEY MANAGE IT AMID THIS ROILING POT OF SEWAGE.
NOR AM I CONVINCED IT IS A POSITIVE TRAIT.

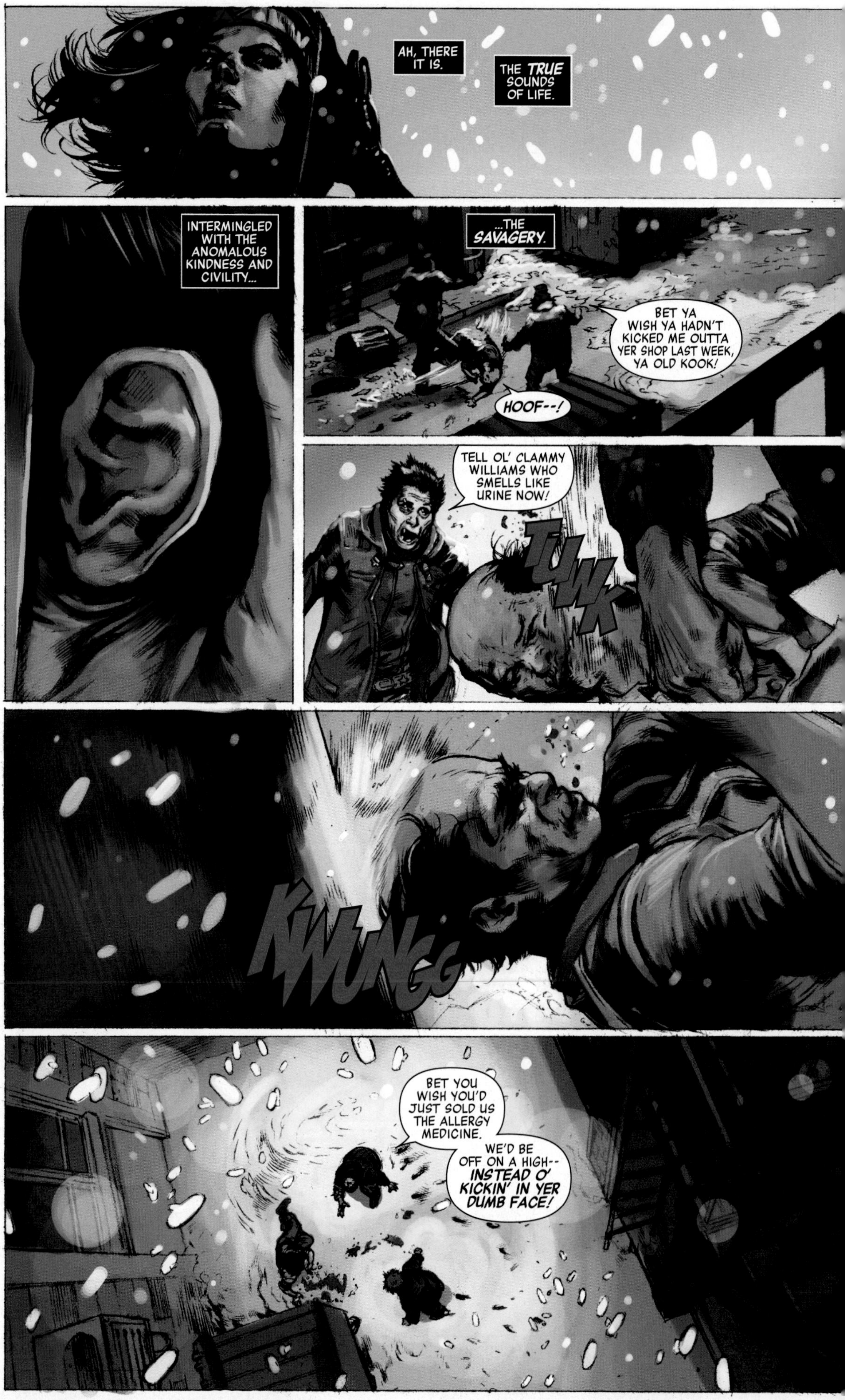
AH, THERE IT IS.
THE TRUE SOUNDS OF LIFE.
INTERMINGLED WITH THE ANOMALOUS KINDNESS AND CIVILITY...
...THE SAVAGERY.
BET YA WISH YA HADN'T KICKED ME OUTTA YER SHOP LAST WEEK, YA OLD KOOK!
HOOF--!
TELL OL' CLAMMY WILLIAMS WHO SMELLS LIKE URINE NOW!
TUNK
KWUNGG
BET YOU WISH YOU'D JUST SOLD US THE ALLERGY MEDICINE.
WE'D BE OFF ON A HIGH-- INSTEAD O' KICKIN' IN YER DUMB FACE!

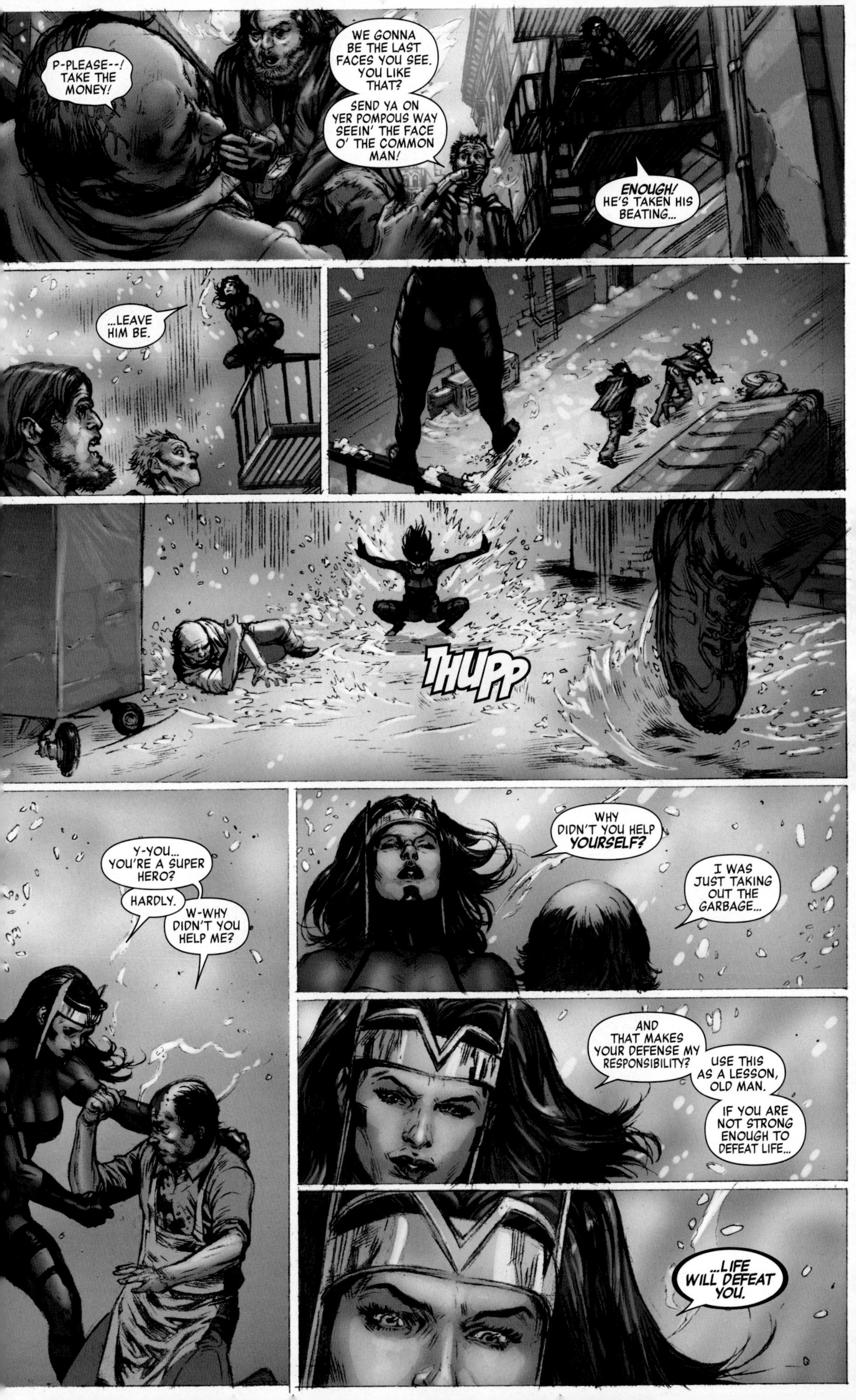
P-PLEASE--! TAKE THE MONEY!
WE GONNA BE THE LAST FACES YOU SEE. YOU LIKE THAT?
SEND YA ON YER POMPOUS WAY SEEIN' THE FACE O' THE COMMON MAN!
ENOUGH! HE'S TAKEN HIS BEATING...
...LEAVE HIM BE.
THUPP
Y-YOU... YOU'RE A SUPER HERO?
HARDLY.
W-WHY DIDN'T YOU HELP ME?
WHY DIDN'T YOU HELP YOURSELF?
I WAS JUST TAKING OUT THE GARBAGE...
AND THAT MAKES YOUR DEFENSE MY RESPONSIBILITY?
USE THIS AS A LESSON, OLD MAN.
IF YOU ARE NOT STRONG ENOUGH TO DEFEAT LIFE...
...LIFE WILL DEFEAT YOU.

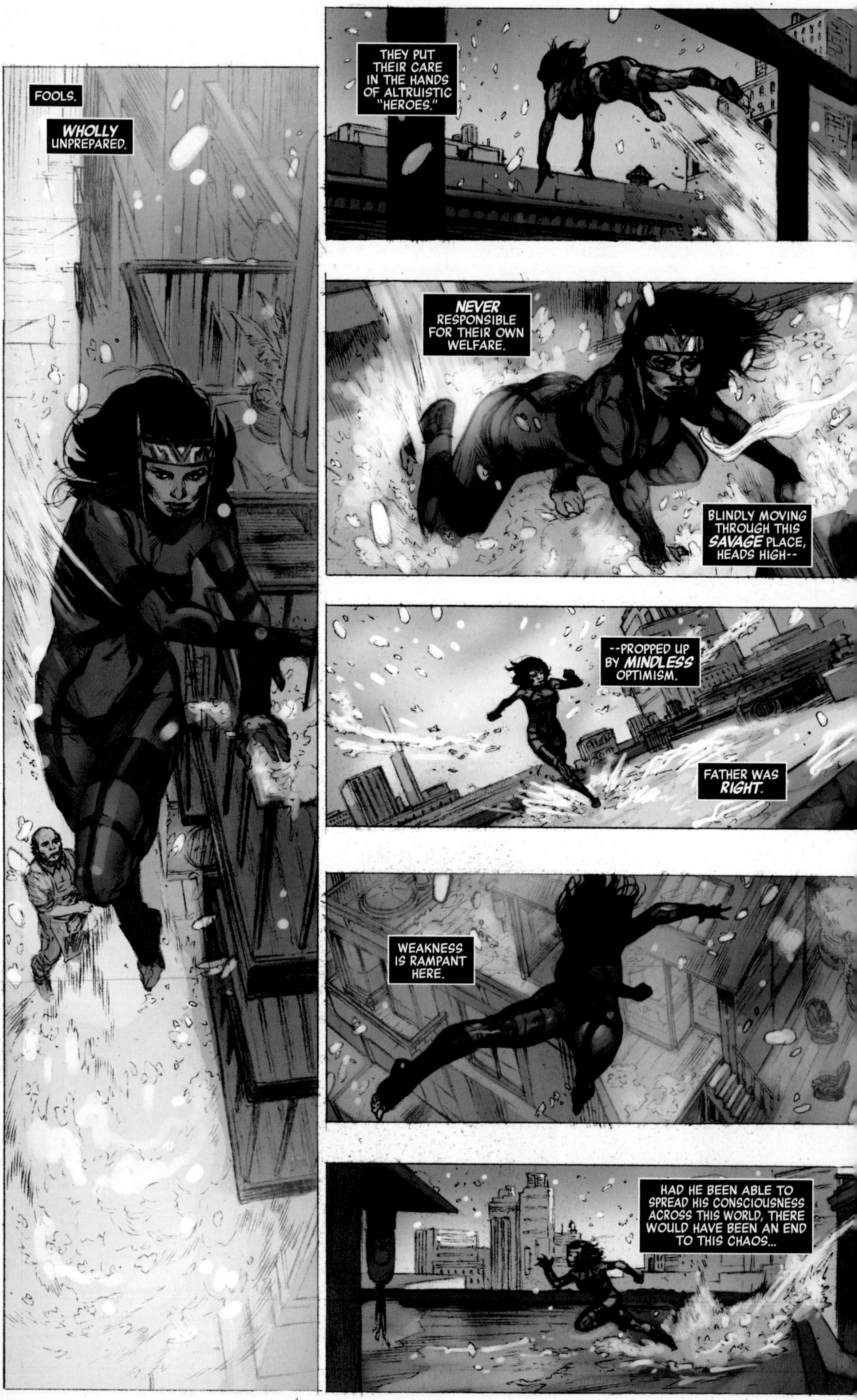
FOOLS.
WHOLLY UNPREPARED.
THEY PUT THEIR CARE IN THE HANDS OF ALTRUISTIC "HEROES."
NEVER RESPONSIBLE FOR THEIR OWN WELFARE.
BLINDLY MOVING THROUGH THIS SAVAGE PLACE, HEADS HIGH--
--PROPPED UP BY MINDLESS OPTIMISM.
FATHER WAS RIGHT.
WEAKNESS IS RAMPANT HERE.
HAD HE BEEN ABLE TO SPREAD HIS CONSCIOUSNESS ACROSS THIS WORLD, THERE WOULD HAVE BEEN AN END TO THIS CHAOS...

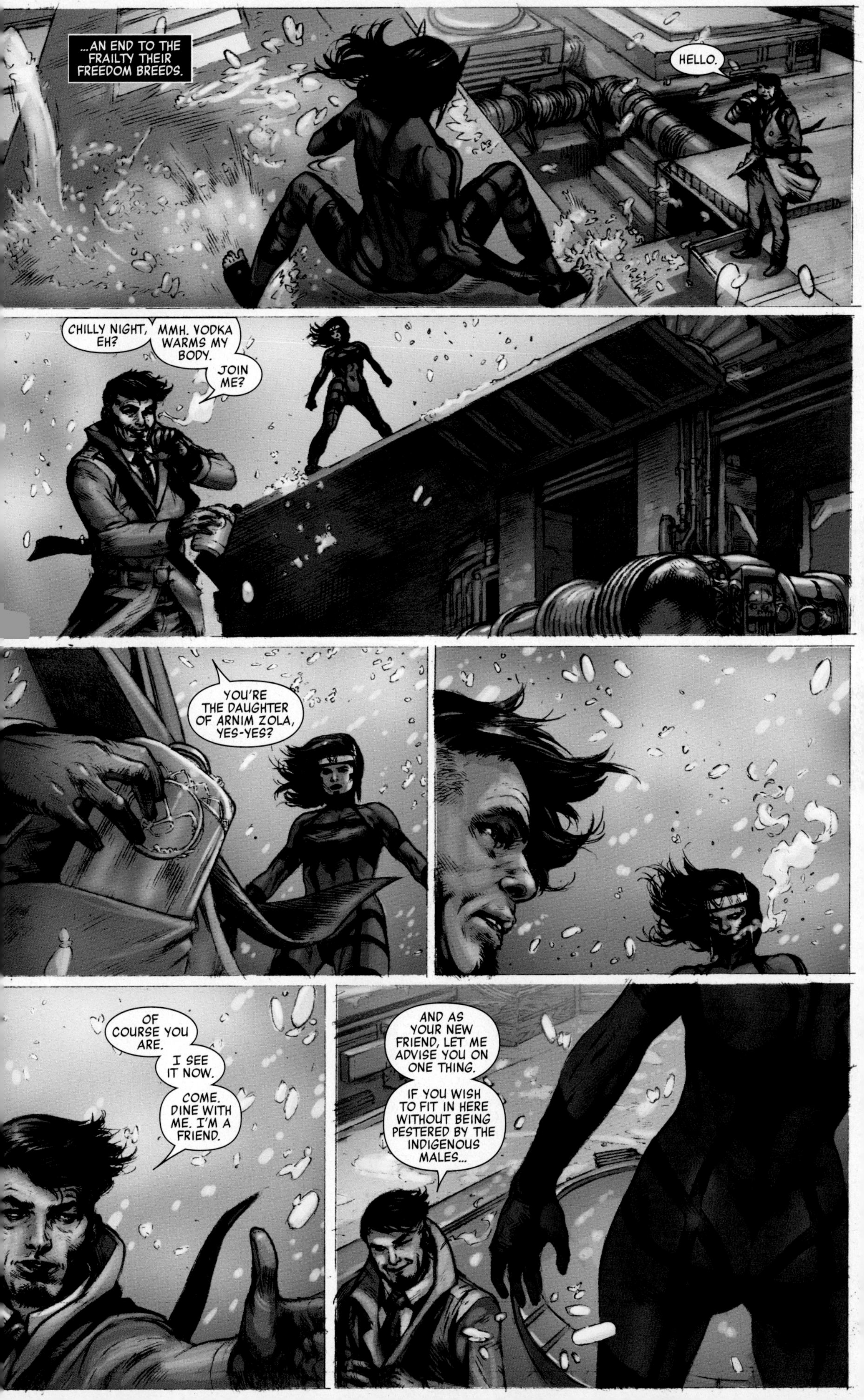
...AN END TO THE FRAILTY THEIR FREEDOM BREEDS.
HELLO.
CHILLY NIGHT, EH?
MMH. VODKA WARMS MY BODY.
JOIN ME?
YOU'RE THE DAUGHTER OF ARNIM ZOLA, YES-YES?
OF COURSE YOU ARE.
I SEE IT NOW.
COME. DINE WITH ME. I'M A FRIEND.
AND AS YOUR NEW FRIEND, LET ME ADVISE YOU ON ONE THING.
IF YOU WISH TO FIT IN HERE WITHOUT BEING PESTERED BY THE INDIGENOUS MALES...

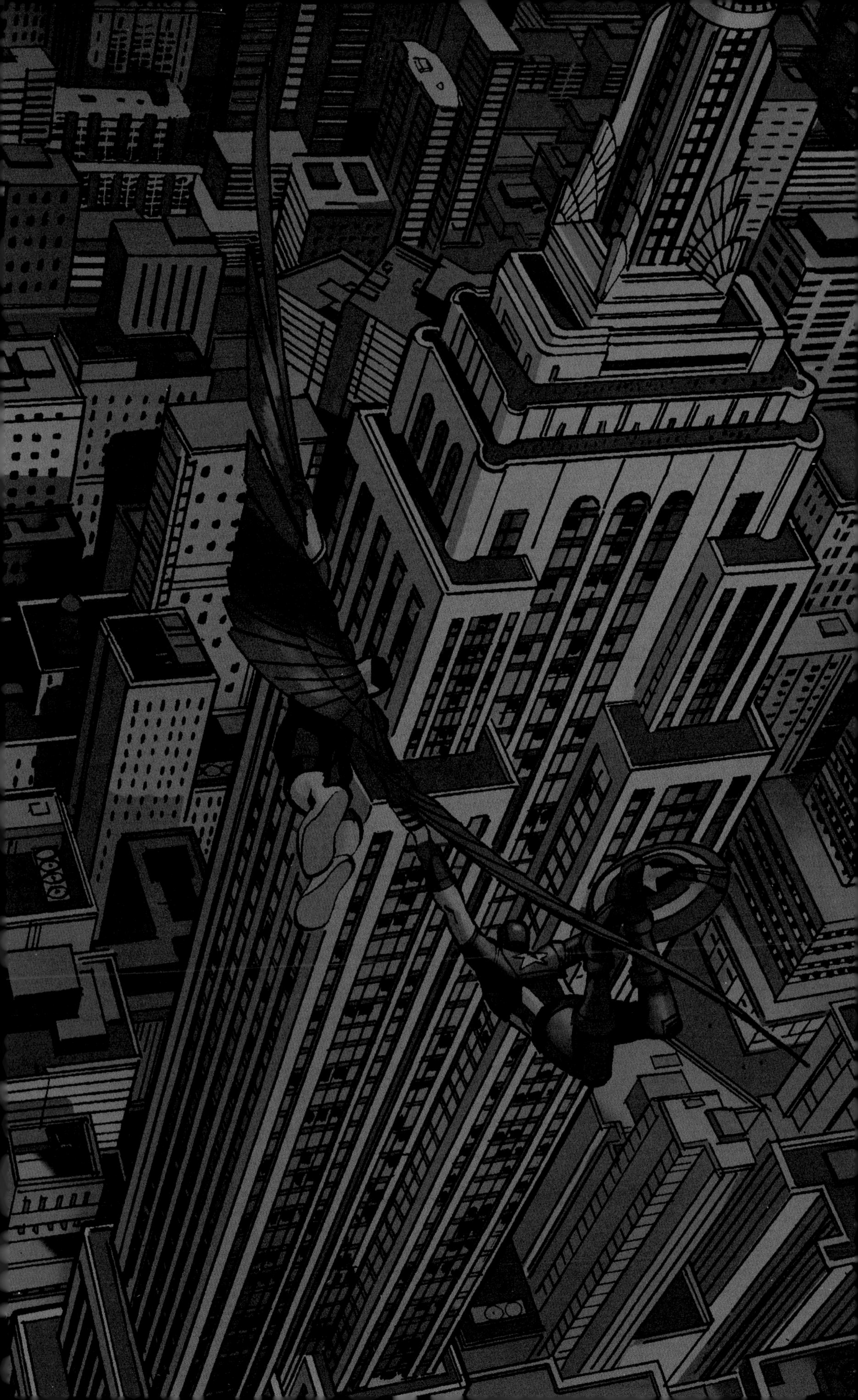

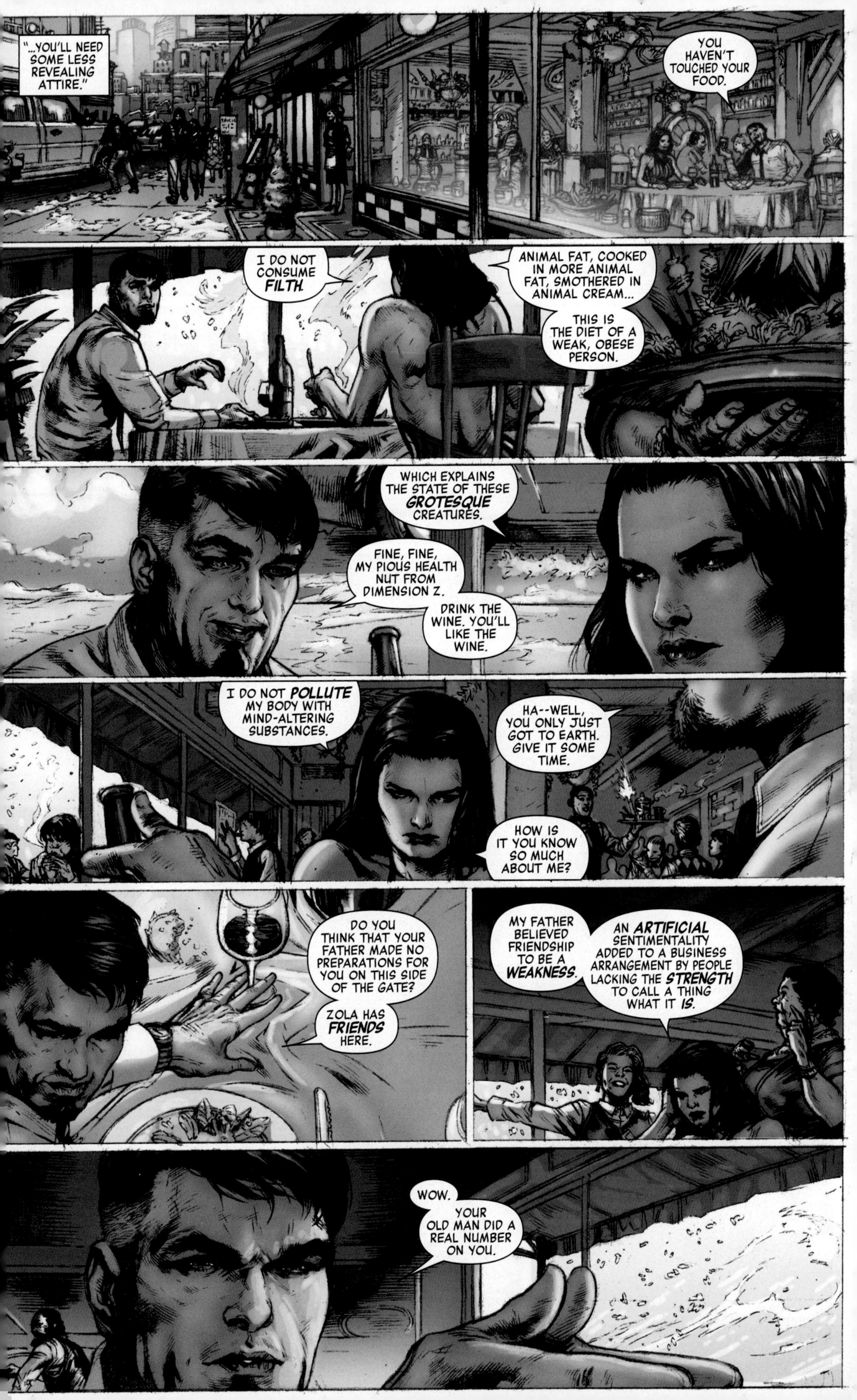
"...YOU'LL NEED SOME LESS REVEALING ATTIRE."
YOU HAVEN'T TOUCHED YOUR FOOD.
I DO NOT CONSUME FILTH.
ANIMAL FAT, COOKED IN MORE ANIMAL FAT, SMOTHERED IN ANIMAL CREAM...
THIS IS THE DIET OF A WEAK, OBESE PERSON.
WHICH EXPLAINS THE STATE OF THESE GROTESQUE CREATURES.
FINE, FINE, MY PIOUS HEALTH NUT FROM DIMENSION Z.
DRINK THE WINE. YOU'LL LIKE THE WINE.
I DO NOT POLLUTE MY BODY WITH MIND-ALTERING SUBSTANCES.
HA--WELL, YOU ONLY JUST GOT TO EARTH. GIVE IT SOME TIME.
HOW IS IT YOU KNOW SO MUCH ABOUT ME?
DO YOU THINK THAT YOUR FATHER MADE NO PREPARATIONS FOR YOU ON THIS SIDE OF THE GATE?
ZOLA HAS FRIENDS HERE.
MY FATHER BELIEVED FRIENDSHIP TO BE A WEAKNESS.
AN ARTIFICIAL SENTIMENTALITY ADDED TO A BUSINESS ARRANGEMENT BY PEOPLE LACKING THE STRENGTH TO CALL A THING WHAT IT IS.
WOW.
YOUR OLD MAN DID A REAL NUMBER ON YOU.

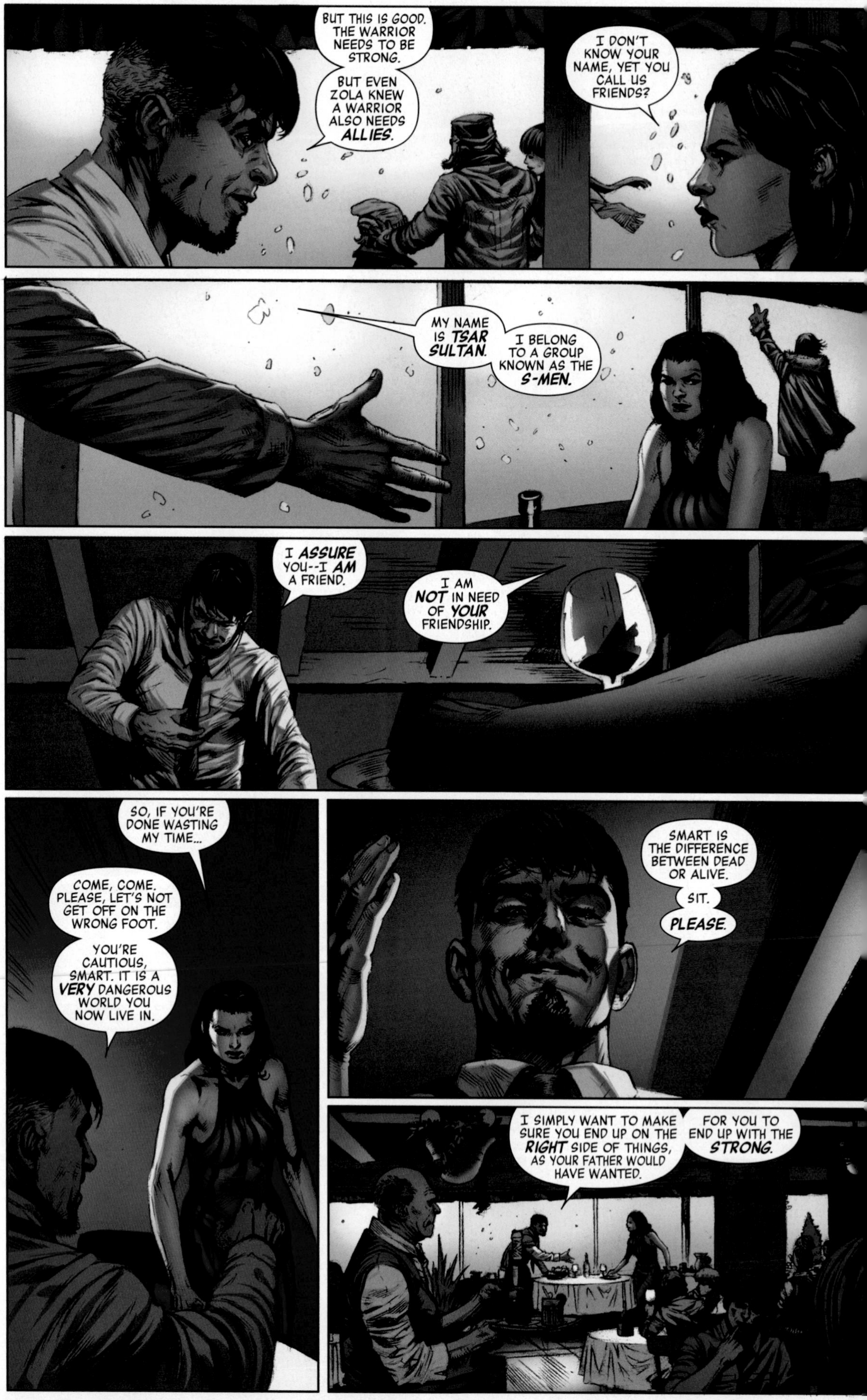
BUT THIS IS GOOD. THE WARRIOR NEEDS TO BE STRONG.
BUT EVEN ZOLA KNEW A WARRIOR ALSO NEEDS **ALLIES**.
I DON'T KNOW YOUR NAME, YET YOU CALL US FRIENDS?
MY NAME IS **TSAR SULTAN**.
I BELONG TO A GROUP KNOWN AS THE **S-MEN**.
I **ASSURE** YOU--I **AM** A FRIEND.
I AM **NOT** IN NEED OF **YOUR** FRIENDSHIP.
SO, IF YOU'RE DONE WASTING MY TIME...
COME, COME. PLEASE, LET'S NOT GET OFF ON THE WRONG FOOT.
YOU'RE CAUTIOUS, SMART. IT IS A **VERY** DANGEROUS WORLD YOU NOW LIVE IN.
SMART IS THE DIFFERENCE BETWEEN DEAD OR ALIVE.
SIT.
PLEASE.
I SIMPLY WANT TO MAKE SURE YOU END UP ON THE **RIGHT** SIDE OF THINGS, AS YOUR FATHER WOULD HAVE WANTED.
FOR YOU TO END UP WITH THE **STRONG**.

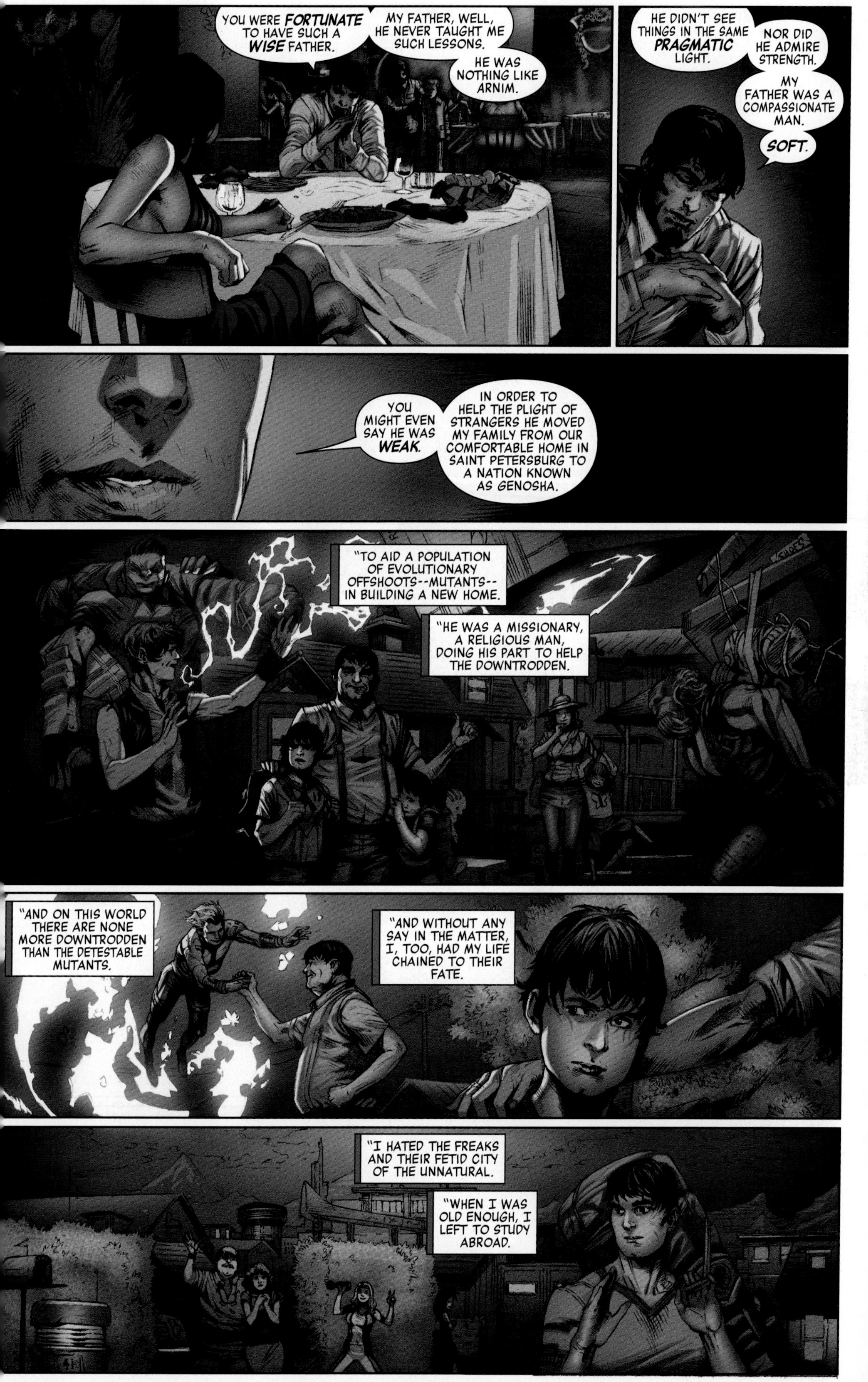

YOU WERE FORTUNATE TO HAVE SUCH A WISE FATHER.
MY FATHER, WELL, HE NEVER TAUGHT ME SUCH LESSONS.
HE WAS NOTHING LIKE ARNIM.
HE DIDN'T SEE THINGS IN THE SAME PRAGMATIC LIGHT.
NOR DID HE ADMIRE STRENGTH.
MY FATHER WAS A COMPASSIONATE MAN.
SOFT.
YOU MIGHT EVEN SAY HE WAS WEAK.
IN ORDER TO HELP THE PLIGHT OF STRANGERS HE MOVED MY FAMILY FROM OUR COMFORTABLE HOME IN SAINT PETERSBURG TO A NATION KNOWN AS GENOSHA.
"TO AID A POPULATION OF EVOLUTIONARY OFFSHOOTS--MUTANTS--IN BUILDING A NEW HOME.
"HE WAS A MISSIONARY, A RELIGIOUS MAN, DOING HIS PART TO HELP THE DOWNTRODDEN.
"AND ON THIS WORLD THERE ARE NONE MORE DOWNTRODDEN THAN THE DETESTABLE MUTANTS.
"AND WITHOUT ANY SAY IN THE MATTER, I, TOO, HAD MY LIFE CHAINED TO THEIR FATE.
"I HATED THE FREAKS AND THEIR FETID CITY OF THE UNNATURAL.
"WHEN I WAS OLD ENOUGH, I LEFT TO STUDY ABROAD.

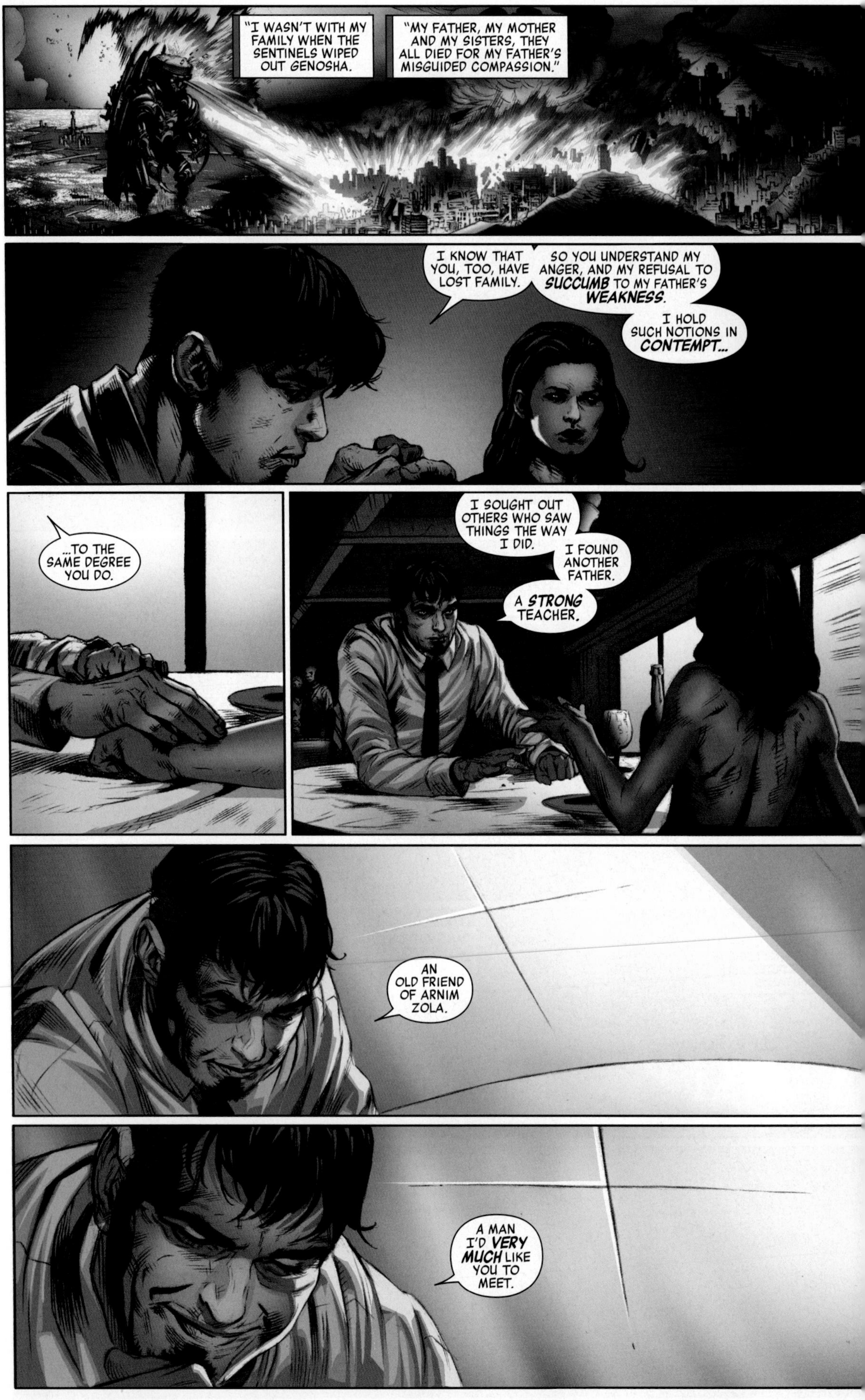
"I WASN'T WITH MY FAMILY WHEN THE SENTINELS WIPED OUT GENOSHA.
"MY FATHER, MY MOTHER AND MY SISTERS, THEY ALL DIED FOR MY FATHER'S MISGUIDED COMPASSION."
I KNOW THAT YOU, TOO, HAVE LOST FAMILY.
SO YOU UNDERSTAND MY ANGER, AND MY REFUSAL TO SUCCUMB TO MY FATHER'S WEAKNESS.
I HOLD SUCH NOTIONS IN CONTEMPT...
...TO THE SAME DEGREE YOU DO.
I SOUGHT OUT OTHERS WHO SAW THINGS THE WAY I DID.
I FOUND ANOTHER FATHER.
A STRONG TEACHER.
AN OLD FRIEND OF ARNIM ZOLA.
A MAN I'D VERY MUCH LIKE YOU TO MEET.

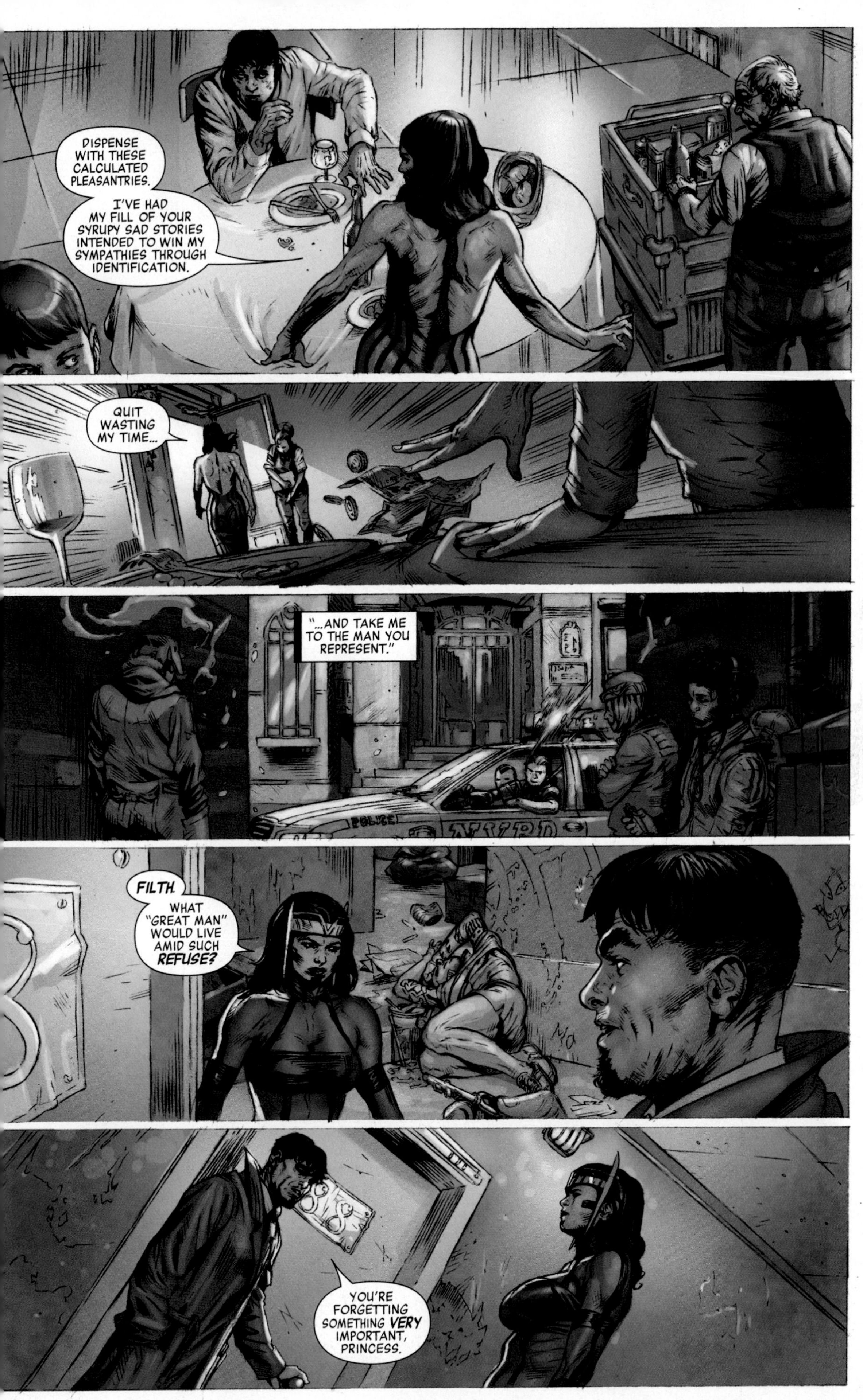
DISPENSE WITH THESE CALCULATED PLEASANTRIES.
I'VE HAD MY FILL OF YOUR SYRUPY SAD STORIES INTENDED TO WIN MY SYMPATHIES THROUGH IDENTIFICATION.
QUIT WASTING MY TIME...
"...AND TAKE ME TO THE MAN YOU REPRESENT."
POLICE
NYPD
FILTH.
WHAT "GREAT MAN" WOULD LIVE AMID SUCH REFUSE?
YOU'RE FORGETTING SOMETHING VERY IMPORTANT, PRINCESS.

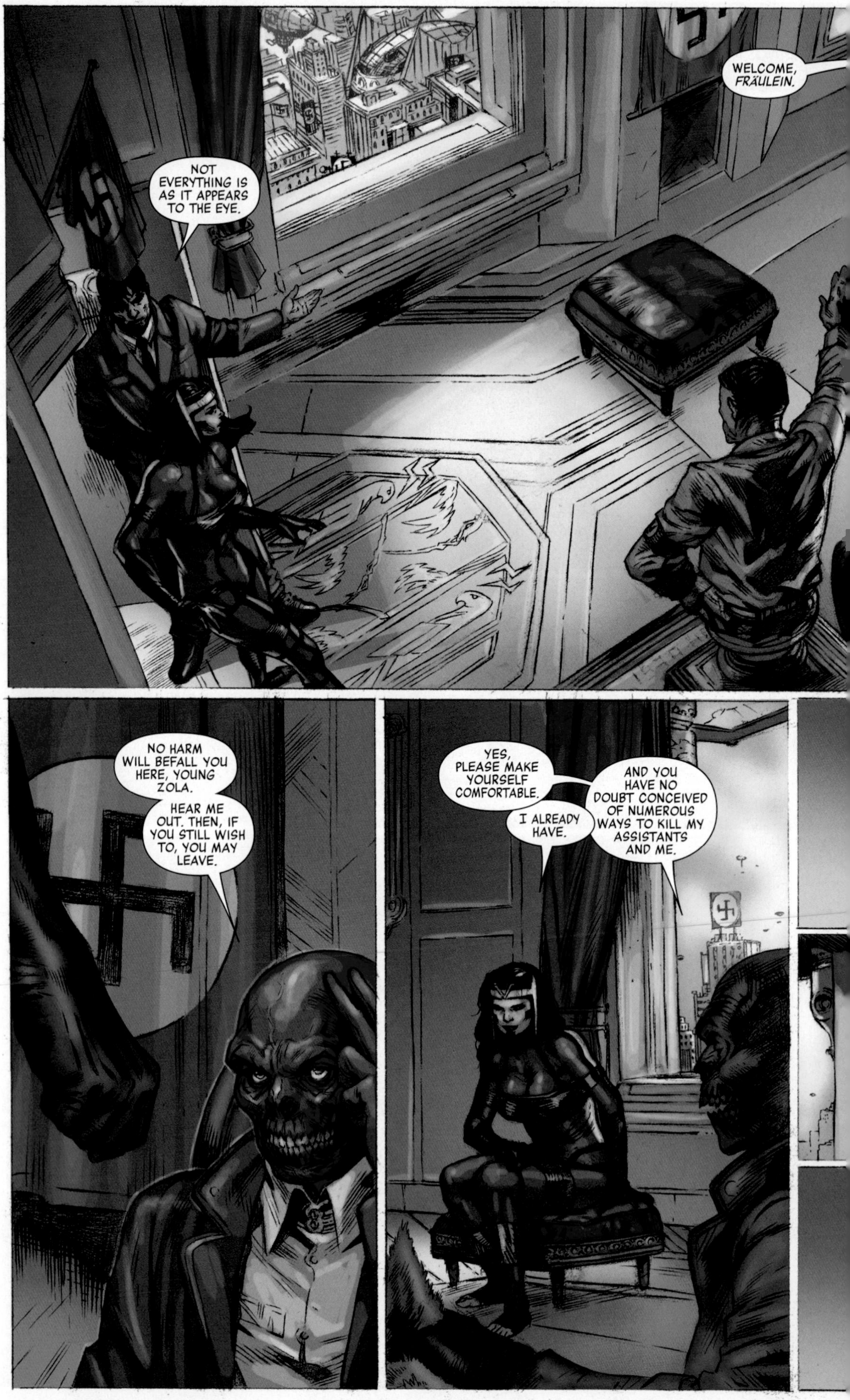
WELCOME, FRÄULEIN.
NOT EVERYTHING IS AS IT APPEARS TO THE EYE.
NO HARM WILL BEFALL YOU HERE, YOUNG ZOLA.
HEAR ME OUT. THEN, IF YOU STILL WISH TO, YOU MAY LEAVE.
YES, PLEASE MAKE YOURSELF COMFORTABLE.
AND YOU HAVE NO DOUBT CONCEIVED OF NUMEROUS WAYS TO KILL MY ASSISTANTS AND ME.
I ALREADY HAVE.

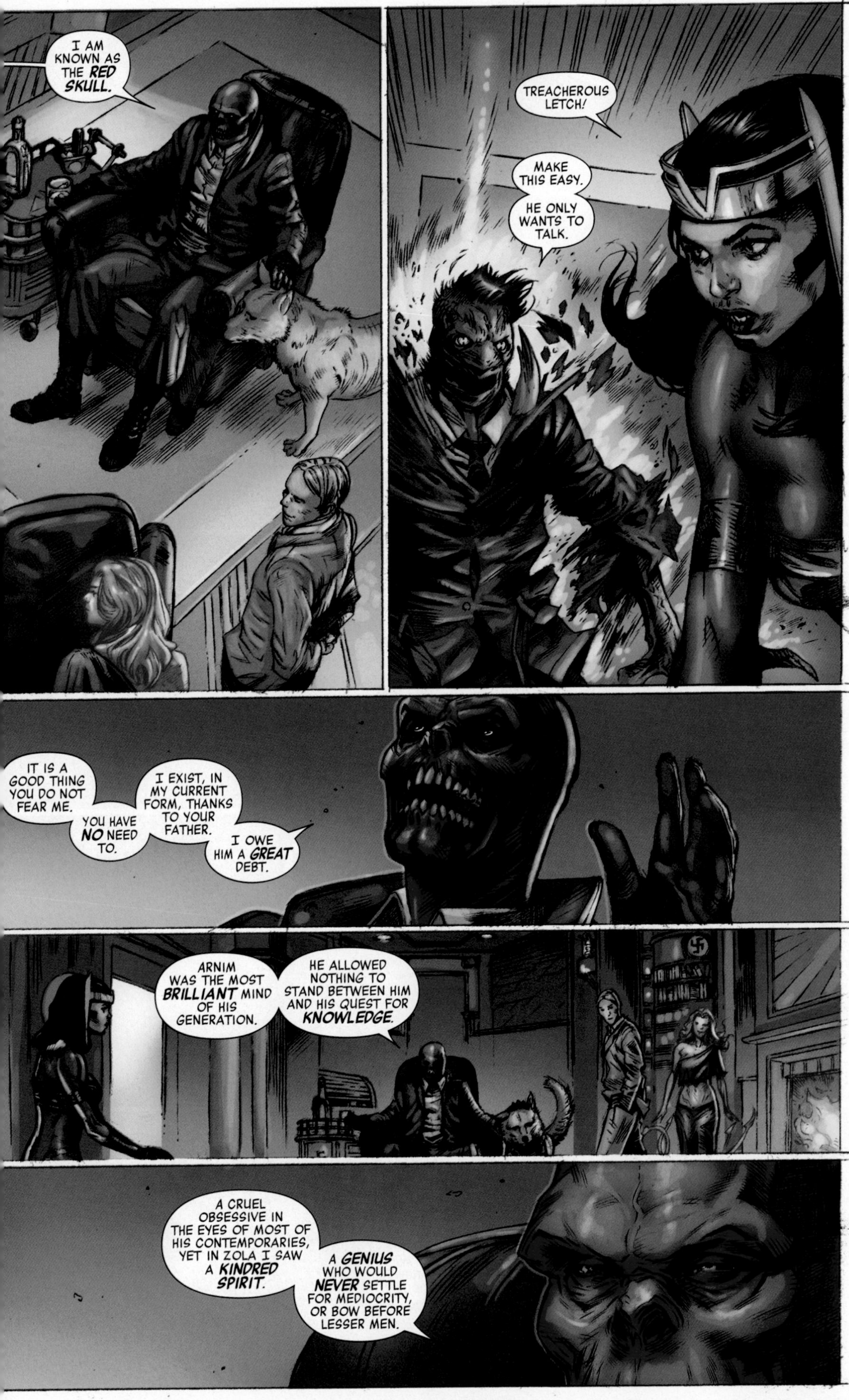
I AM KNOWN AS THE RED SKULL.
TREACHEROUS LETCH!
MAKE THIS EASY.
HE ONLY WANTS TO TALK.
IT IS A GOOD THING YOU DO NOT FEAR ME.
YOU HAVE NO NEED TO.
I EXIST, IN MY CURRENT FORM, THANKS TO YOUR FATHER.
I OWE HIM A GREAT DEBT.
ARNIM WAS THE MOST BRILLIANT MIND OF HIS GENERATION.
HE ALLOWED NOTHING TO STAND BETWEEN HIM AND HIS QUEST FOR KNOWLEDGE.
A CRUEL OBSESSIVE IN THE EYES OF MOST OF HIS CONTEMPORARIES, YET IN ZOLA I SAW A KINDRED SPIRIT.
A GENIUS WHO WOULD NEVER SETTLE FOR MEDIOCRITY, OR BOW BEFORE LESSER MEN.

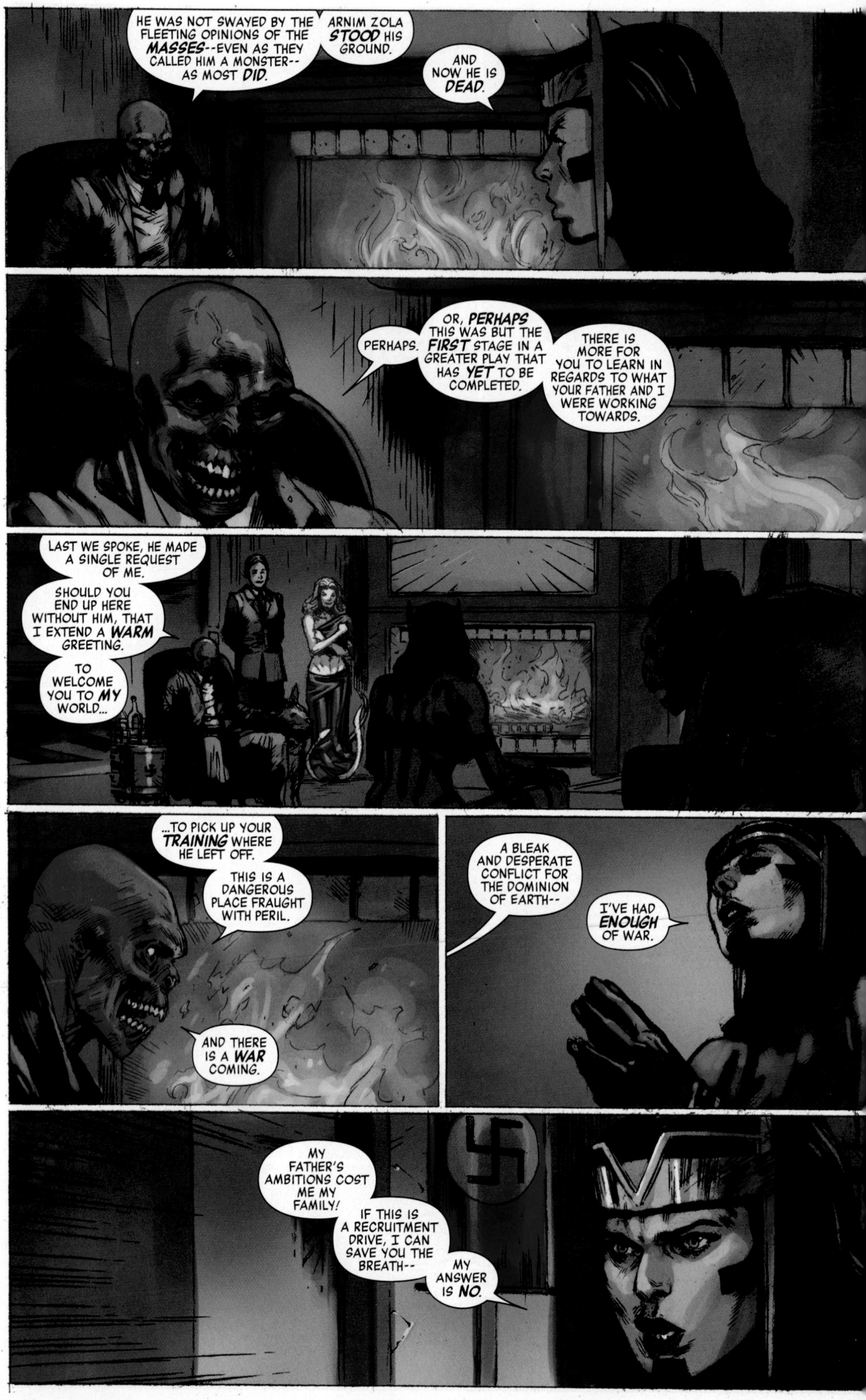
HE WAS NOT SWAYED BY THE FLEETING OPINIONS OF THE MASSES--EVEN AS THEY CALLED HIM A MONSTER--AS MOST DID.
ARNIM ZOLA STOOD HIS GROUND.
AND NOW HE IS DEAD.
PERHAPS.
OR, PERHAPS THIS WAS BUT THE FIRST STAGE IN A GREATER PLAY THAT HAS YET TO BE COMPLETED.
THERE IS MORE FOR YOU TO LEARN IN REGARDS TO WHAT YOUR FATHER AND I WERE WORKING TOWARDS.
LAST WE SPOKE, HE MADE A SINGLE REQUEST OF ME.
SHOULD YOU END UP HERE WITHOUT HIM, THAT I EXTEND A WARM GREETING.
TO WELCOME YOU TO MY WORLD...
...TO PICK UP YOUR TRAINING WHERE HE LEFT OFF.
THIS IS A DANGEROUS PLACE FRAUGHT WITH PERIL.
AND THERE IS A WAR COMING.
A BLEAK AND DESPERATE CONFLICT FOR THE DOMINION OF EARTH--
I'VE HAD ENOUGH OF WAR.
MY FATHER'S AMBITIONS COST ME MY FAMILY!
IF THIS IS A RECRUITMENT DRIVE, I CAN SAVE YOU THE BREATH--
MY ANSWER IS NO.

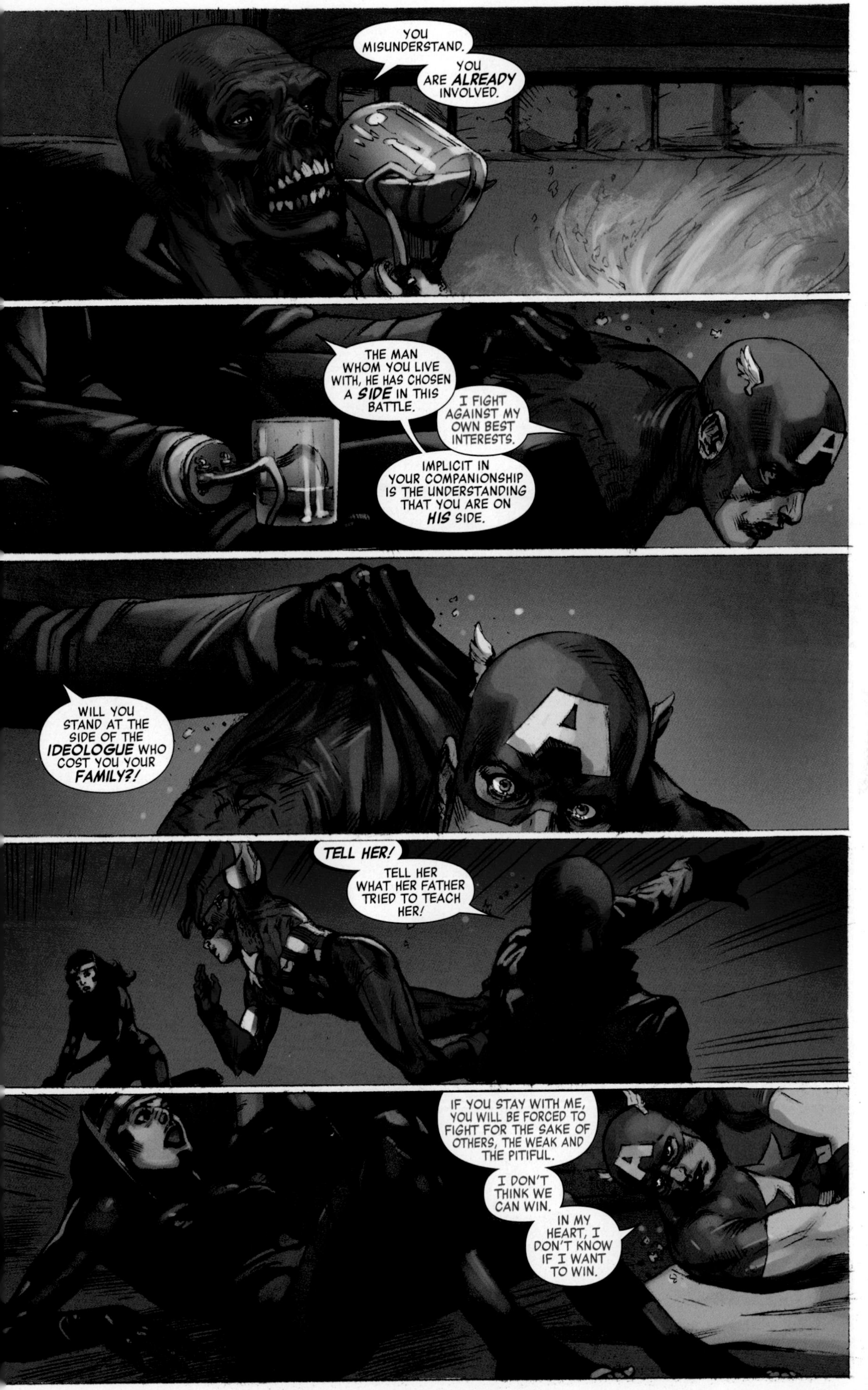

YOU MISUNDERSTAND.
YOU ARE ALREADY INVOLVED.
THE MAN WHOM YOU LIVE WITH, HE HAS CHOSEN A SIDE IN THIS BATTLE.
I FIGHT AGAINST MY OWN BEST INTERESTS.
IMPLICIT IN YOUR COMPANIONSHIP IS THE UNDERSTANDING THAT YOU ARE ON HIS SIDE.
WILL YOU STAND AT THE SIDE OF THE IDEOLOGUE WHO COST YOU YOUR FAMILY?!
TELL HER!
TELL HER WHAT HER FATHER TRIED TO TEACH HER!
IF YOU STAY WITH ME, YOU WILL BE FORCED TO FIGHT FOR THE SAKE OF OTHERS, THE WEAK AND THE PITIFUL.
I DON'T THINK WE CAN WIN.
IN MY HEART, I DON'T KNOW IF I WANT TO WIN.

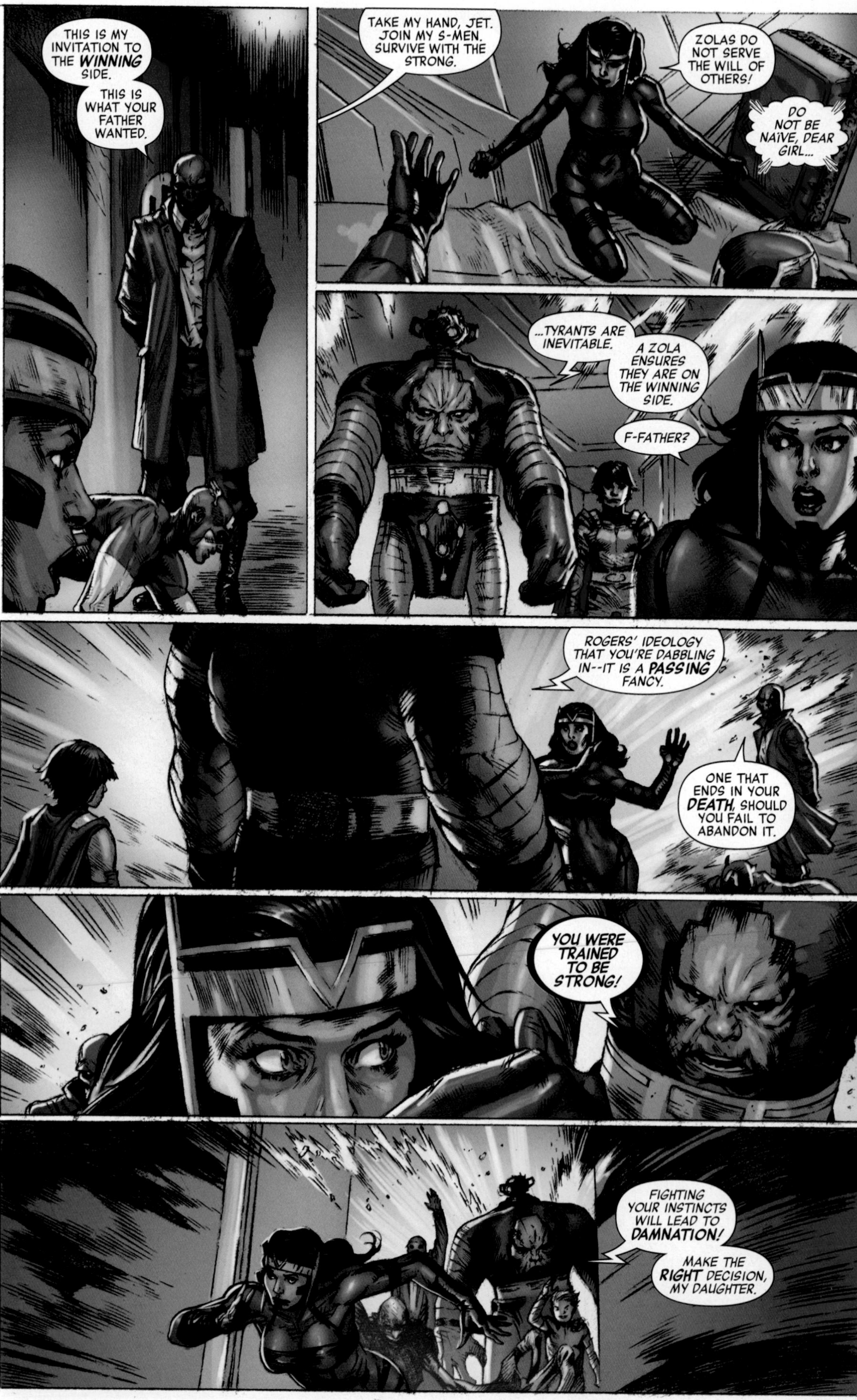
THIS IS MY INVITATION TO THE WINNING SIDE.
THIS IS WHAT YOUR FATHER WANTED.
TAKE MY HAND, JET. JOIN MY S-MEN. SURVIVE WITH THE STRONG.
ZOLAS DO NOT SERVE THE WILL OF OTHERS!
DO NOT BE NAÏVE, DEAR GIRL...
...TYRANTS ARE INEVITABLE.
A ZOLA ENSURES THEY ARE ON THE WINNING SIDE.
F-FATHER?
ROGERS' IDEOLOGY THAT YOU'RE DABBLING IN--IT IS A PASSING FANCY.
ONE THAT ENDS IN YOUR DEATH, SHOULD YOU FAIL TO ABANDON IT.
YOU WERE TRAINED TO BE STRONG!
FIGHTING YOUR INSTINCTS WILL LEAD TO DAMNATION!
MAKE THE RIGHT DECISION, MY DAUGHTER.

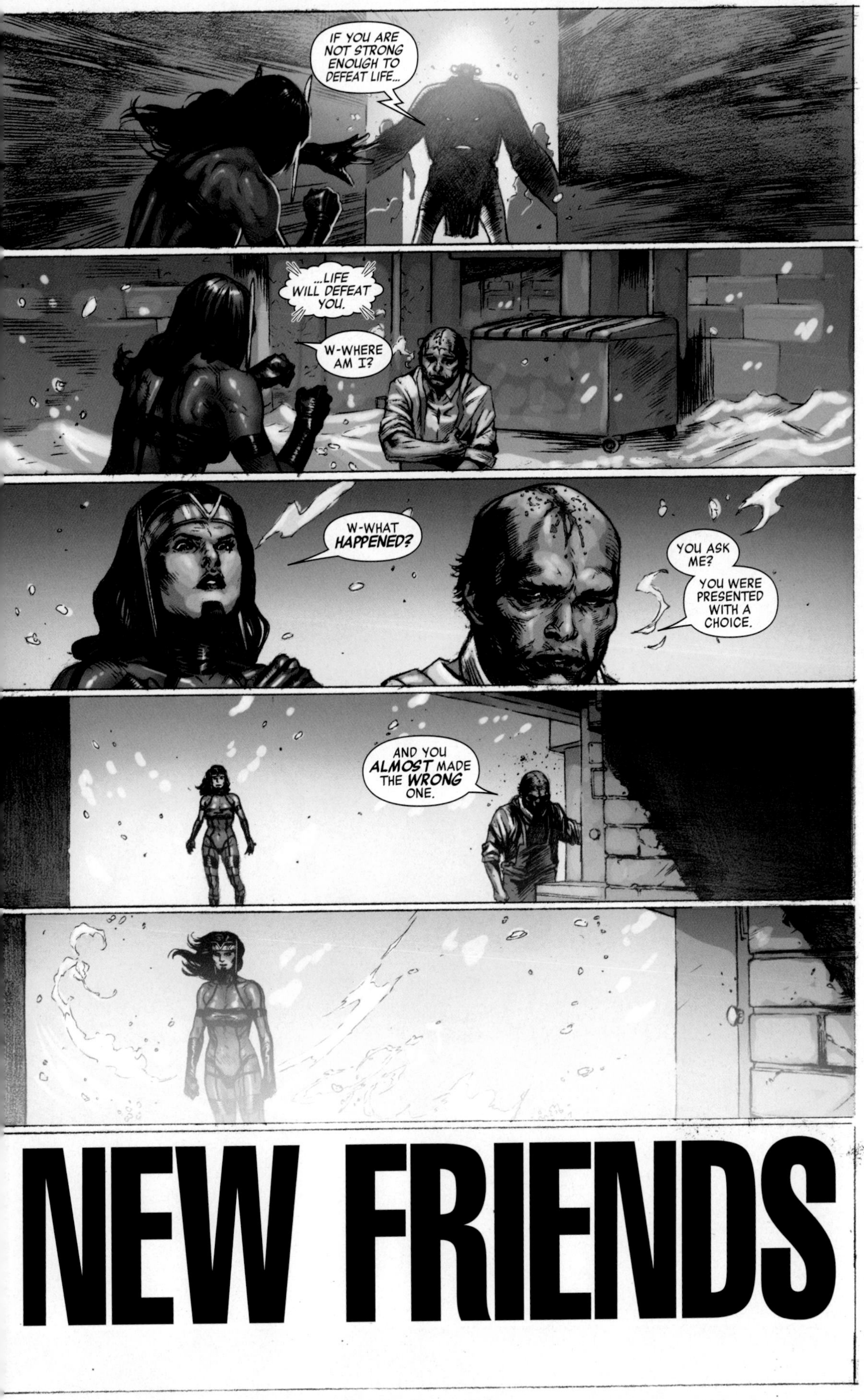
IF YOU ARE NOT STRONG ENOUGH TO DEFEAT LIFE...
...LIFE WILL DEFEAT YOU.
W-WHERE AM I?
W-WHAT HAPPENED?
YOU ASK ME?
YOU WERE PRESENTED WITH A CHOICE.
AND YOU ALMOST MADE THE WRONG ONE.

NEW FRIENDS

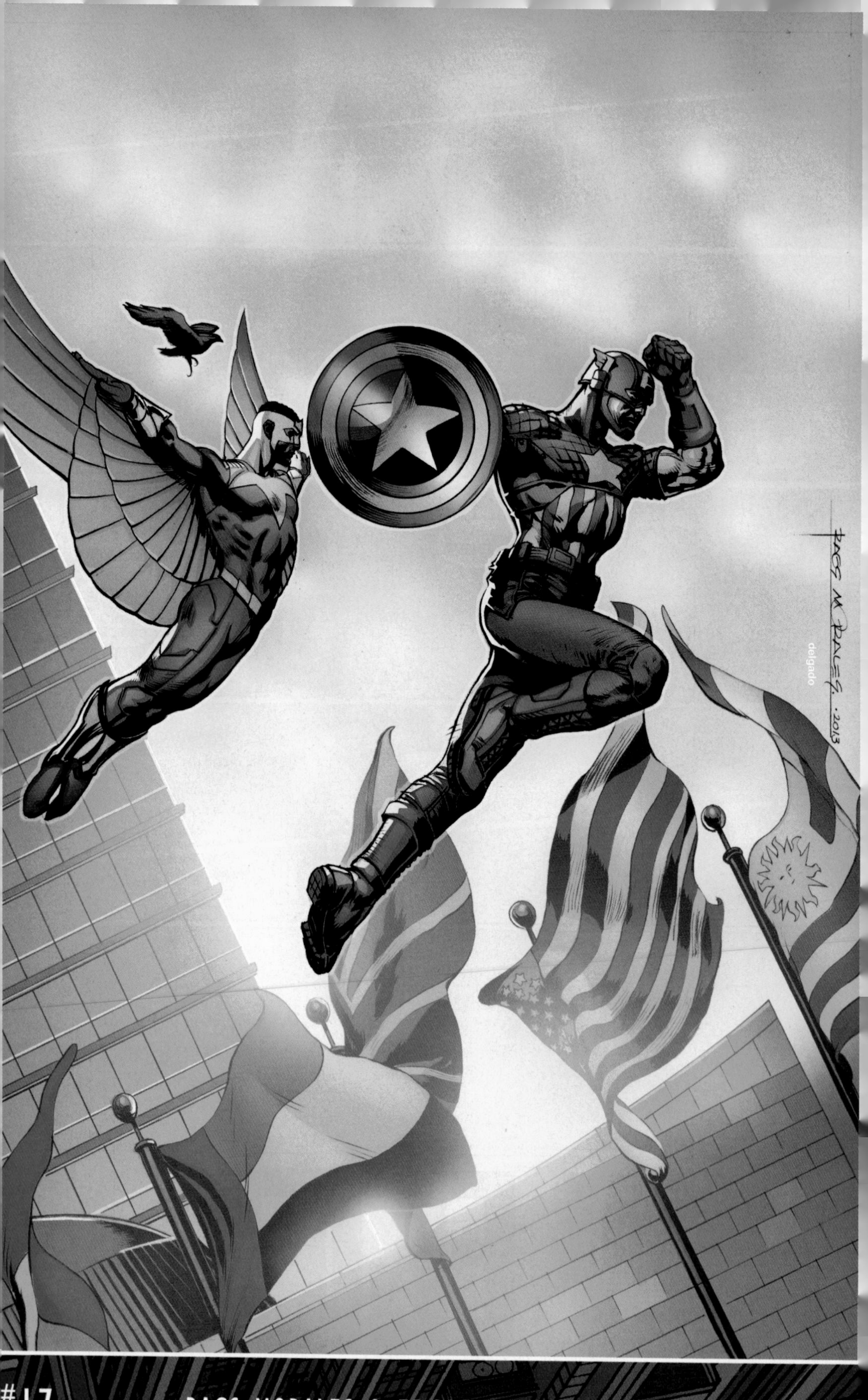
delgado

#17 VARIANT BY RAGS MORALES & EDGAR DELGADO

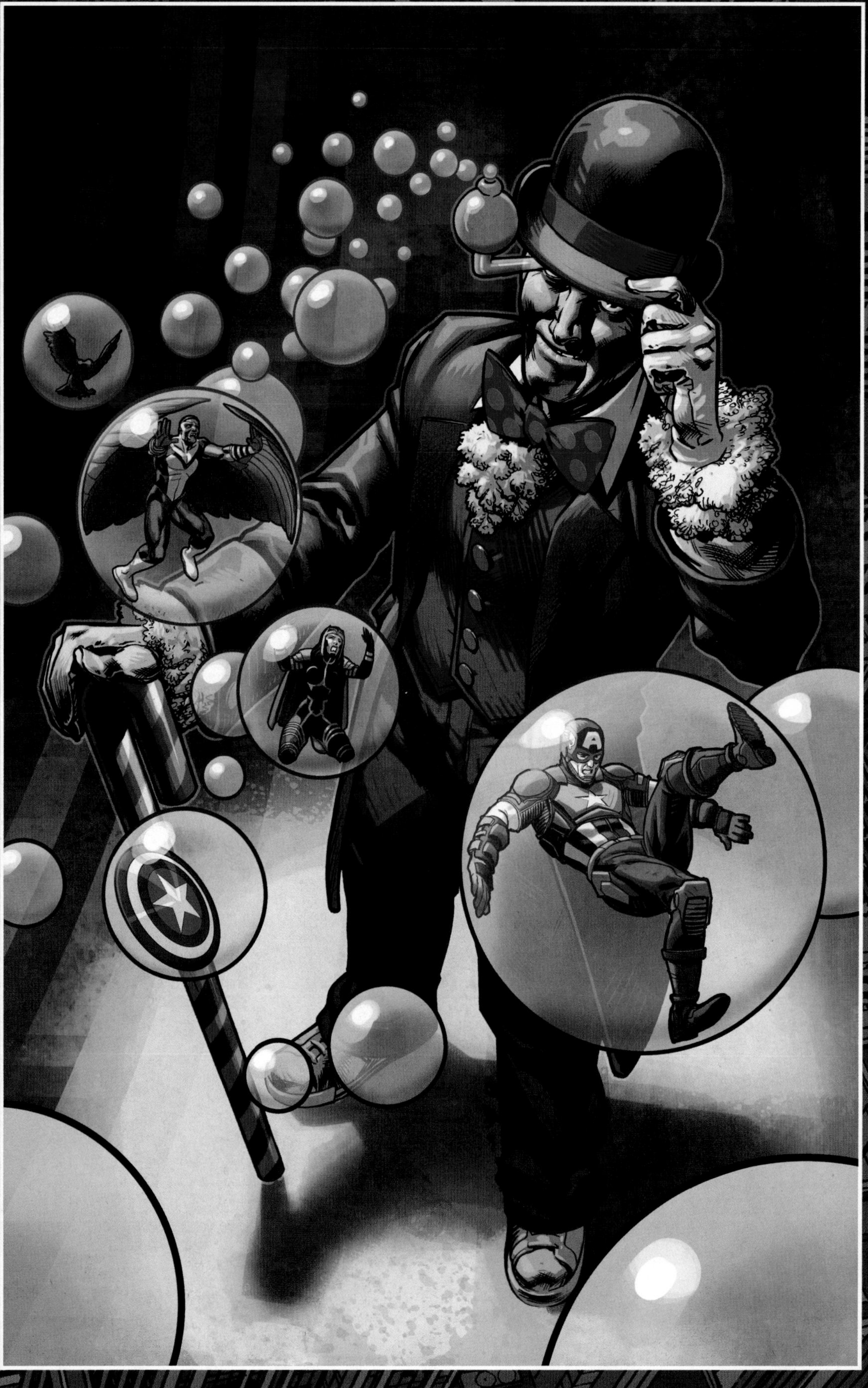

SEVENTEEN

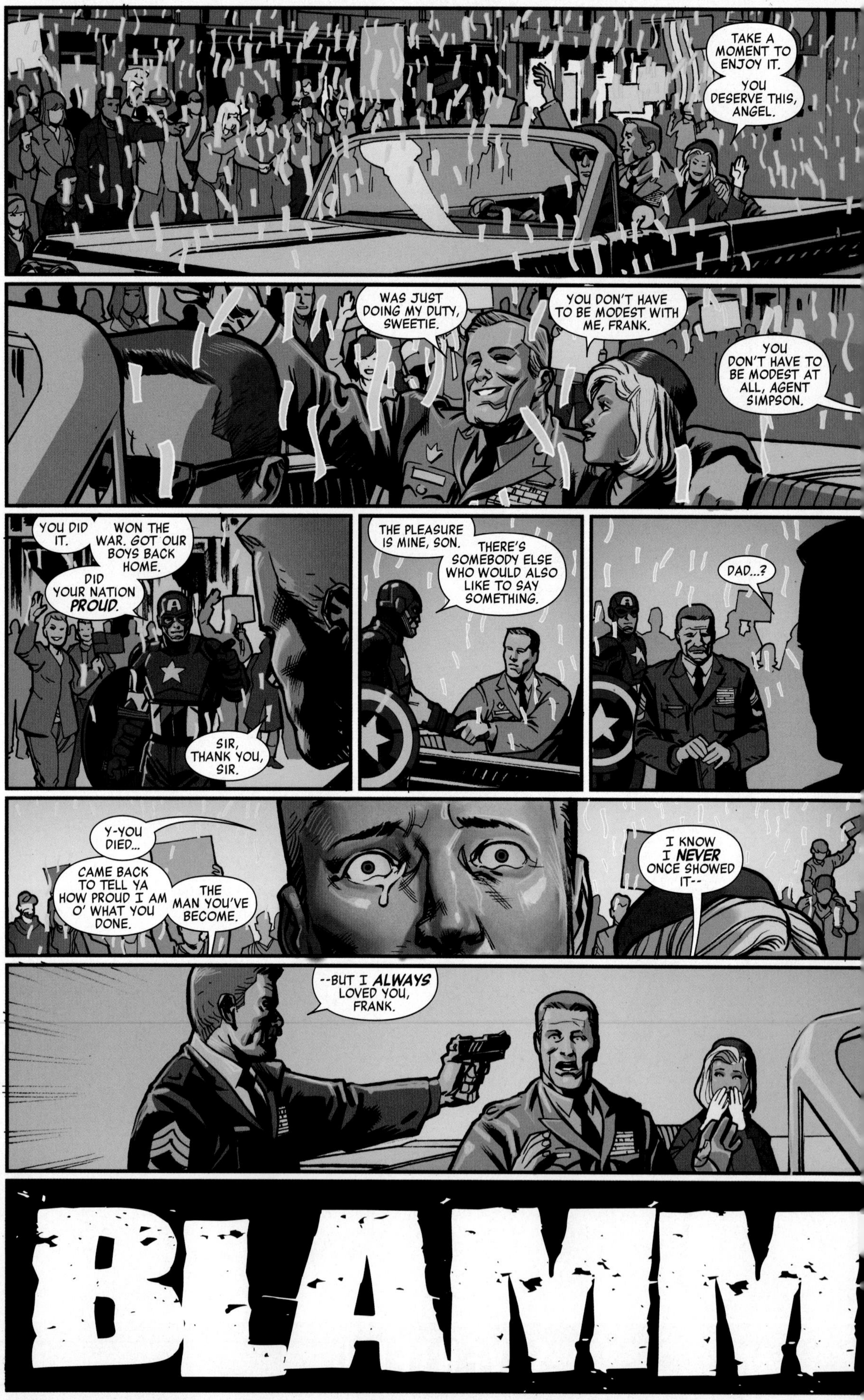
TAKE A MOMENT TO ENJOY IT.
YOU DESERVE THIS, ANGEL.
WAS JUST DOING MY DUTY, SWEETIE.
YOU DON'T HAVE TO BE MODEST WITH ME, FRANK.
YOU DON'T HAVE TO BE MODEST AT ALL, AGENT SIMPSON.
YOU DID IT.
WON THE WAR. GOT OUR BOYS BACK HOME.
DID YOUR NATION PROUD.
SIR, THANK YOU, SIR.
THE PLEASURE IS MINE, SON.
THERE'S SOMEBODY ELSE WHO WOULD ALSO LIKE TO SAY SOMETHING.
DAD...?
Y-YOU DIED...
CAME BACK TO TELL YA HOW PROUD I AM O' WHAT YOU DONE.
THE MAN YOU'VE BECOME.
I KNOW I NEVER ONCE SHOWED IT--
--BUT I ALWAYS LOVED YOU, FRANK.
BLAMM

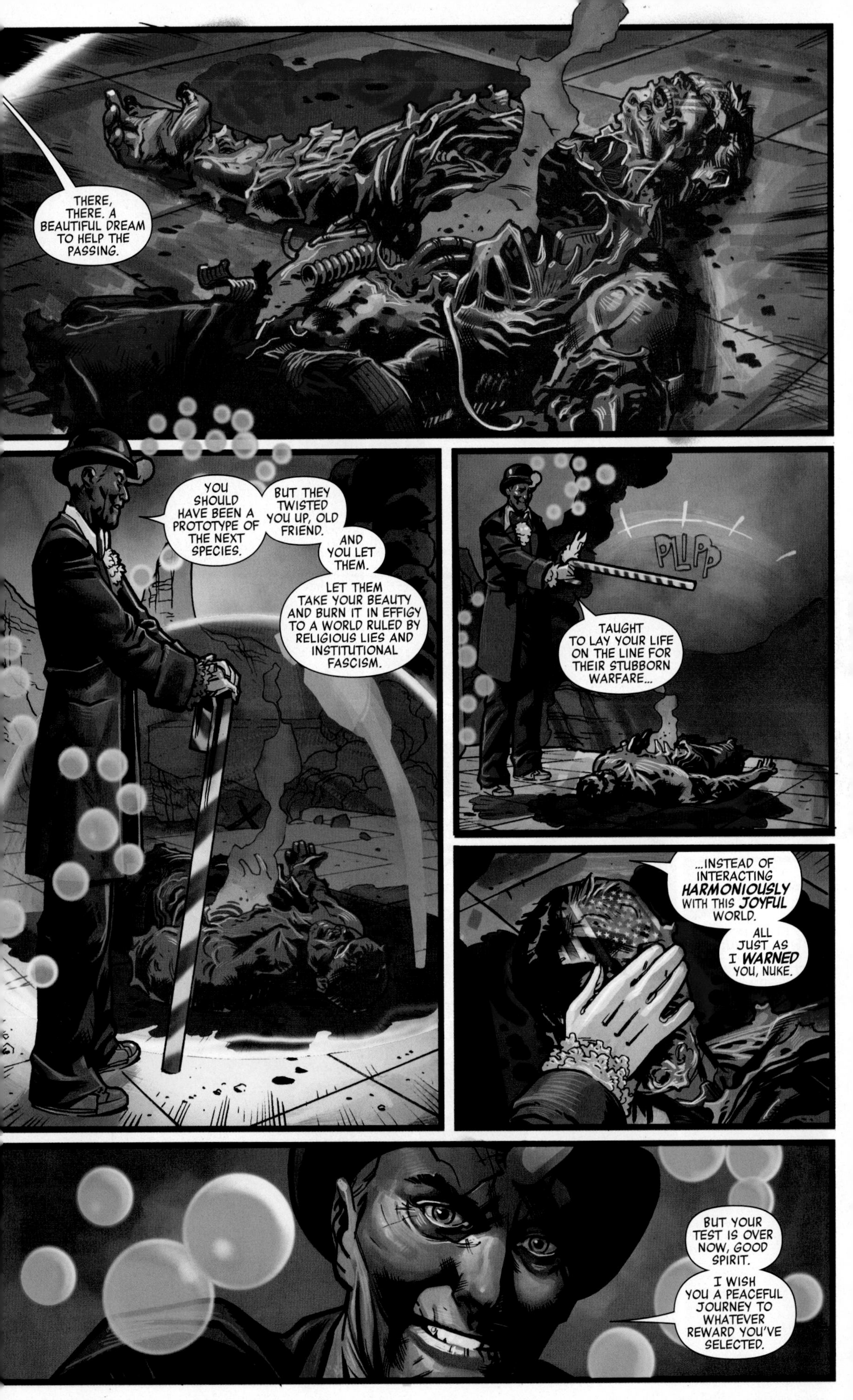
THERE, THERE. A BEAUTIFUL DREAM TO HELP THE PASSING.
YOU SHOULD HAVE BEEN A PROTOTYPE OF THE NEXT SPECIES.
BUT THEY TWISTED YOU UP, OLD FRIEND.
AND YOU LET THEM.
LET THEM TAKE YOUR BEAUTY AND BURN IT IN EFFIGY TO A WORLD RULED BY RELIGIOUS LIES AND INSTITUTIONAL FASCISM.
PLIPP
TAUGHT TO LAY YOUR LIFE ON THE LINE FOR THEIR STUBBORN WARFARE...
...INSTEAD OF INTERACTING HARMONIOUSLY WITH THIS JOYFUL WORLD.
ALL JUST AS I WARNED YOU, NUKE.
BUT YOUR TEST IS OVER NOW, GOOD SPIRIT.
I WISH YOU A PEACEFUL JOURNEY TO WHATEVER REWARD YOU'VE SELECTED.

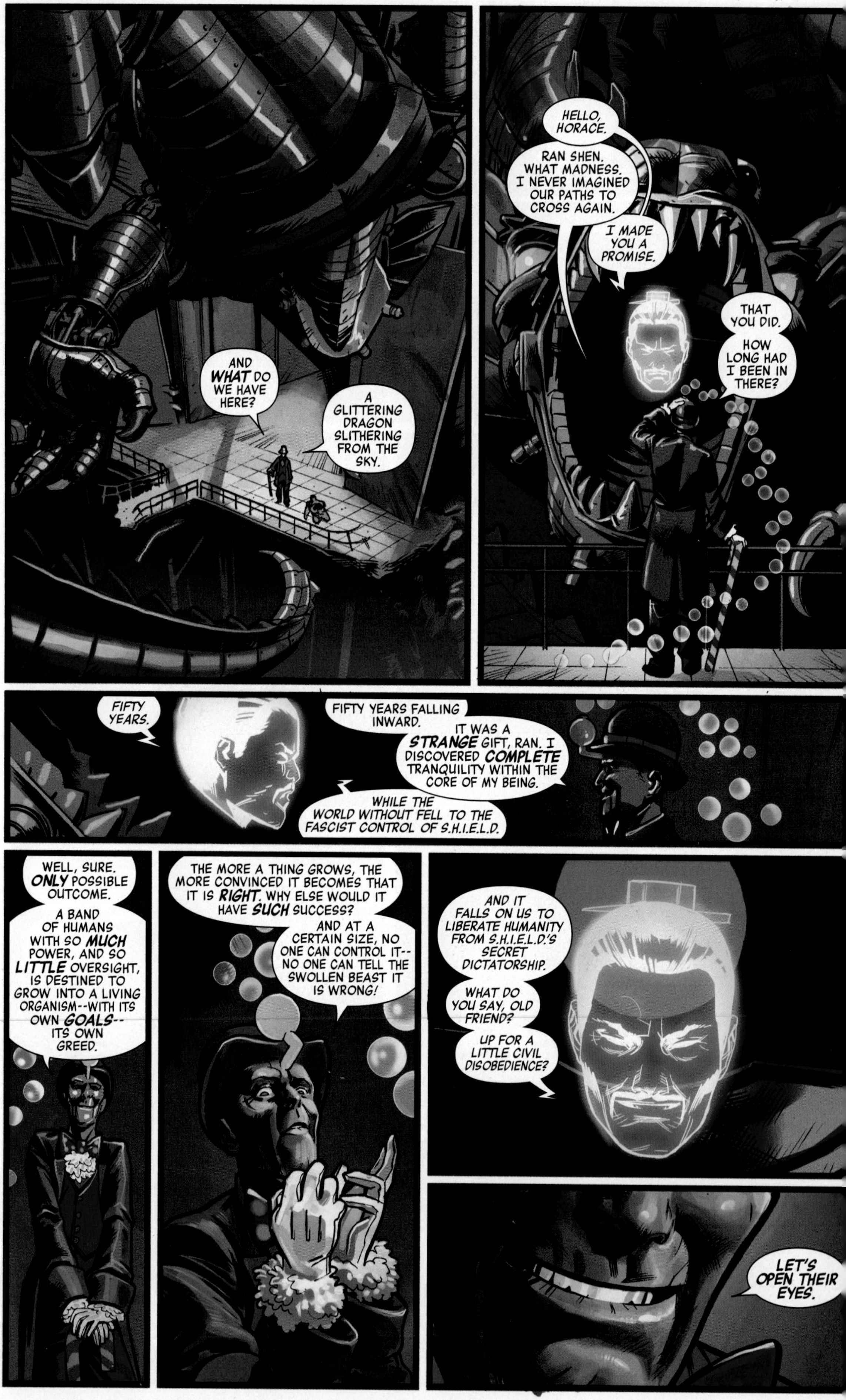
AND WHAT DO WE HAVE HERE?
A GLITTERING DRAGON SLITHERING FROM THE SKY.
HELLO, HORACE.
RAN SHEN. WHAT MADNESS. I NEVER IMAGINED OUR PATHS TO CROSS AGAIN.
I MADE YOU A PROMISE.
THAT YOU DID.
HOW LONG HAD I BEEN IN THERE?
FIFTY YEARS.
FIFTY YEARS FALLING INWARD.
IT WAS A STRANGE GIFT, RAN. I DISCOVERED COMPLETE TRANQUILITY WITHIN THE CORE OF MY BEING.
WHILE THE WORLD WITHOUT FELL TO THE FASCIST CONTROL OF S.H.I.E.L.D.
WELL, SURE. ONLY POSSIBLE OUTCOME.
A BAND OF HUMANS WITH SO MUCH POWER, AND SO LITTLE OVERSIGHT, IS DESTINED TO GROW INTO A LIVING ORGANISM--WITH ITS OWN GOALS-- ITS OWN GREED.
THE MORE A THING GROWS, THE MORE CONVINCED IT BECOMES THAT IT IS RIGHT. WHY ELSE WOULD IT HAVE SUCH SUCCESS?
AND AT A CERTAIN SIZE, NO ONE CAN CONTROL IT-- NO ONE CAN TELL THE SWOLLEN BEAST IT IS WRONG!
AND IT FALLS ON US TO LIBERATE HUMANITY FROM S.H.I.E.L.D.'S SECRET DICTATORSHIP.
WHAT DO YOU SAY, OLD FRIEND?
UP FOR A LITTLE CIVIL DISOBEDIENCE?
LET'S OPEN THEIR EYES.

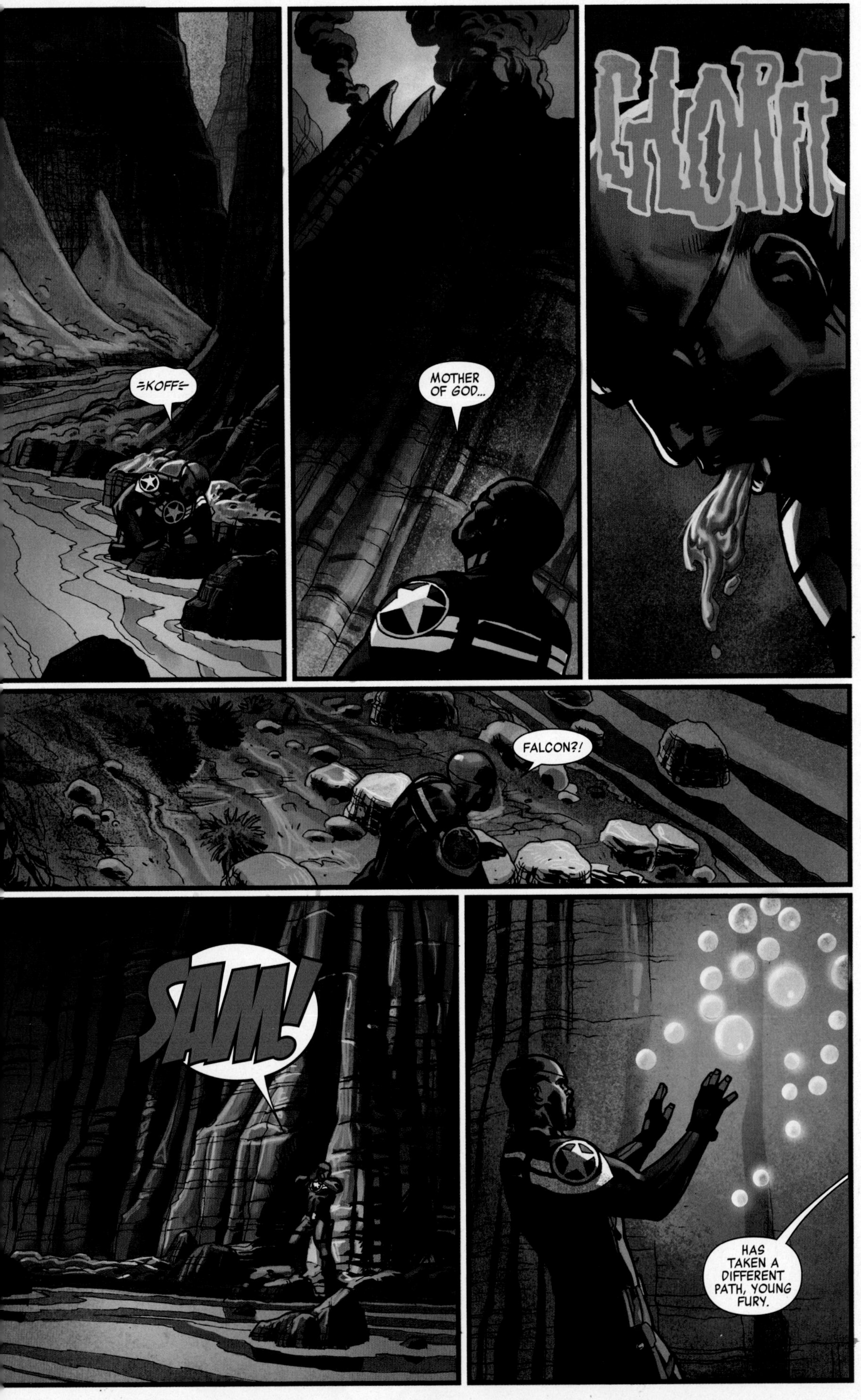

KOFF
MOTHER OF GOD...
GHORF
FALCON?!
SAM!
HAS TAKEN A DIFFERENT PATH, YOUNG FURY.

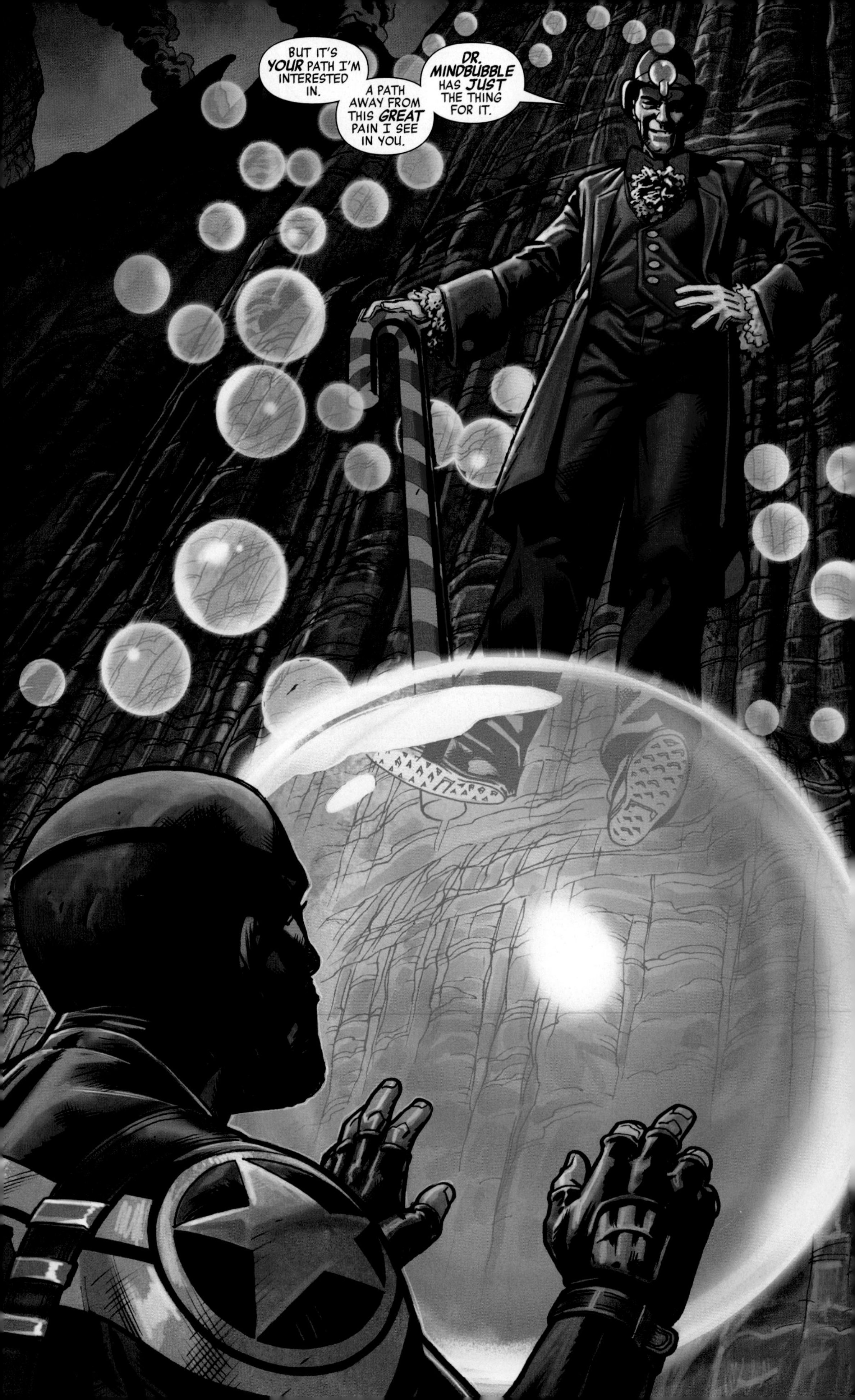
BUT IT'S YOUR PATH I'M INTERESTED IN.
A PATH AWAY FROM THIS GREAT PAIN I SEE IN YOU.
DR. MINDBUBBLE HAS JUST THE THING FOR IT.

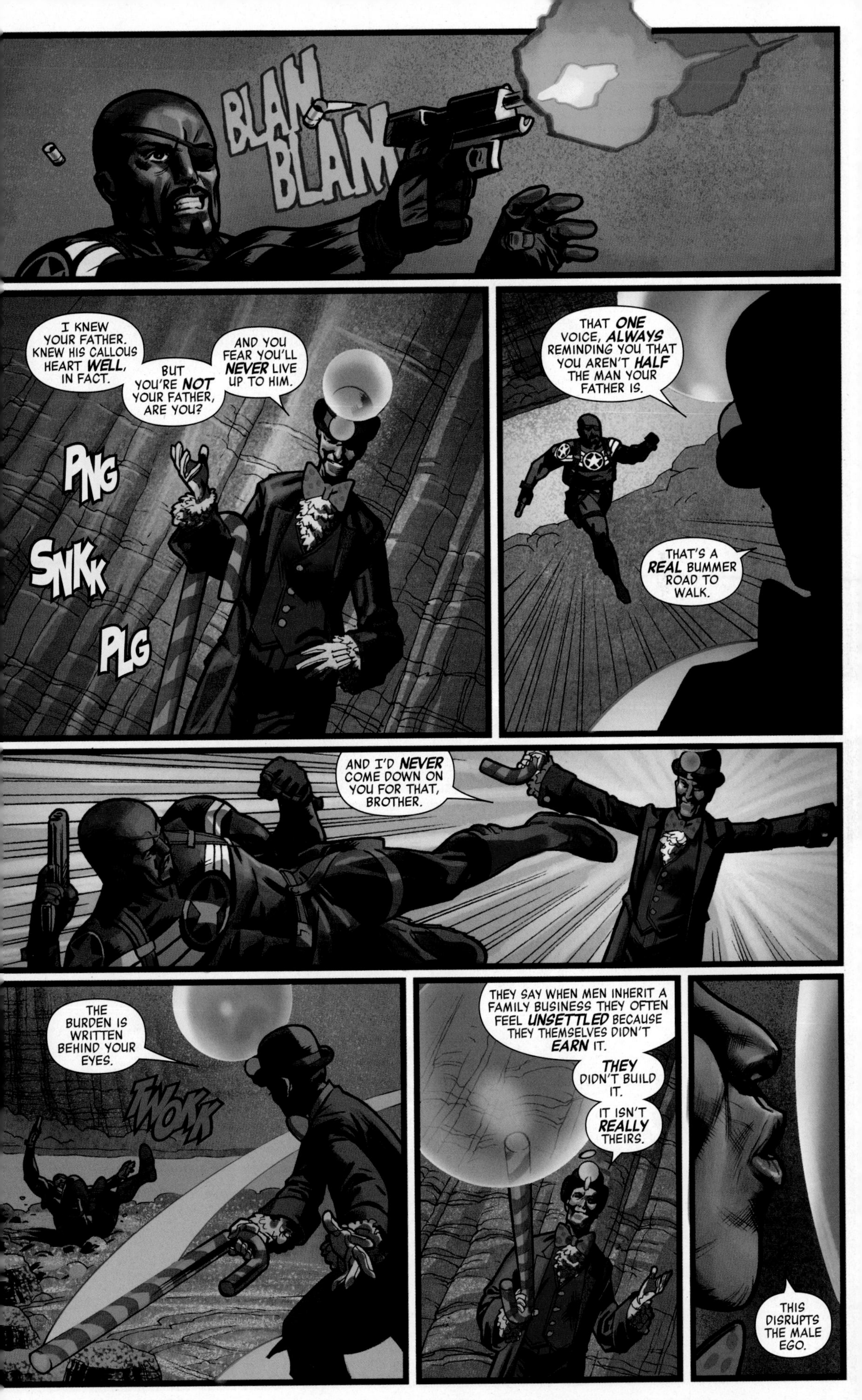
BLAM BLAM
I KNEW YOUR FATHER. KNEW HIS CALLOUS HEART WELL, IN FACT.
BUT YOU'RE NOT YOUR FATHER, ARE YOU?
AND YOU FEAR YOU'LL NEVER LIVE UP TO HIM.
PNG
SNKK
PLG
THAT ONE VOICE, ALWAYS REMINDING YOU THAT YOU AREN'T HALF THE MAN YOUR FATHER IS.
THAT'S A REAL BUMMER ROAD TO WALK.
AND I'D NEVER COME DOWN ON YOU FOR THAT, BROTHER.
THE BURDEN IS WRITTEN BEHIND YOUR EYES.
TWOKK
THEY SAY WHEN MEN INHERIT A FAMILY BUSINESS THEY OFTEN FEEL UNSETTLED BECAUSE THEY THEMSELVES DIDN'T EARN IT.
THEY DIDN'T BUILD IT.
IT ISN'T REALLY THEIRS.
THIS DISRUPTS THE MALE EGO.

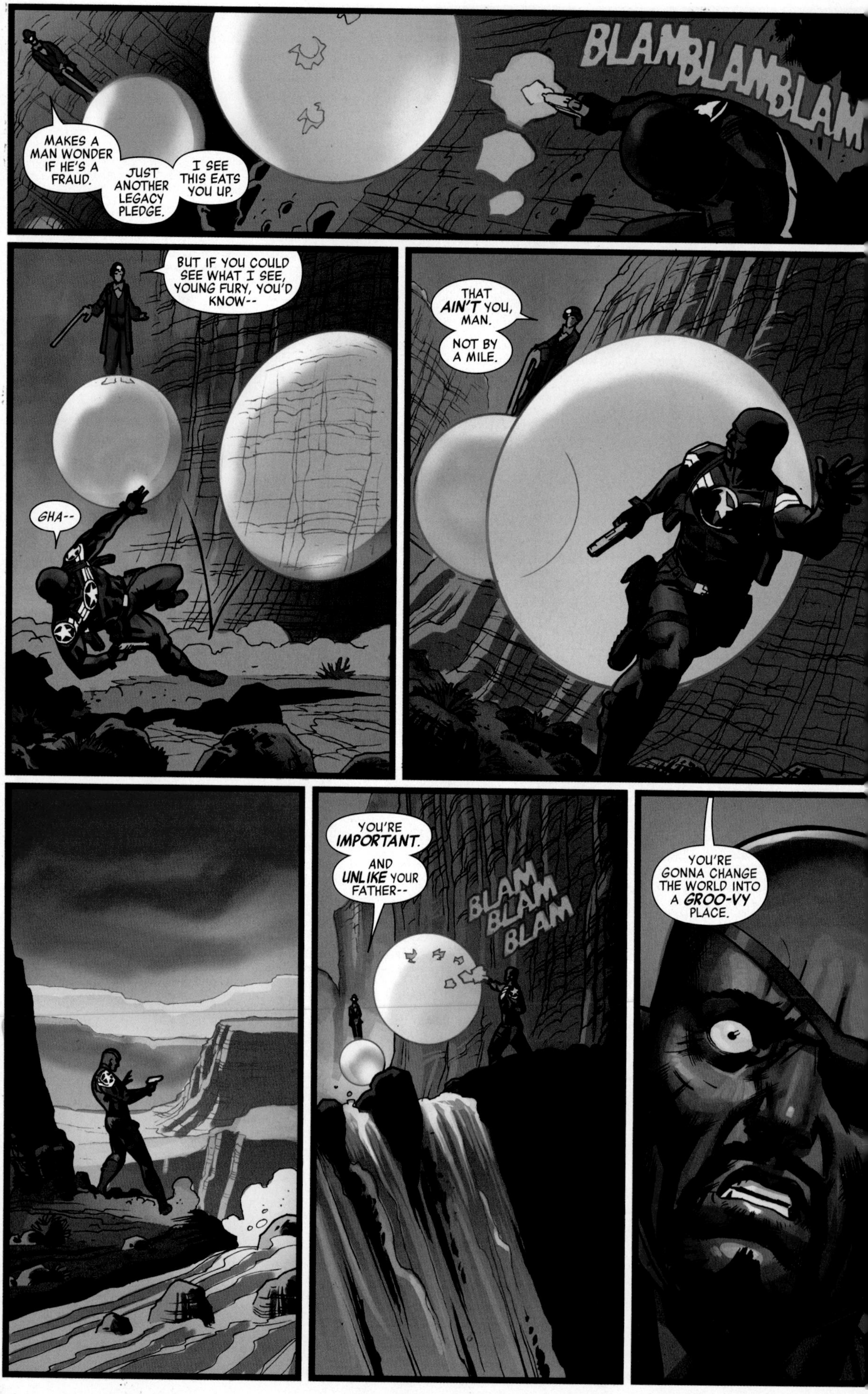
MAKES A MAN WONDER IF HE'S A FRAUD.
JUST ANOTHER LEGACY PLEDGE.
I SEE THIS EATS YOU UP.
BLAMBLAMBLAM
BUT IF YOU COULD SEE WHAT I SEE, YOUNG FURY, YOU'D KNOW--
GHA--
THAT AIN'T YOU, MAN.
NOT BY A MILE.
YOU'RE IMPORTANT.
AND UNLIKE YOUR FATHER--
BLAM BLAM BLAM
YOU'RE GONNA CHANGE THE WORLD INTO A GROO-VY PLACE.

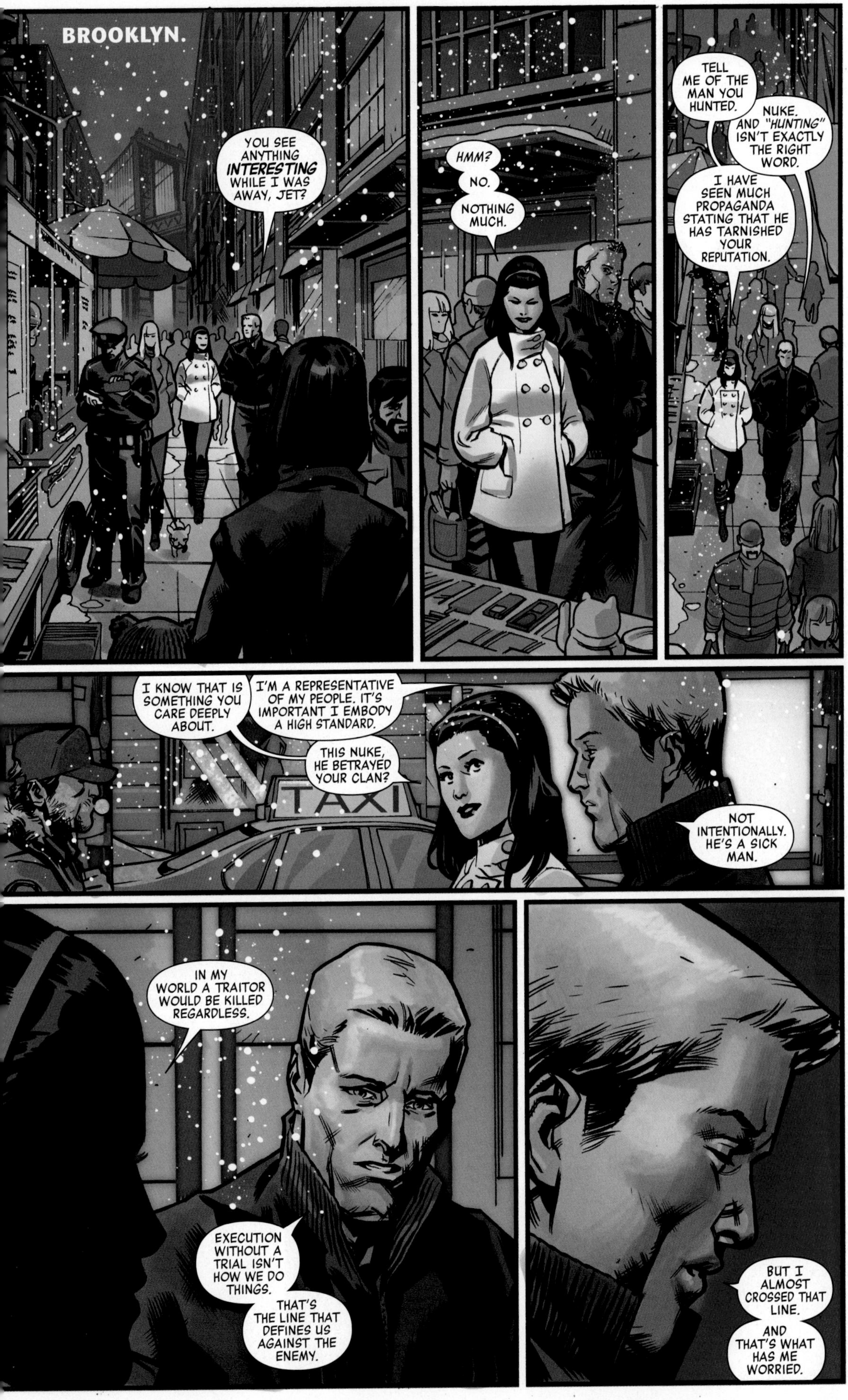
BROOKLYN.
YOU SEE ANYTHING INTERESTING WHILE I WAS AWAY, JET?
HMM?
NO.
NOTHING MUCH.
TELL ME OF THE MAN YOU HUNTED.
NUKE. AND "HUNTING" ISN'T EXACTLY THE RIGHT WORD.
I HAVE SEEN MUCH PROPAGANDA STATING THAT HE HAS TARNISHED YOUR REPUTATION.
I'M A REPRESENTATIVE OF MY PEOPLE. IT'S IMPORTANT I EMBODY A HIGH STANDARD.
I KNOW THAT IS SOMETHING YOU CARE DEEPLY ABOUT.
THIS NUKE, HE BETRAYED YOUR CLAN?
TAXI
NOT INTENTIONALLY. HE'S A SICK MAN.
IN MY WORLD A TRAITOR WOULD BE KILLED REGARDLESS.
EXECUTION WITHOUT A TRIAL ISN'T HOW WE DO THINGS.
THAT'S THE LINE THAT DEFINES US AGAINST THE ENEMY.
BUT I ALMOST CROSSED THAT LINE.
AND THAT'S WHAT HAS ME WORRIED.

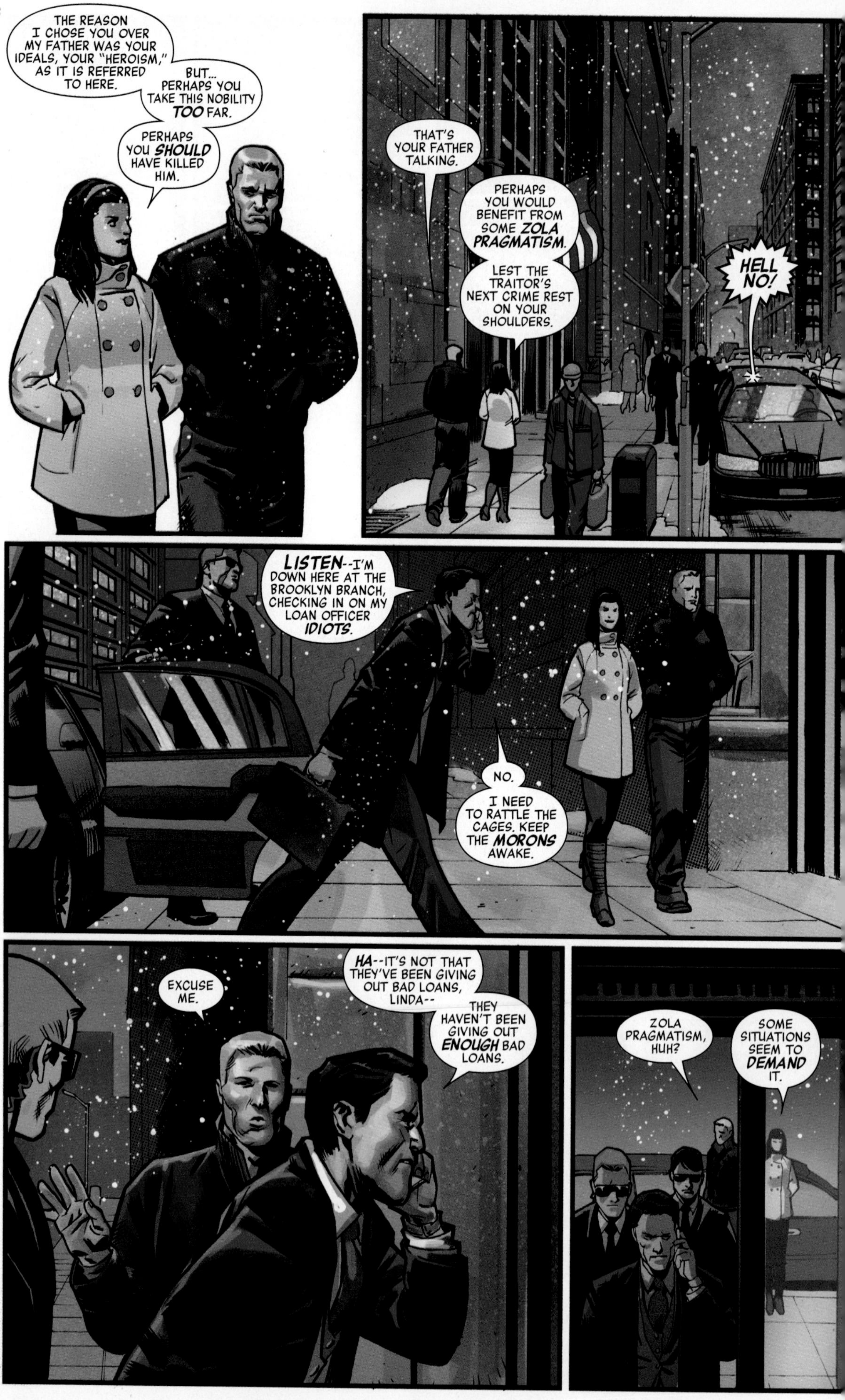
THE REASON I CHOSE YOU OVER MY FATHER WAS YOUR IDEALS, YOUR "HEROISM," AS IT IS REFERRED TO HERE.
BUT... PERHAPS YOU TAKE THIS NOBILITY TOO FAR.
PERHAPS YOU SHOULD HAVE KILLED HIM.
THAT'S YOUR FATHER TALKING.
PERHAPS YOU WOULD BENEFIT FROM SOME ZOLA PRAGMATISM.
LEST THE TRAITOR'S NEXT CRIME REST ON YOUR SHOULDERS.
HELL NO!
LISTEN--I'M DOWN HERE AT THE BROOKLYN BRANCH, CHECKING IN ON MY LOAN OFFICER IDIOTS.
NO.
I NEED TO RATTLE THE CAGES. KEEP THE MORONS AWAKE.
EXCUSE ME.
HA--IT'S NOT THAT THEY'VE BEEN GIVING OUT BAD LOANS, LINDA--
THEY HAVEN'T BEEN GIVING OUT ENOUGH BAD LOANS.
ZOLA PRAGMATISM, HUH?
SOME SITUATIONS SEEM TO DEMAND IT.

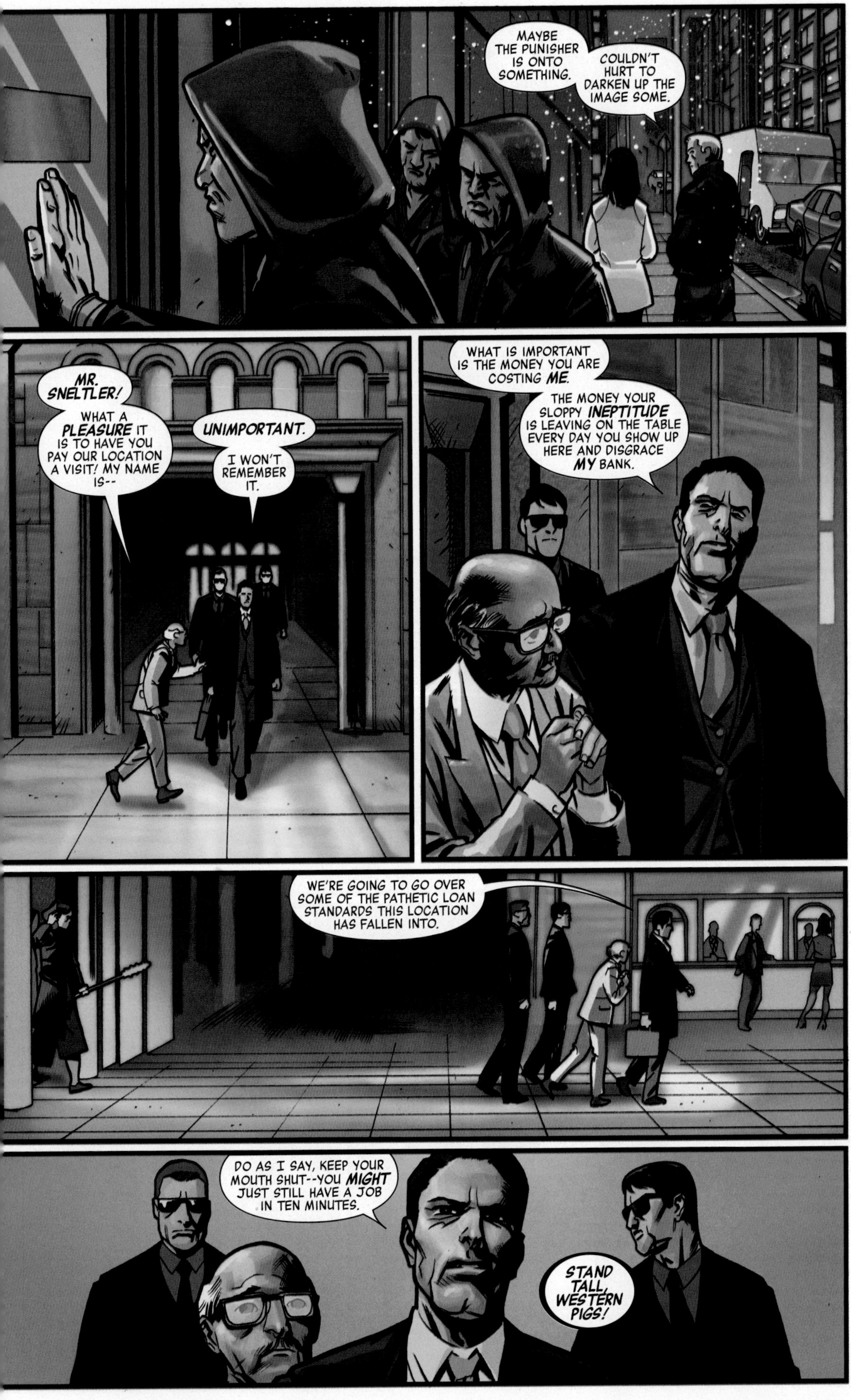
MAYBE THE PUNISHER IS ONTO SOMETHING.
COULDN'T HURT TO DARKEN UP THE IMAGE SOME.
MR. SNELTLER!
WHAT A PLEASURE IT IS TO HAVE YOU PAY OUR LOCATION A VISIT! MY NAME IS--
UNIMPORTANT.
I WON'T REMEMBER IT.
WHAT IS IMPORTANT IS THE MONEY YOU ARE COSTING ME.
THE MONEY YOUR SLOPPY INEPTITUDE IS LEAVING ON THE TABLE EVERY DAY YOU SHOW UP HERE AND DISGRACE MY BANK.
WE'RE GOING TO GO OVER SOME OF THE PATHETIC LOAN STANDARDS THIS LOCATION HAS FALLEN INTO.
DO AS I SAY, KEEP YOUR MOUTH SHUT--YOU MIGHT JUST STILL HAVE A JOB IN TEN MINUTES.
STAND TALL, WESTERN PIGS!

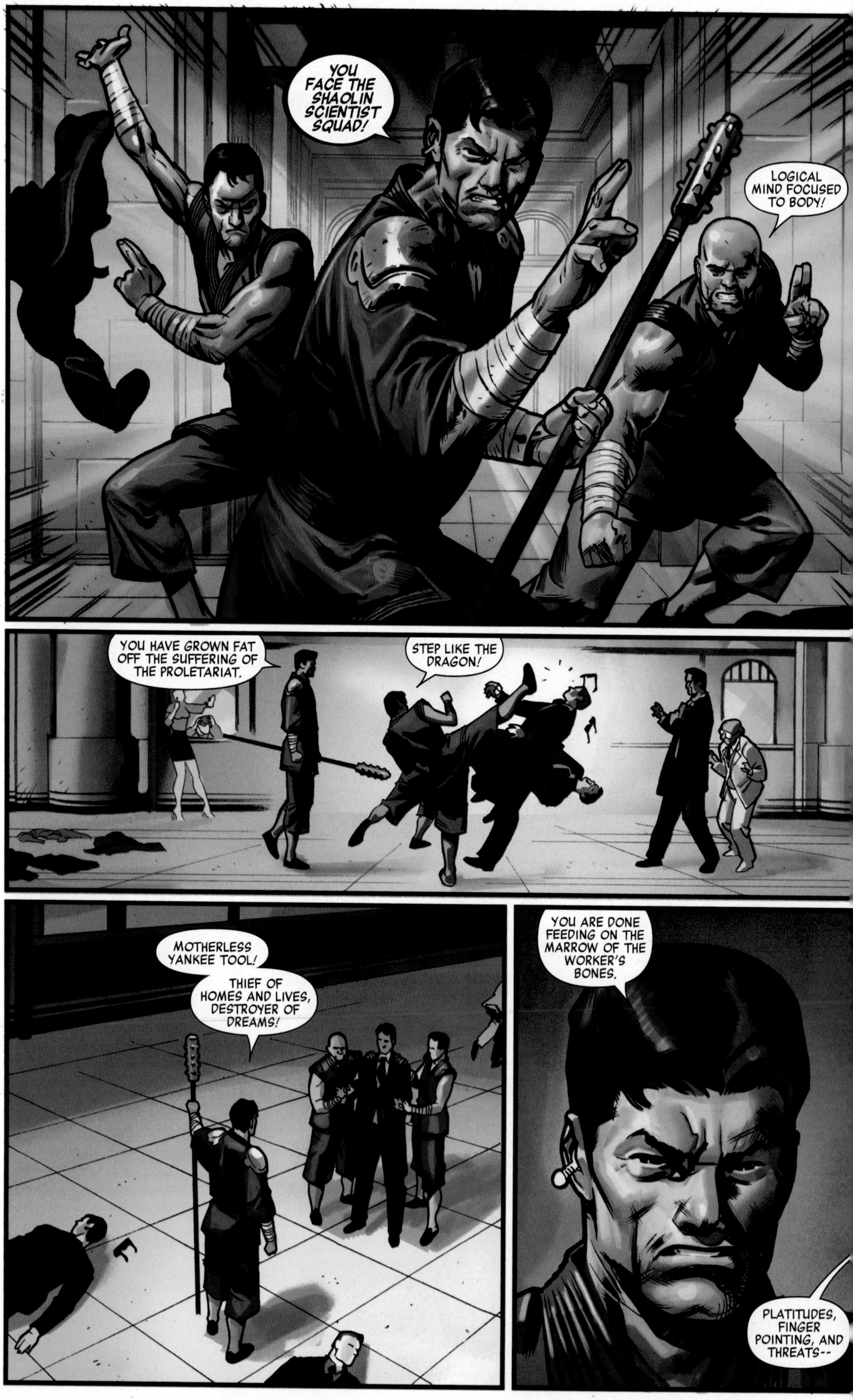
YOU FACE THE SHAOLIN SCIENTIST SQUAD!
LOGICAL MIND FOCUSED TO BODY!
YOU HAVE GROWN FAT OFF THE SUFFERING OF THE PROLETARIAT.
STEP LIKE THE DRAGON!
MOTHERLESS YANKEE TOOL!
THIEF OF HOMES AND LIVES, DESTROYER OF DREAMS!
YOU ARE DONE FEEDING ON THE MARROW OF THE WORKER'S BONES.
PLATITUDES, FINGER POINTING, AND THREATS--

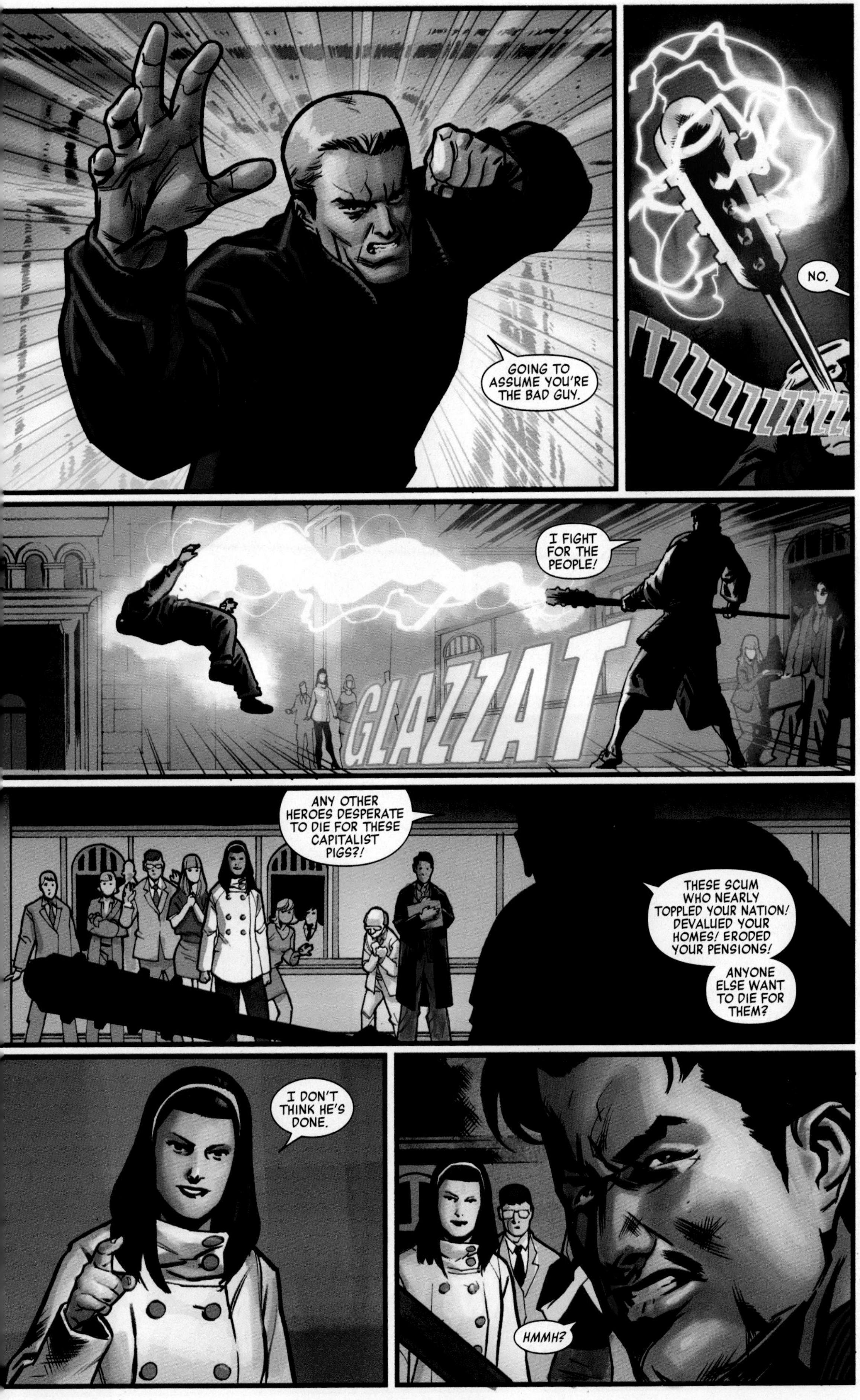

GOING TO ASSUME YOU'RE THE BAD GUY.
NO.
TZZZZZZZZZZZ
I FIGHT FOR THE PEOPLE!
GLAZZAT
ANY OTHER HEROES DESPERATE TO DIE FOR THESE CAPITALIST PIGS?!
THESE SCUM WHO NEARLY TOPPLED YOUR NATION! DEVALUED YOUR HOMES! ERODED YOUR PENSIONS!
ANYONE ELSE WANT TO DIE FOR THEM?
I DON'T THINK HE'S DONE.
HMMH?

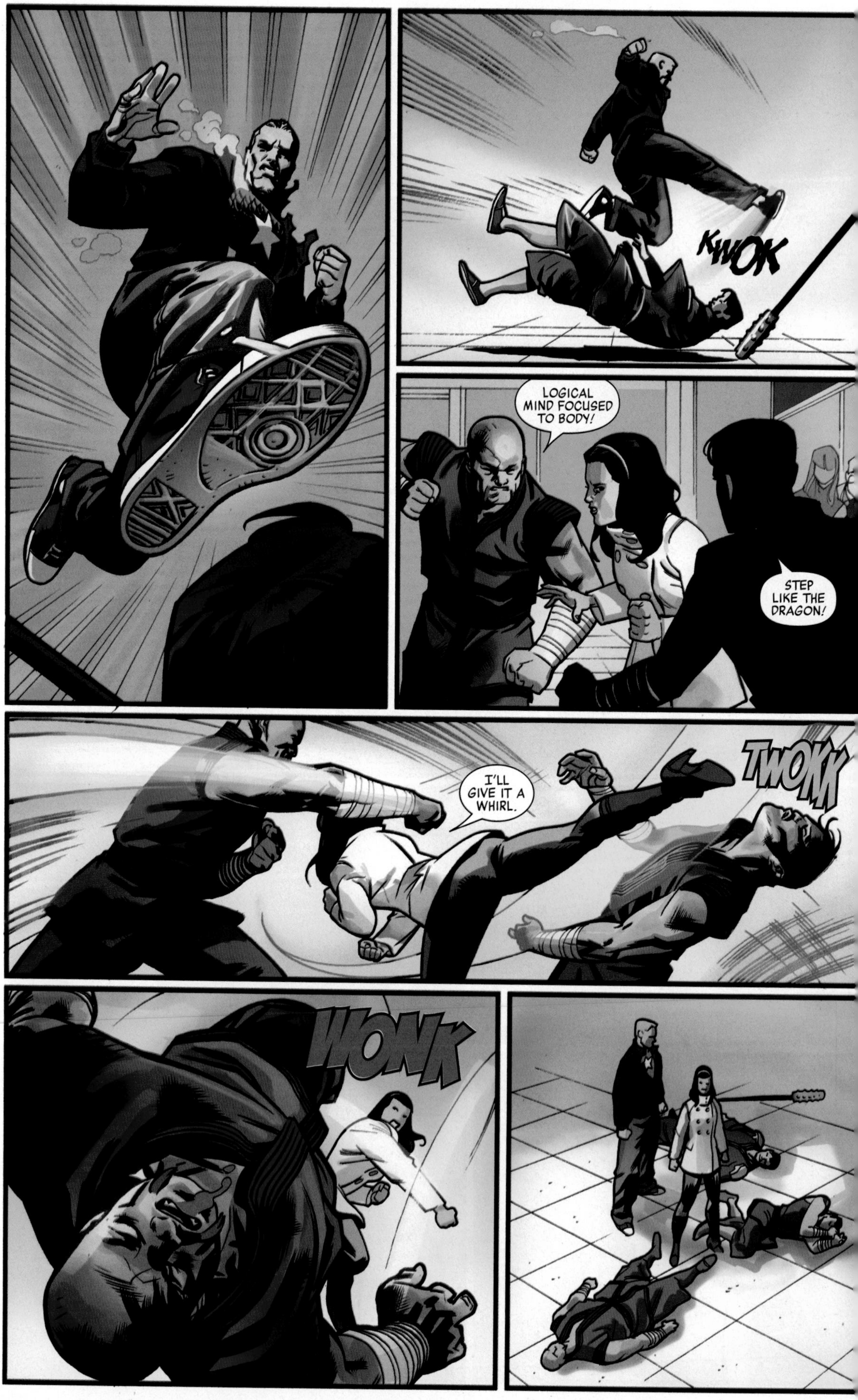

KWOK
LOGICAL MIND FOCUSED TO BODY!
STEP LIKE THE DRAGON!
I'LL GIVE IT A WHIRL.
TWOKK
WONK

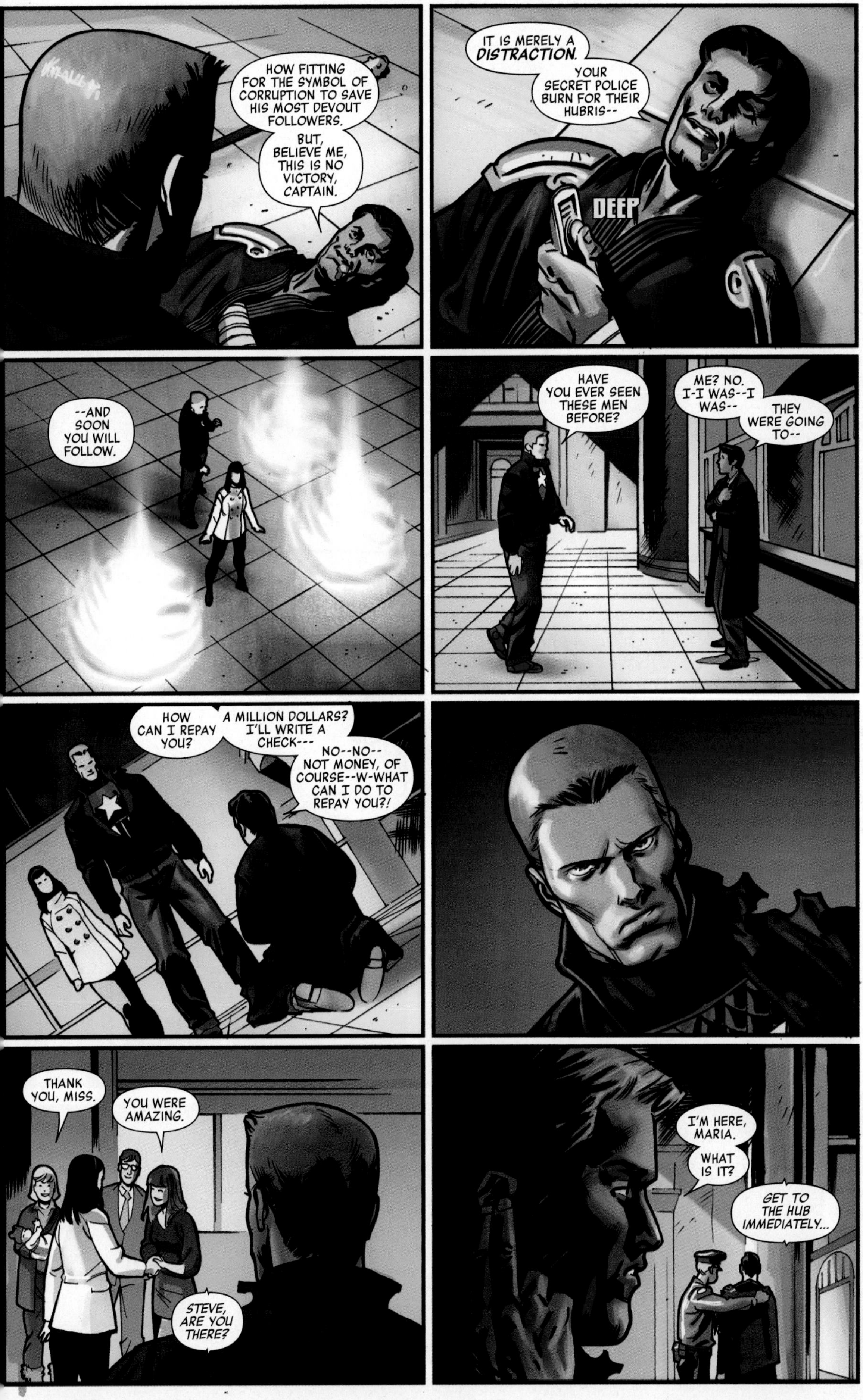
HOW FITTING FOR THE SYMBOL OF CORRUPTION TO SAVE HIS MOST DEVOUT FOLLOWERS.
BUT, BELIEVE ME, THIS IS NO VICTORY, CAPTAIN.
IT IS MERELY A DISTRACTION.
YOUR SECRET POLICE BURN FOR THEIR HUBRIS--
DEEP
--AND SOON YOU WILL FOLLOW.
HAVE YOU EVER SEEN THESE MEN BEFORE?
ME? NO. I-I WAS--I WAS--
THEY WERE GOING TO--
HOW CAN I REPAY YOU?
A MILLION DOLLARS? I'LL WRITE A CHECK---
NO--NO--NOT MONEY, OF COURSE--W-WHAT CAN I DO TO REPAY YOU?!
THANK YOU, MISS.
YOU WERE AMAZING.
STEVE, ARE YOU THERE?
I'M HERE, MARIA.
WHAT IS IT?
GET TO THE HUB IMMEDIATELY...

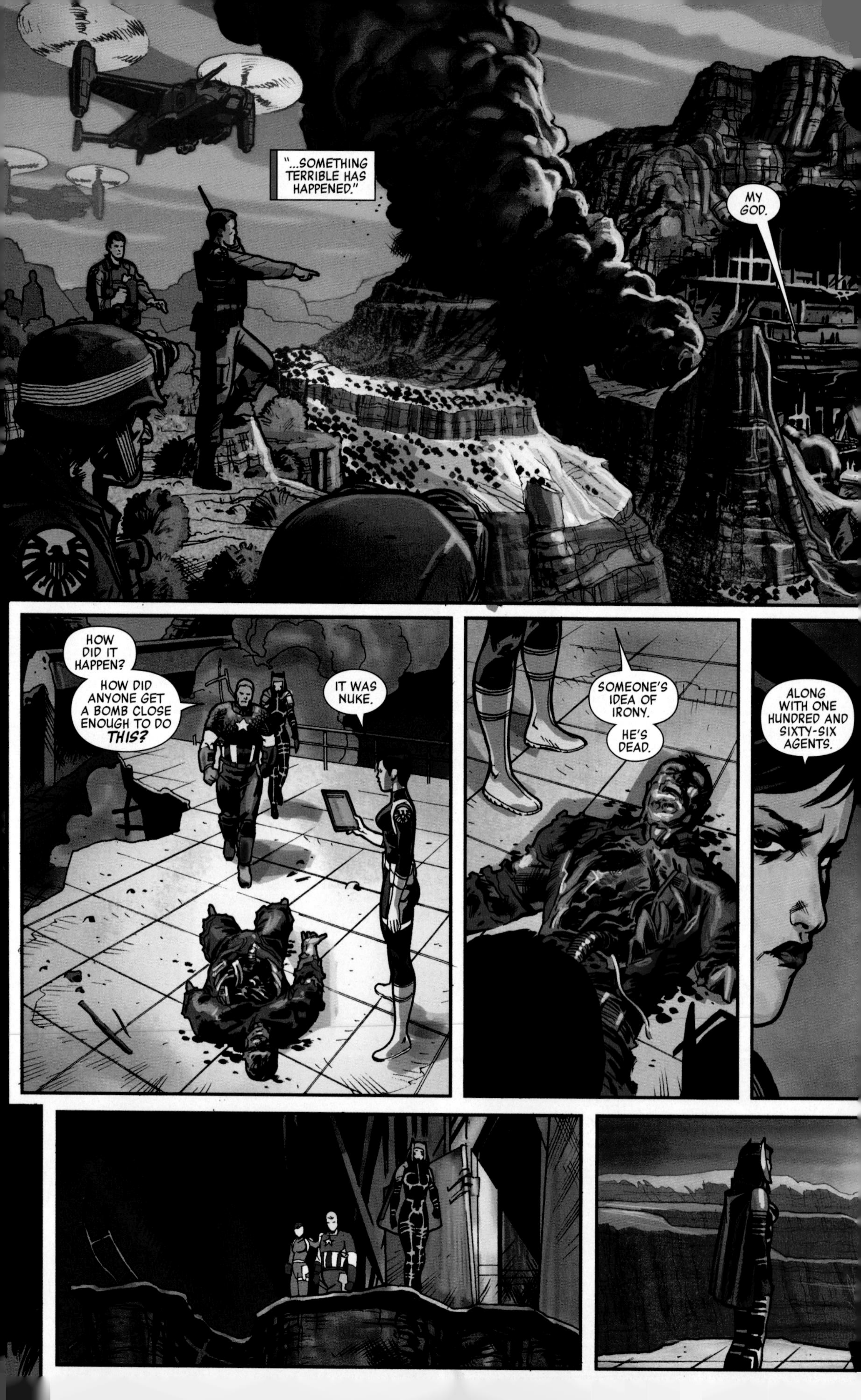
"...SOMETHING TERRIBLE HAS HAPPENED."
MY GOD.
HOW DID IT HAPPEN?
HOW DID ANYONE GET A BOMB CLOSE ENOUGH TO DO **THIS?**
IT WAS NUKE.
SOMEONE'S IDEA OF IRONY.
HE'S DEAD.
ALONG WITH ONE HUNDRED AND SIXTY-SIX AGENTS.

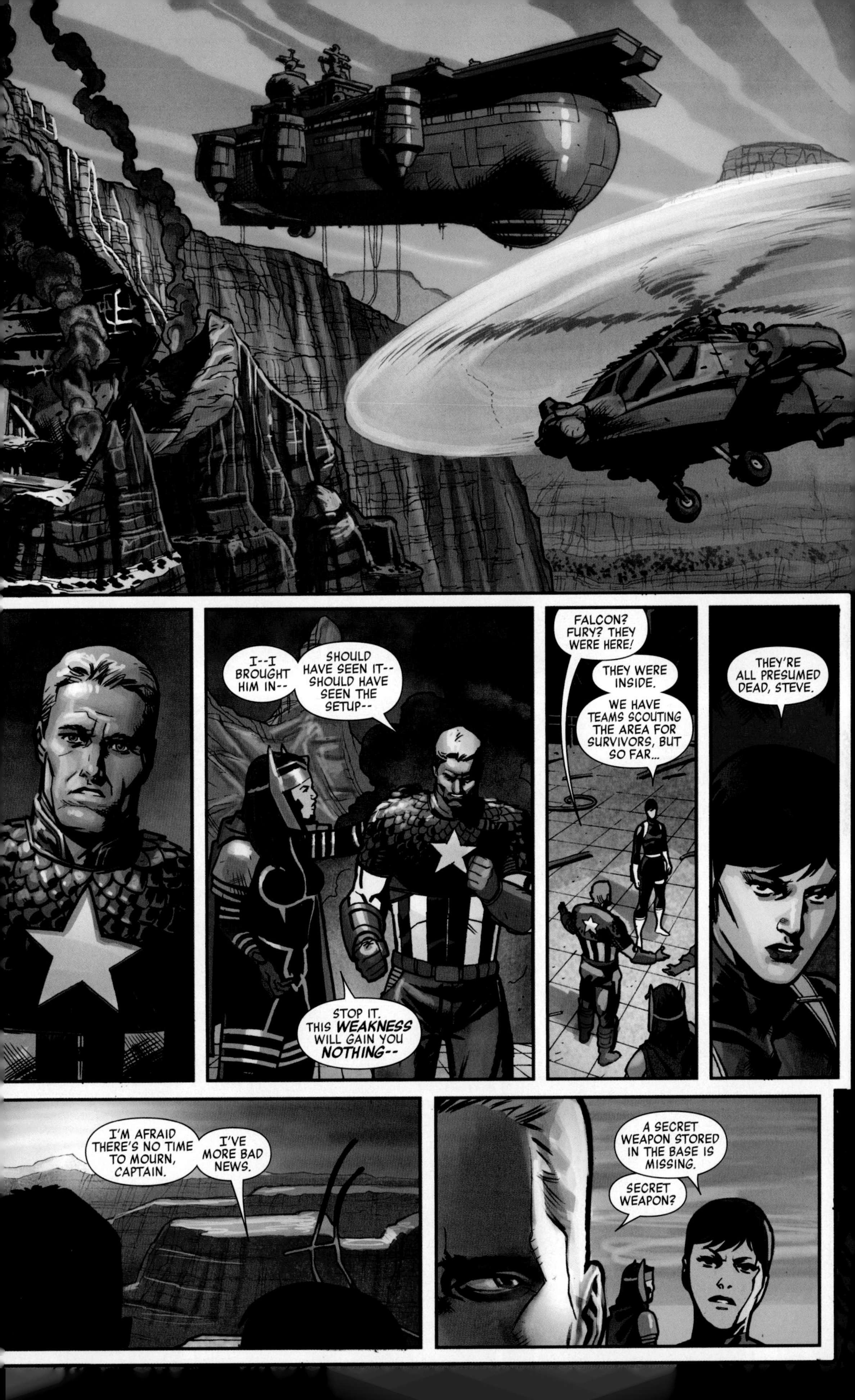
I--I BROUGHT HIM IN--
SHOULD HAVE SEEN IT-- SHOULD HAVE SEEN THE SETUP--
STOP IT. THIS WEAKNESS WILL GAIN YOU NOTHING--
FALCON? FURY? THEY WERE HERE!
THEY WERE INSIDE.
WE HAVE TEAMS SCOUTING THE AREA FOR SURVIVORS, BUT SO FAR...
THEY'RE ALL PRESUMED DEAD, STEVE.
I'M AFRAID THERE'S NO TIME TO MOURN, CAPTAIN.
I'VE MORE BAD NEWS.
A SECRET WEAPON STORED IN THE BASE IS MISSING.
SECRET WEAPON?

WEAPON MINUS IS FREE.

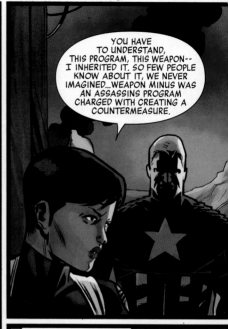

YOU HAVE TO UNDERSTAND, THIS PROGRAM, THIS WEAPON-- I INHERITED IT. SO FEW PEOPLE KNOW ABOUT IT, WE NEVER IMAGINED...WEAPON MINUS WAS AN ASSASSINS PROGRAM CHARGED WITH CREATING A COUNTERMEASURE.

A COUNTERMEASURE TO *WHAT*, MARIA?

YOU, STEVE.

YOU AND NUKE AND WOLVERINE AND EVERY PROJECT OF THE WEAPON PLUS PROGRAM.

YOUR FRIEND ISN'T DEAD.

WHAT?

THE FALCON.

HE LIES TWO MILES DOWNSTREAM, WITH A SEVERE CONCUSSION.

IF YOU HURRY HE CAN BE SAVED.

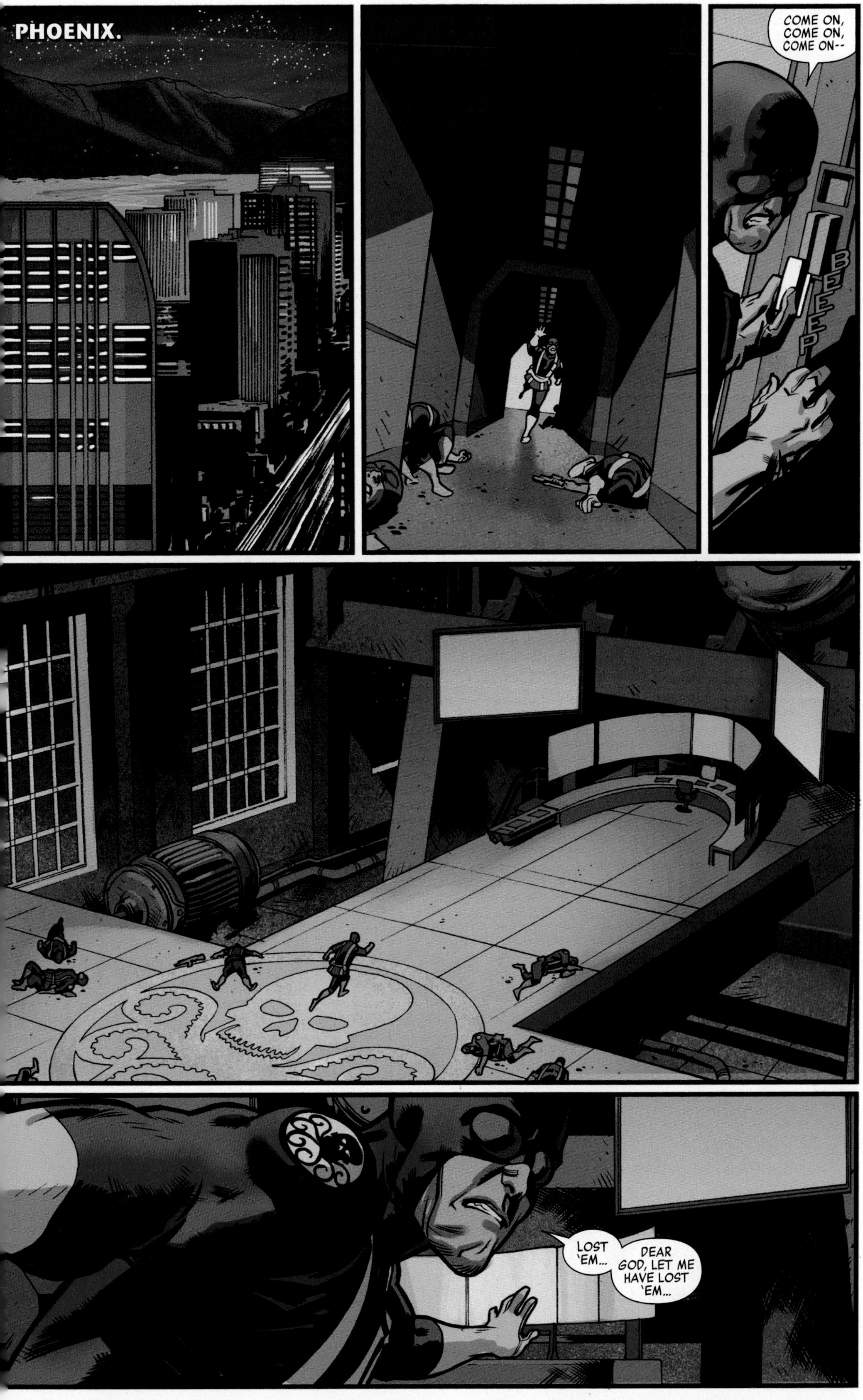
PHOENIX.
COME ON, COME ON, COME ON--
BEEEP
LOST 'EM...
DEAR GOD, LET ME HAVE LOST 'EM...

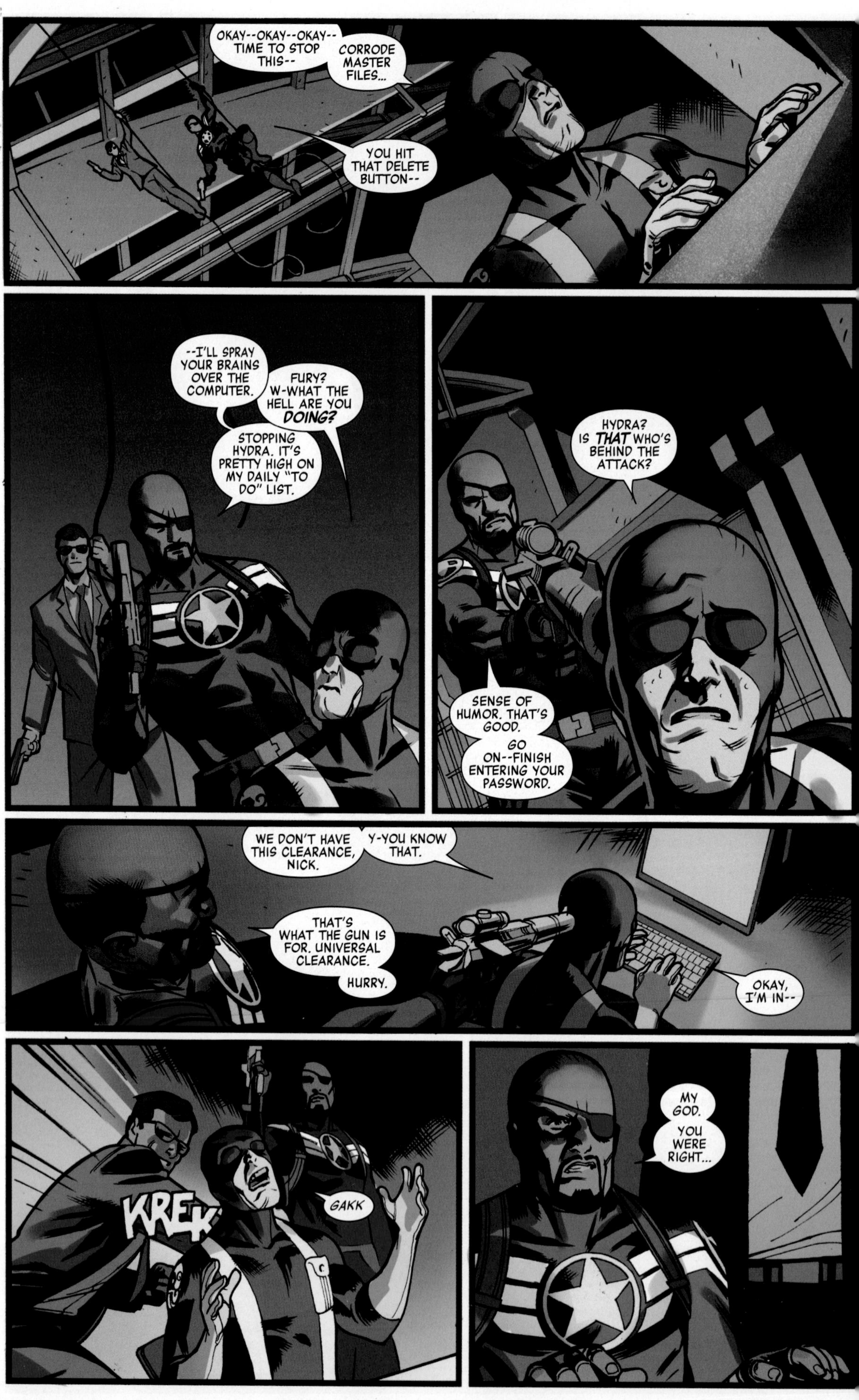
OKAY--OKAY--OKAY--
TIME TO STOP
THIS--
CORRODE
MASTER
FILES...
YOU HIT
THAT DELETE
BUTTON--
--I'LL SPRAY
YOUR BRAINS
OVER THE
COMPUTER.
FURY?
W-WHAT THE
HELL ARE YOU
DOING?
STOPPING
HYDRA. IT'S
PRETTY HIGH ON
MY DAILY "TO
DO" LIST.
HYDRA?
IS THAT WHO'S
BEHIND THE
ATTACK?
SENSE OF
HUMOR. THAT'S
GOOD.
GO
ON--FINISH
ENTERING YOUR
PASSWORD.
WE DON'T HAVE
THIS CLEARANCE,
NICK.
Y-YOU KNOW
THAT.
THAT'S
WHAT THE GUN IS
FOR. UNIVERSAL
CLEARANCE.
HURRY.
OKAY,
I'M IN--
KREK
GAKK
MY
GOD.
YOU
WERE
RIGHT...

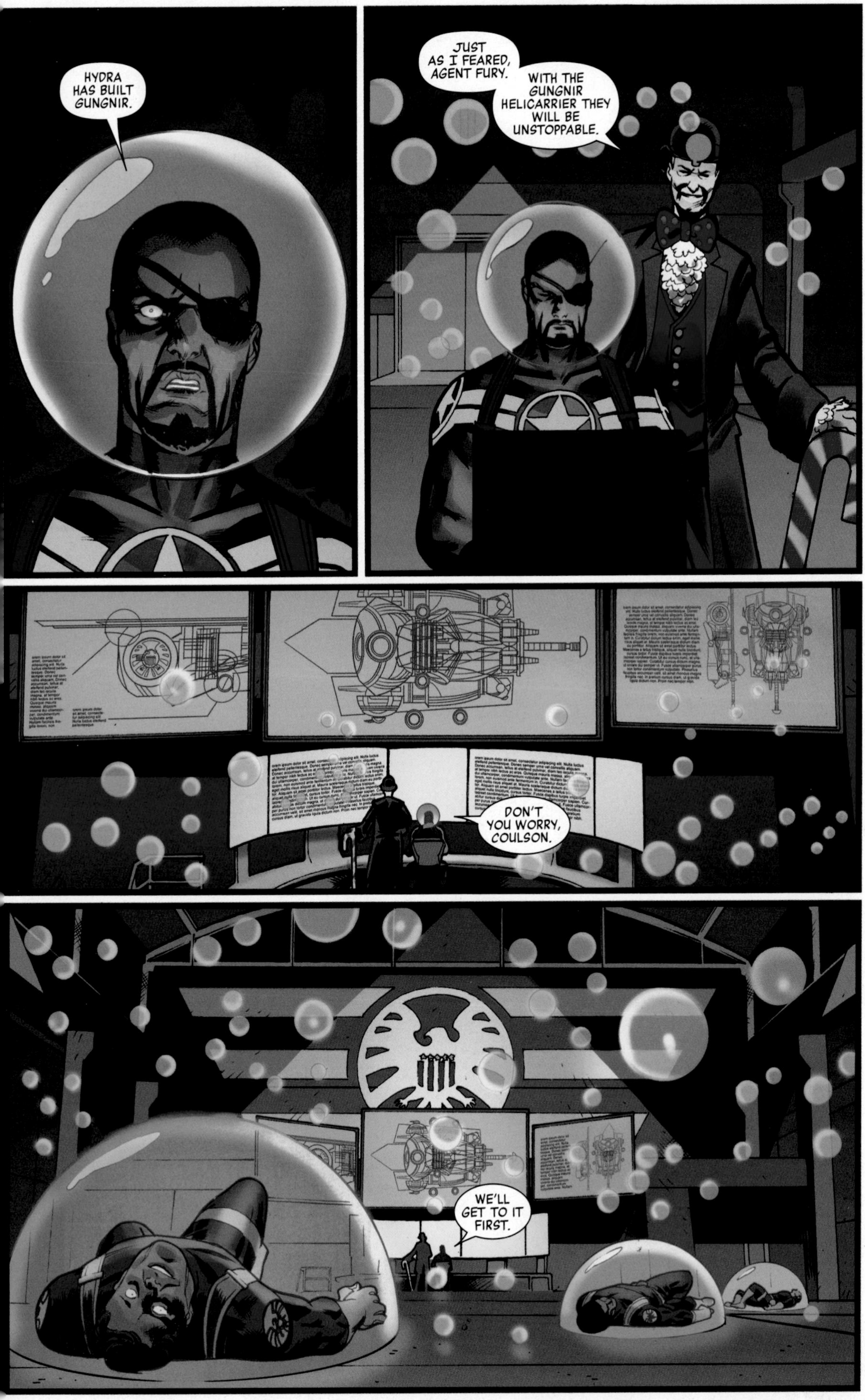
HYDRA HAS BUILT GUNGNIR.
JUST AS I FEARED, AGENT FURY.
WITH THE GUNGNIR HELICARRIER THEY WILL BE UNSTOPPABLE.
DON'T YOU WORRY, COULSON.
WE'LL GET TO IT FIRST.

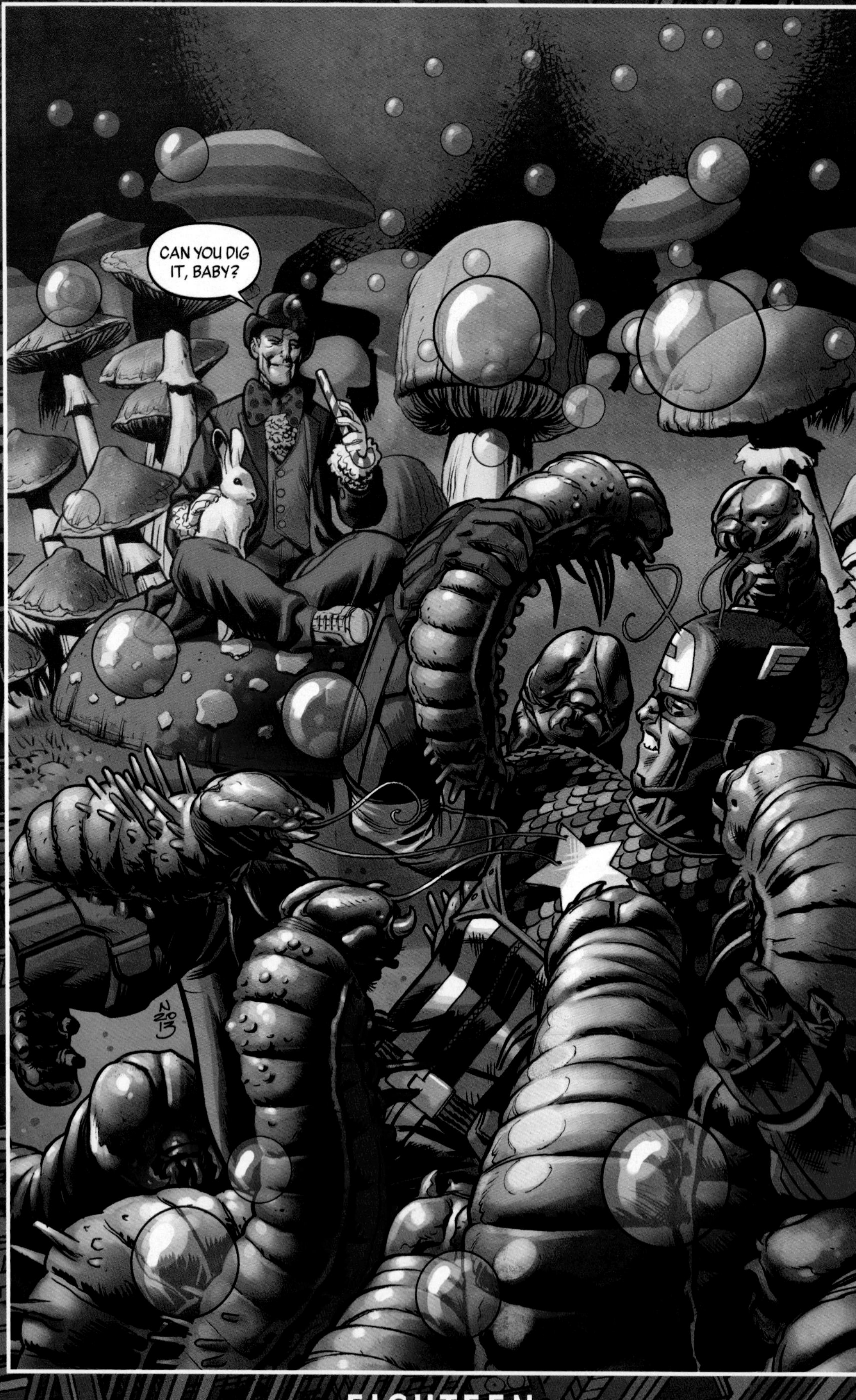
CAN YOU DIG IT, BABY?

EIGHTEEN

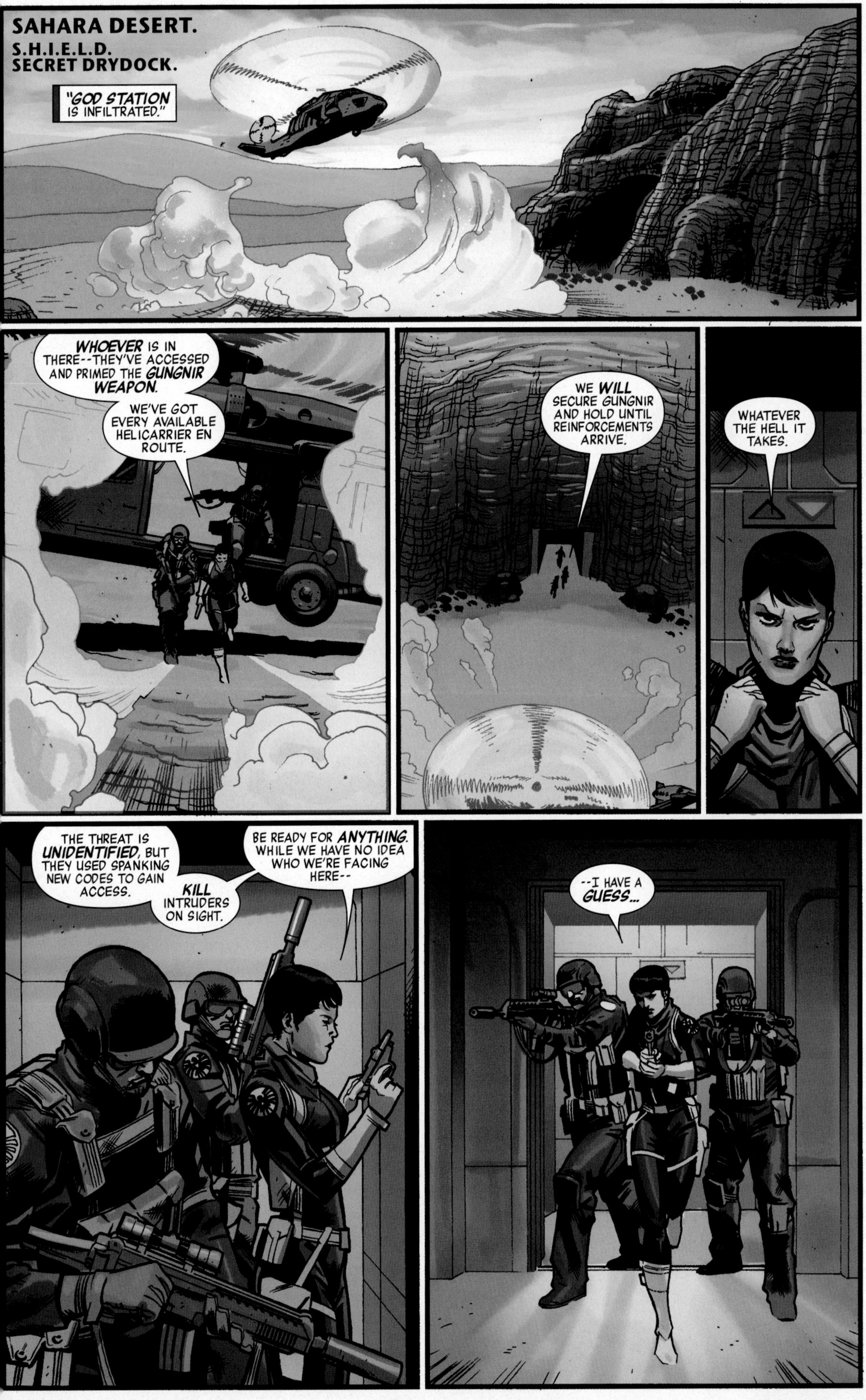
SAHARA DESERT.
S.H.I.E.L.D. SECRET DRYDOCK.
"GOD STATION IS INFILTRATED."
WHOEVER IS IN THERE--THEY'VE ACCESSED AND PRIMED THE GUNGNIR WEAPON.
WE'VE GOT EVERY AVAILABLE HELICARRIER EN ROUTE.
WE WILL SECURE GUNGNIR AND HOLD UNTIL REINFORCEMENTS ARRIVE.
WHATEVER THE HELL IT TAKES.
THE THREAT IS UNIDENTIFIED, BUT THEY USED SPANKING NEW CODES TO GAIN ACCESS.
KILL INTRUDERS ON SIGHT.
BE READY FOR ANYTHING. WHILE WE HAVE NO IDEA WHO WE'RE FACING HERE--
--I HAVE A GUESS...

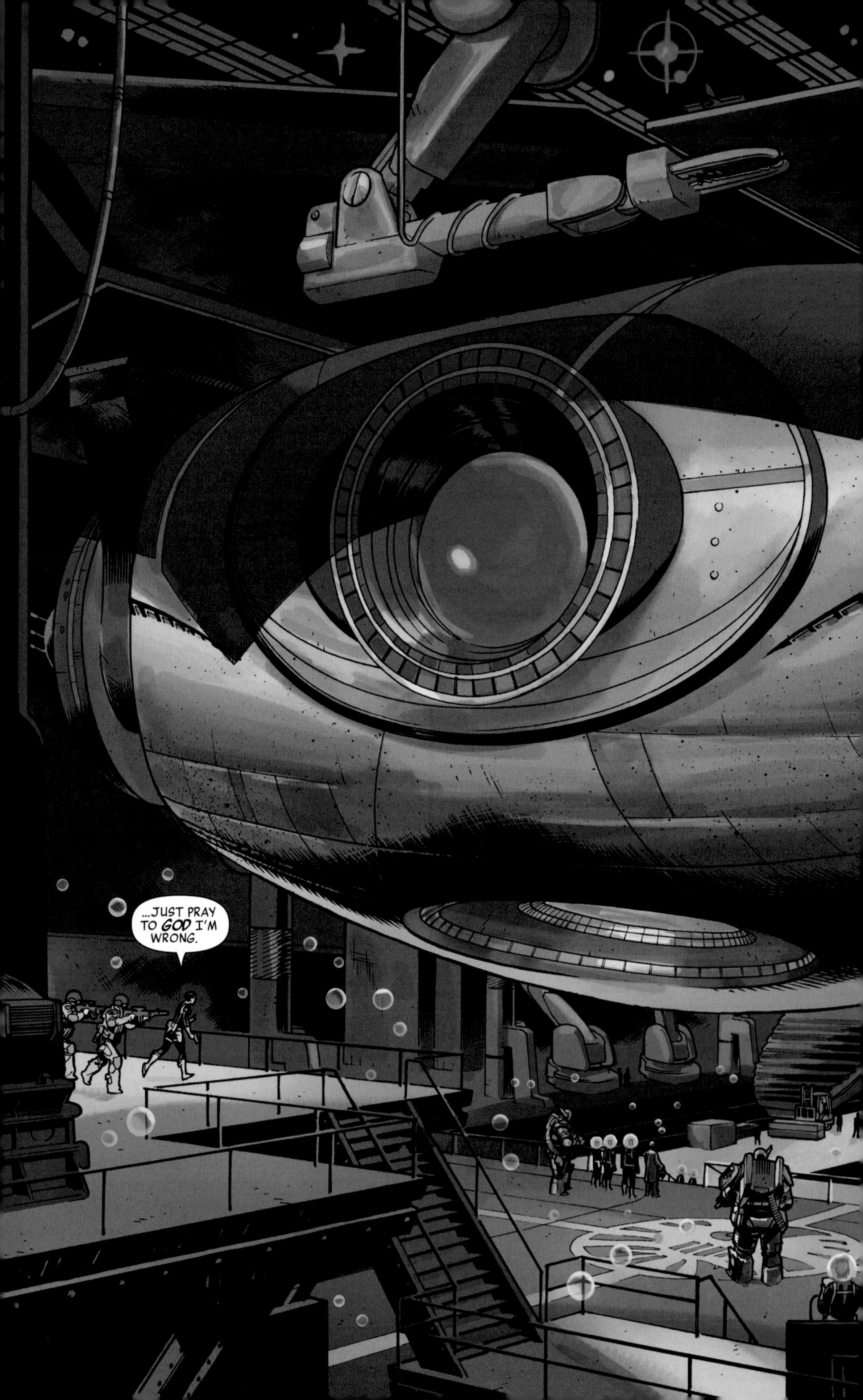
...JUST PRAY TO GOD I'M WRONG.

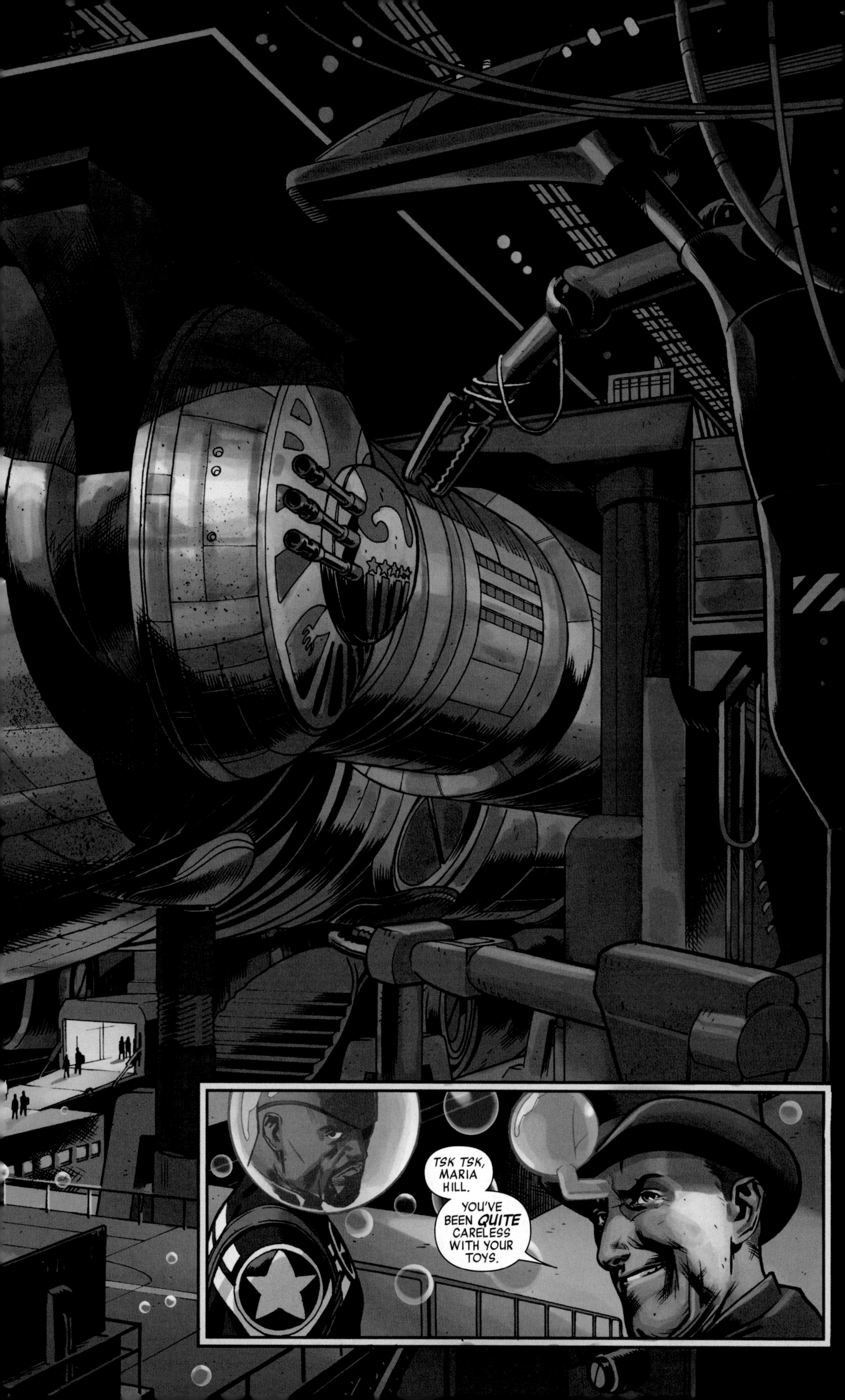
TSK TSK, MARIA HILL.
YOU'VE BEEN QUITE CARELESS WITH YOUR TOYS.

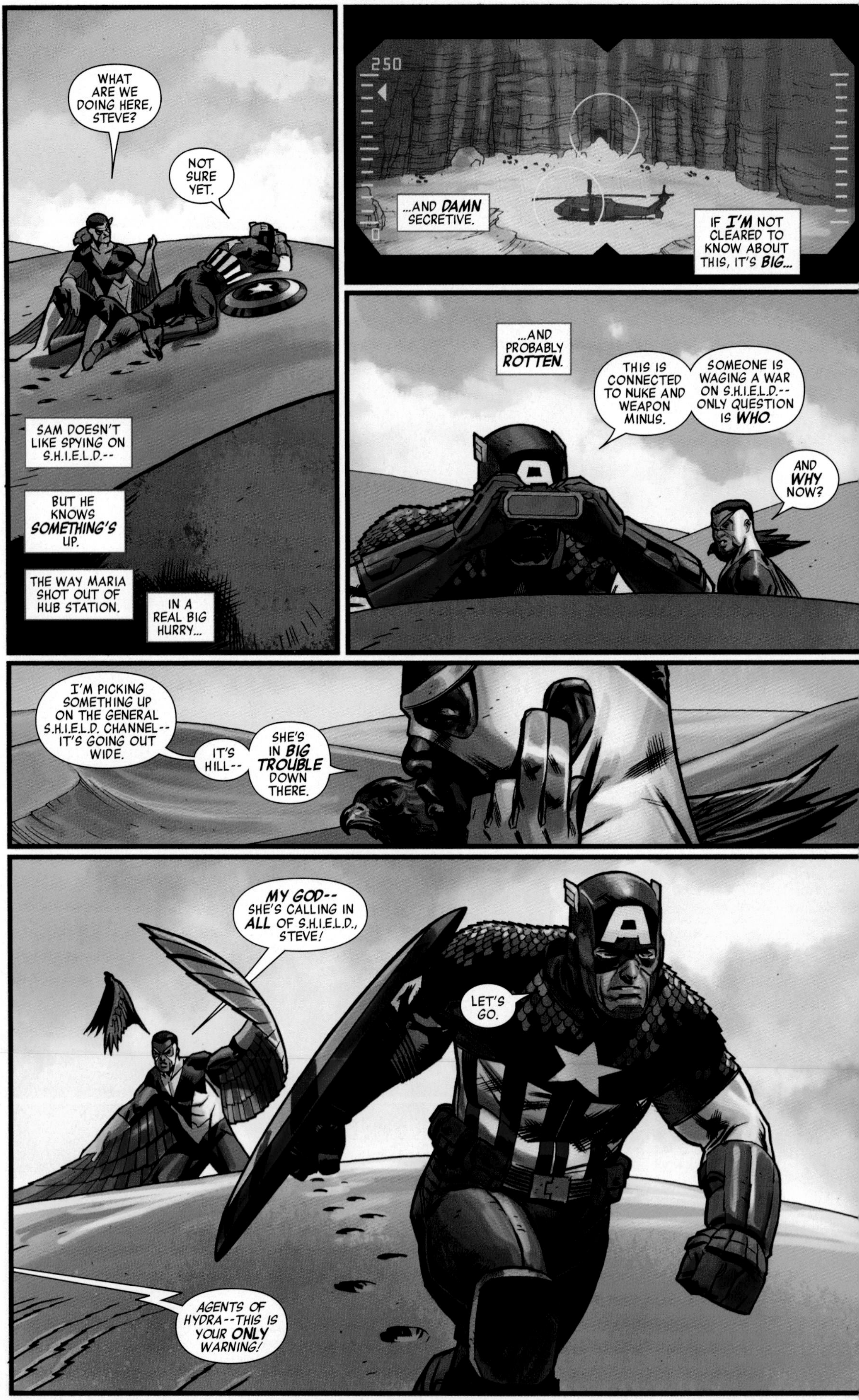

WHAT ARE WE DOING HERE, STEVE?
NOT SURE YET.
SAM DOESN'T LIKE SPYING ON S.H.I.E.L.D.--
BUT HE KNOWS SOMETHING'S UP.
THE WAY MARIA SHOT OUT OF HUB STATION.
IN A REAL BIG HURRY...
250
...AND DAMN SECRETIVE.
IF I'M NOT CLEARED TO KNOW ABOUT THIS, IT'S BIG...
...AND PROBABLY ROTTEN.
THIS IS CONNECTED TO NUKE AND WEAPON MINUS.
SOMEONE IS WAGING A WAR ON S.H.I.E.L.D.-- ONLY QUESTION IS WHO.
AND WHY NOW?
I'M PICKING SOMETHING UP ON THE GENERAL S.H.I.E.L.D. CHANNEL-- IT'S GOING OUT WIDE.
IT'S HILL--
SHE'S IN BIG TROUBLE DOWN THERE.
MY GOD-- SHE'S CALLING IN ALL OF S.H.I.E.L.D., STEVE!
LET'S GO.
AGENTS OF HYDRA--THIS IS YOUR ONLY WARNING!

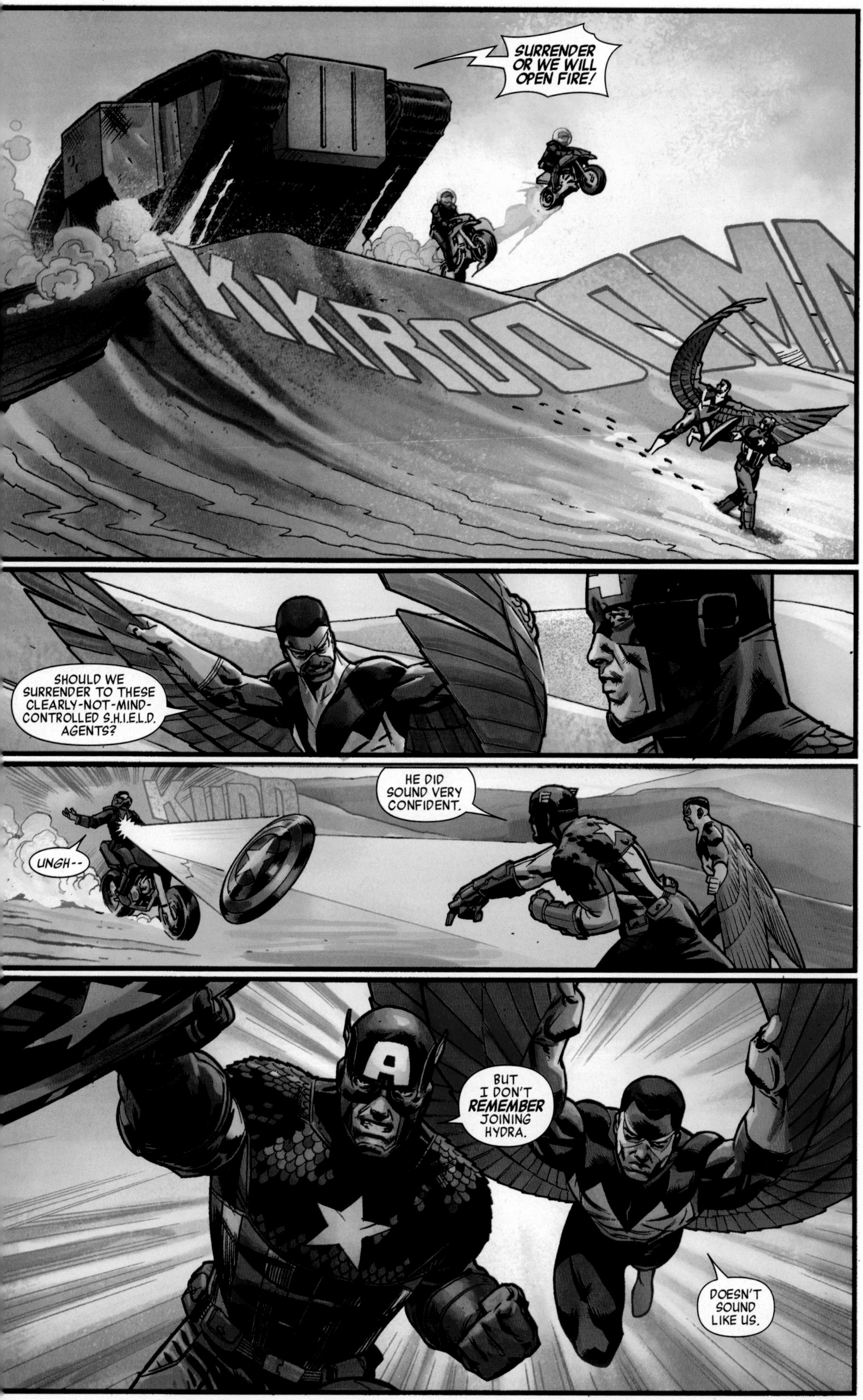
SURRENDER OR WE WILL OPEN FIRE!
KKROOOM
SHOULD WE SURRENDER TO THESE CLEARLY-NOT-MIND-CONTROLLED S.H.I.E.L.D. AGENTS?
KUDD
UNGH--
HE DID SOUND VERY CONFIDENT.
BUT I DON'T REMEMBER JOINING HYDRA.
DOESN'T SOUND LIKE US.

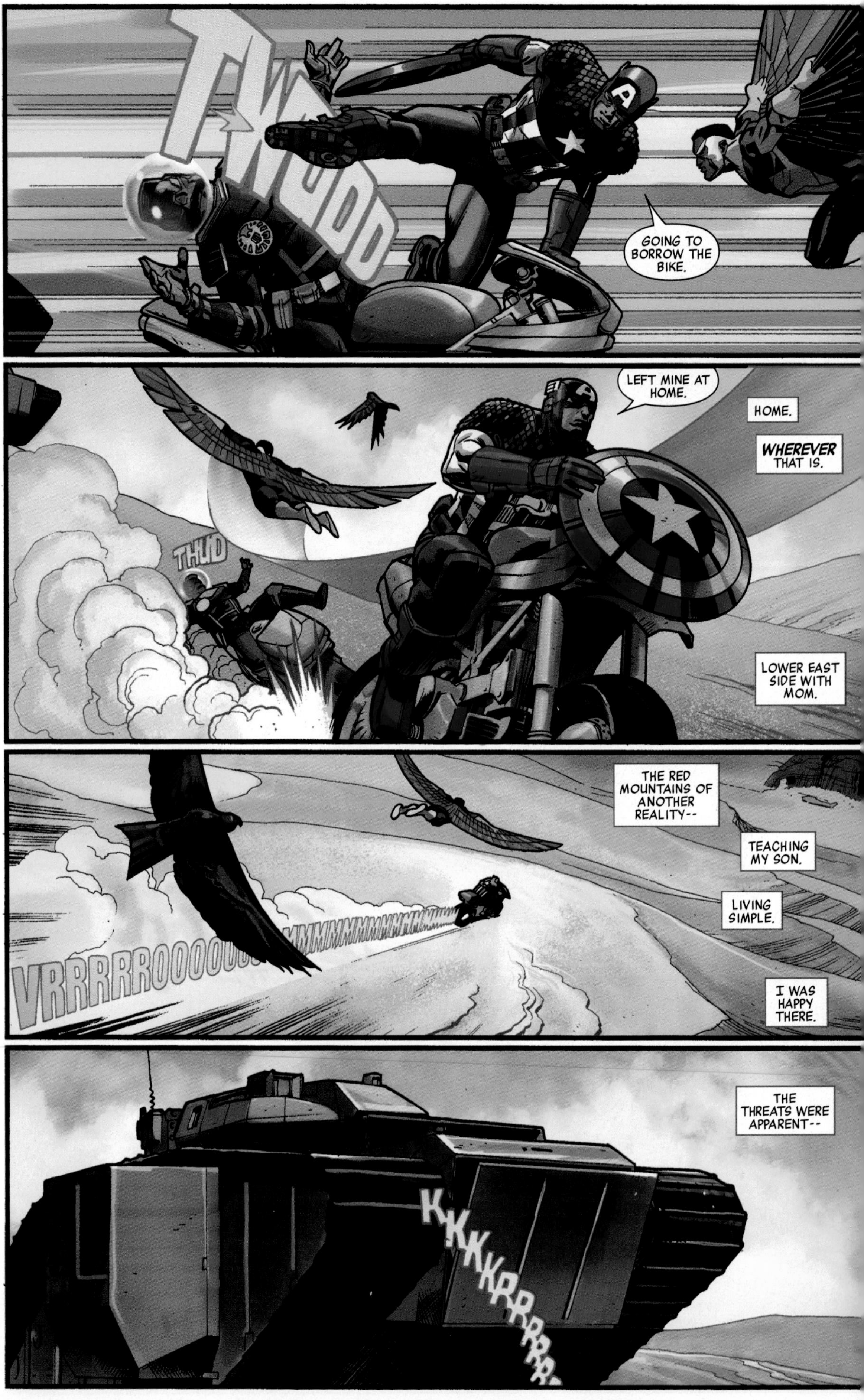

THWUDD
GOING TO BORROW THE BIKE.
LEFT MINE AT HOME.
HOME.
WHEREVER THAT IS.
THUD
LOWER EAST SIDE WITH MOM.
THE RED MOUNTAINS OF ANOTHER REALITY--
TEACHING MY SON.
LIVING SIMPLE.
I WAS HAPPY THERE.
THE THREATS WERE APPARENT--

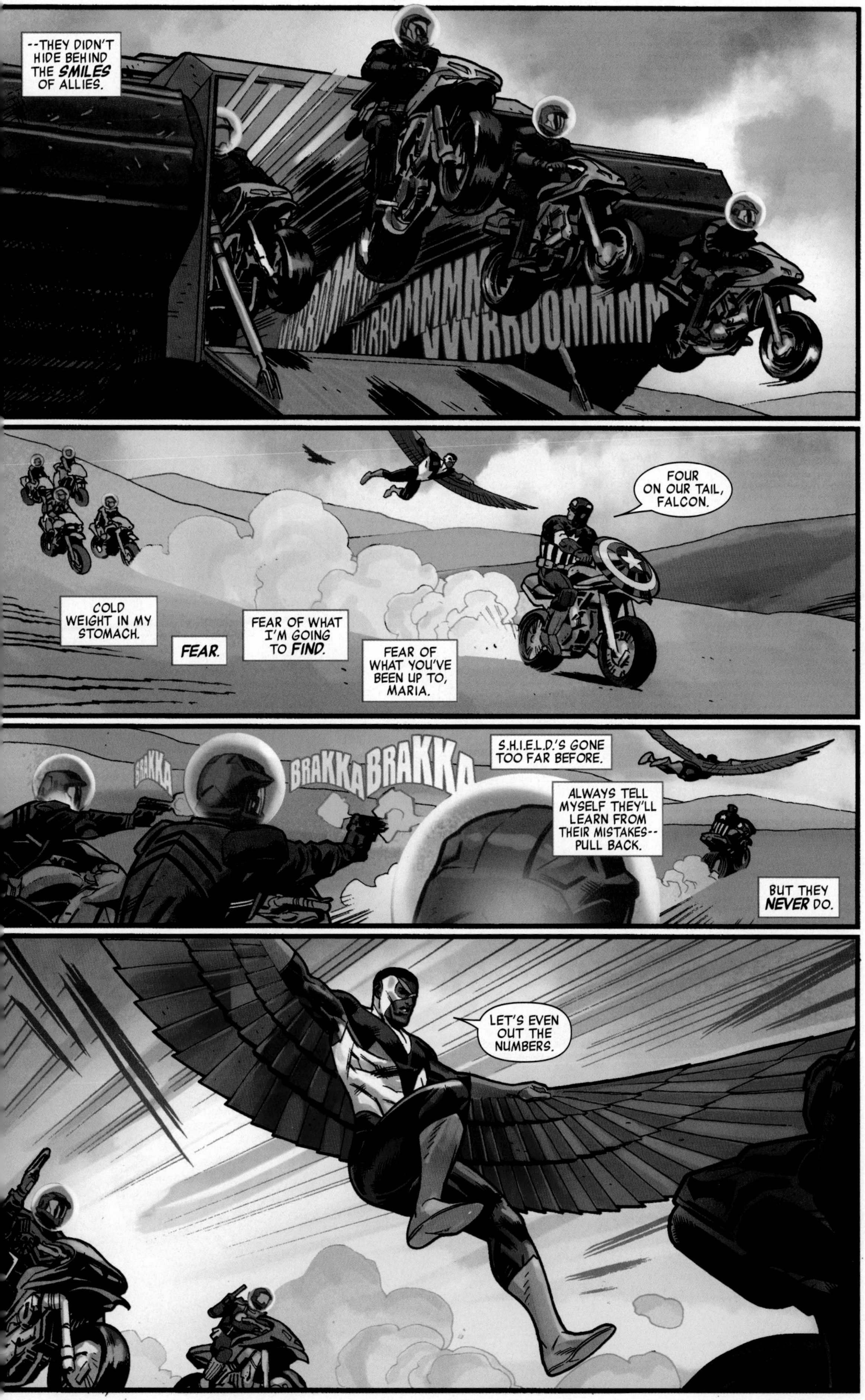
--THEY DIDN'T HIDE BEHIND THE **SMILES** OF ALLIES.
VVRROOMMMM
FOUR ON OUR TAIL, FALCON.
COLD WEIGHT IN MY STOMACH.
FEAR.
FEAR OF WHAT I'M GOING TO **FIND**.
FEAR OF WHAT YOU'VE BEEN UP TO, MARIA.
BRAKKA
BRAKKA BRAKKA
S.H.I.E.L.D.'S GONE TOO FAR BEFORE.
ALWAYS TELL MYSELF THEY'LL LEARN FROM THEIR MISTAKES-- PULL BACK.
BUT THEY **NEVER** DO.
LET'S EVEN OUT THE NUMBERS.

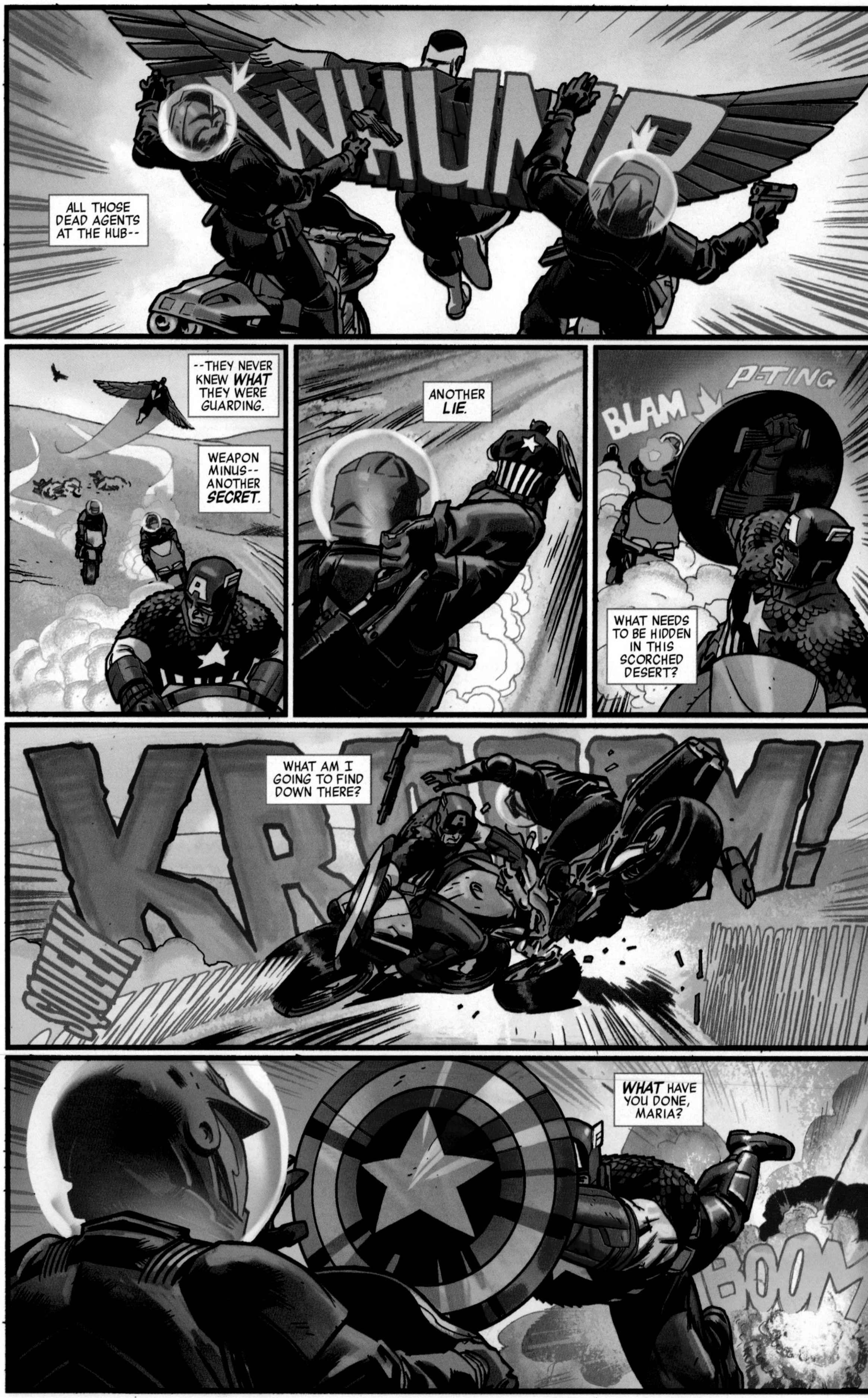
WHUMP
ALL THOSE DEAD AGENTS AT THE HUB--
--THEY NEVER KNEW WHAT THEY WERE GUARDING.
WEAPON MINUS-- ANOTHER SECRET.
ANOTHER LIE.
BLAM
P-TING
WHAT NEEDS TO BE HIDDEN IN THIS SCORCHED DESERT?
WHAT AM I GOING TO FIND DOWN THERE?
WHAT HAVE YOU DONE, MARIA?
BOOM

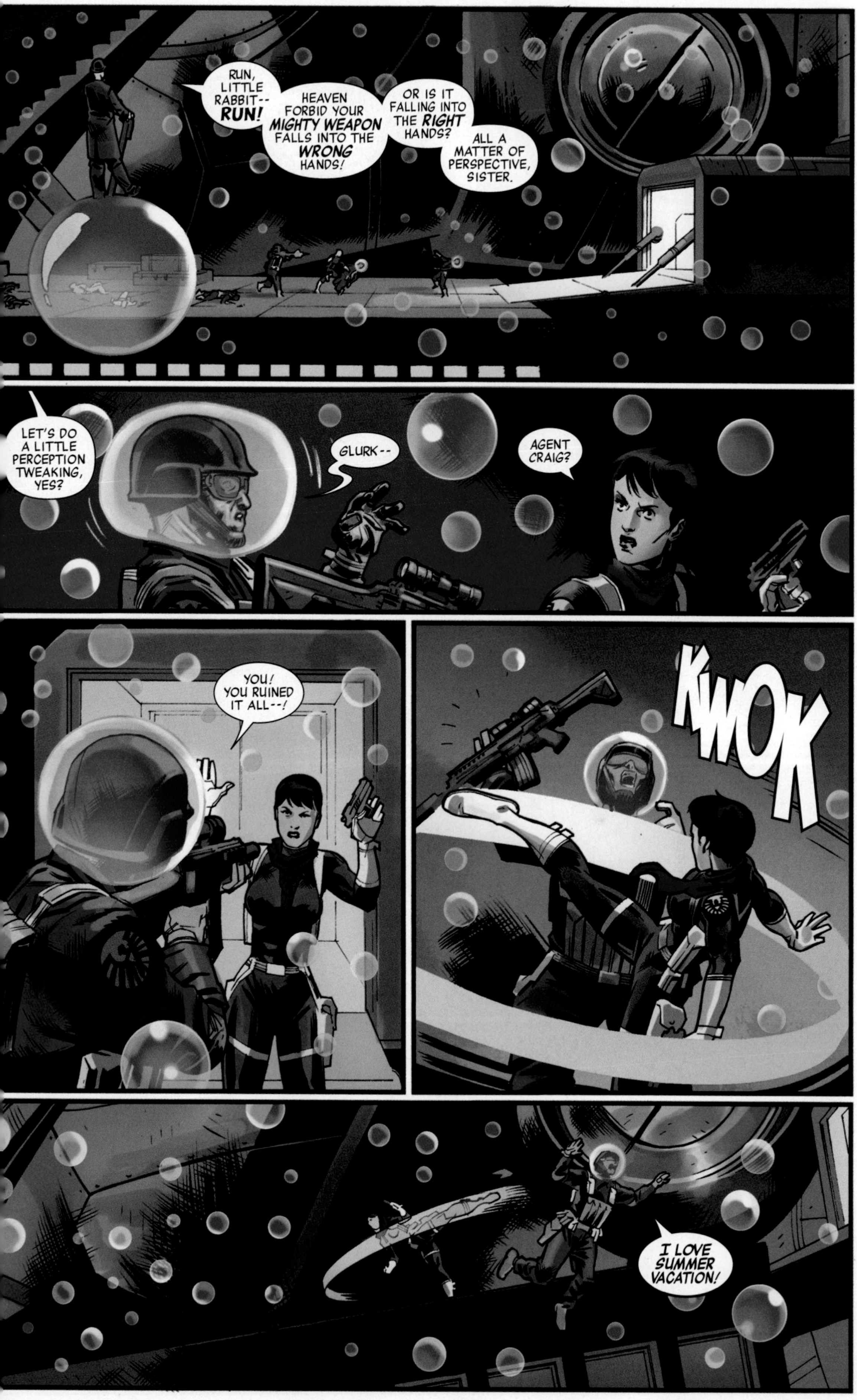
RUN, LITTLE RABBIT-- **RUN!**
HEAVEN FORBID YOUR **MIGHTY WEAPON** FALLS INTO THE **WRONG** HANDS!
OR IS IT FALLING INTO THE **RIGHT** HANDS?
ALL A MATTER OF PERSPECTIVE, SISTER.
LET'S DO A LITTLE PERCEPTION TWEAKING, YES?
GLURK--
AGENT CRAIG?
YOU! YOU RUINED IT ALL--!
KWOK
I LOVE SUMMER VACATION!

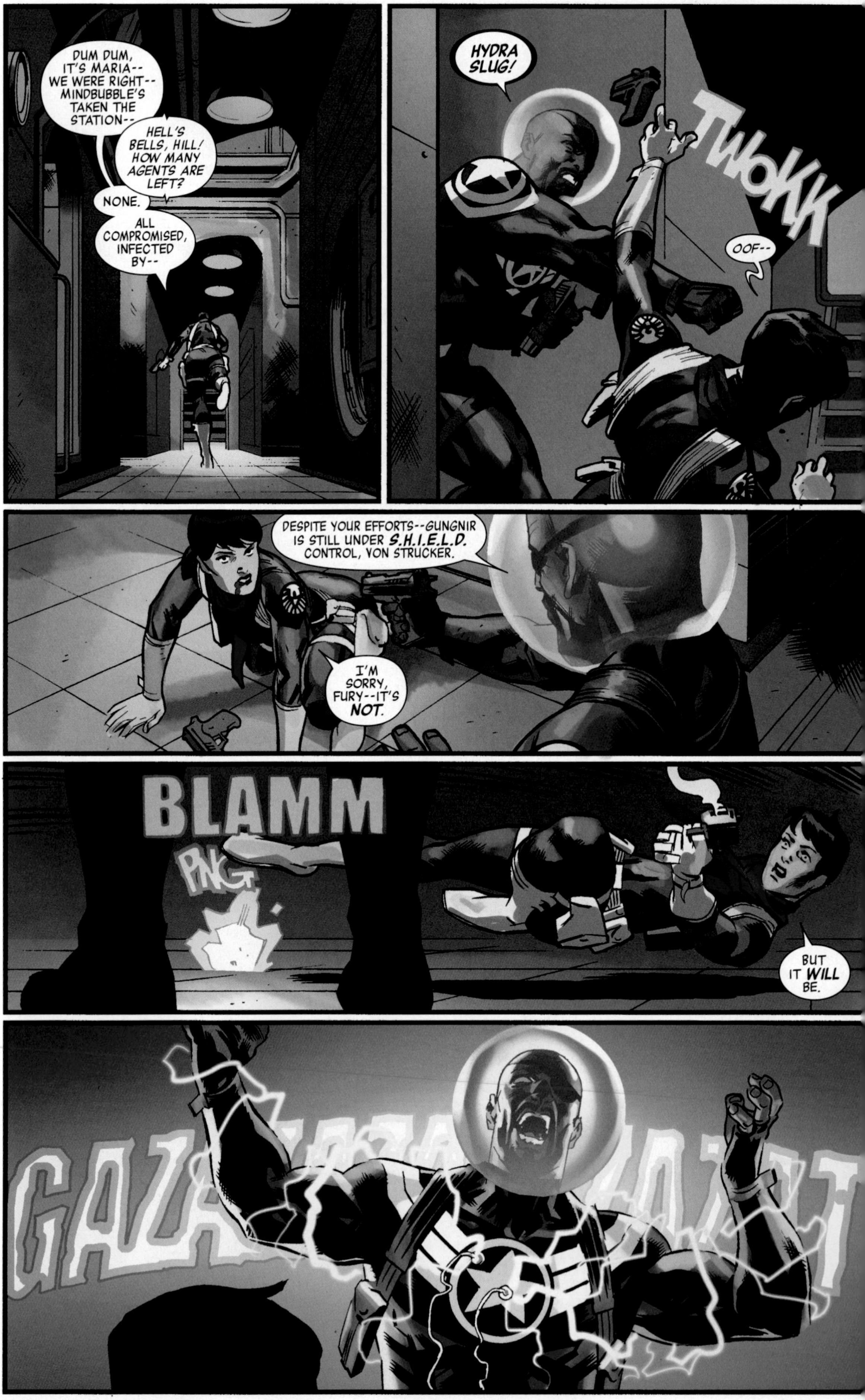
DUM DUM, IT'S MARIA-- WE WERE RIGHT-- MINDBUBBLE'S TAKEN THE STATION--
HELL'S BELLS, HILL! HOW MANY AGENTS ARE LEFT?
NONE.
ALL COMPROMISED, INFECTED BY--
HYDRA SLUG!
TWOKK
OOF--
DESPITE YOUR EFFORTS--GUNGNIR IS STILL UNDER S.H.I.E.L.D. CONTROL, VON STRUCKER.
I'M SORRY, FURY--IT'S NOT.
BLAMM
PING
BUT IT WILL BE.

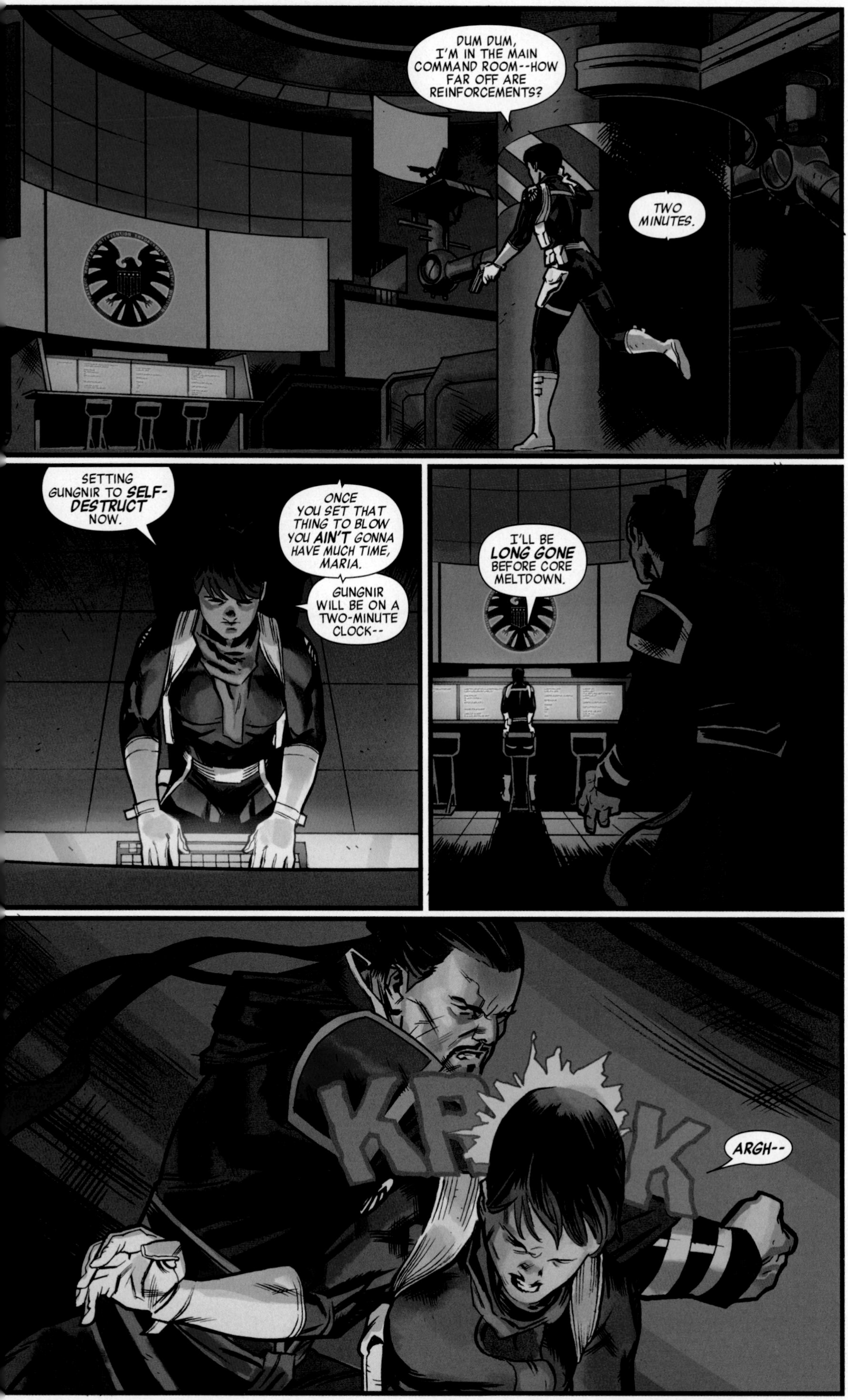
DUM DUM, I'M IN THE MAIN COMMAND ROOM--HOW FAR OFF ARE REINFORCEMENTS?
TWO MINUTES.
SETTING GUNGNIR TO SELF-DESTRUCT NOW.
ONCE YOU SET THAT THING TO BLOW YOU AIN'T GONNA HAVE MUCH TIME, MARIA.
GUNGNIR WILL BE ON A TWO-MINUTE CLOCK--
I'LL BE LONG GONE BEFORE CORE MELTDOWN.
ARGH--

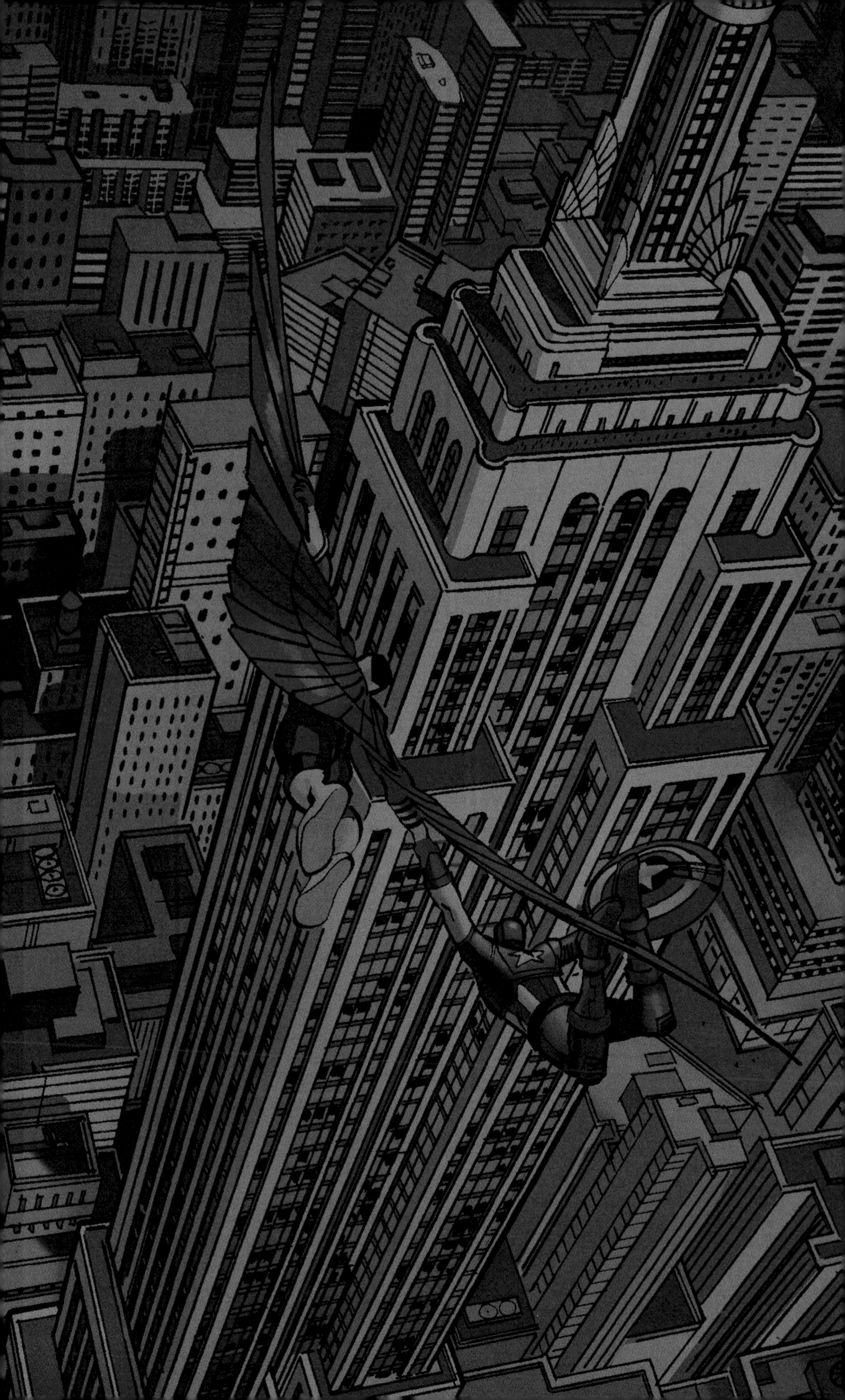

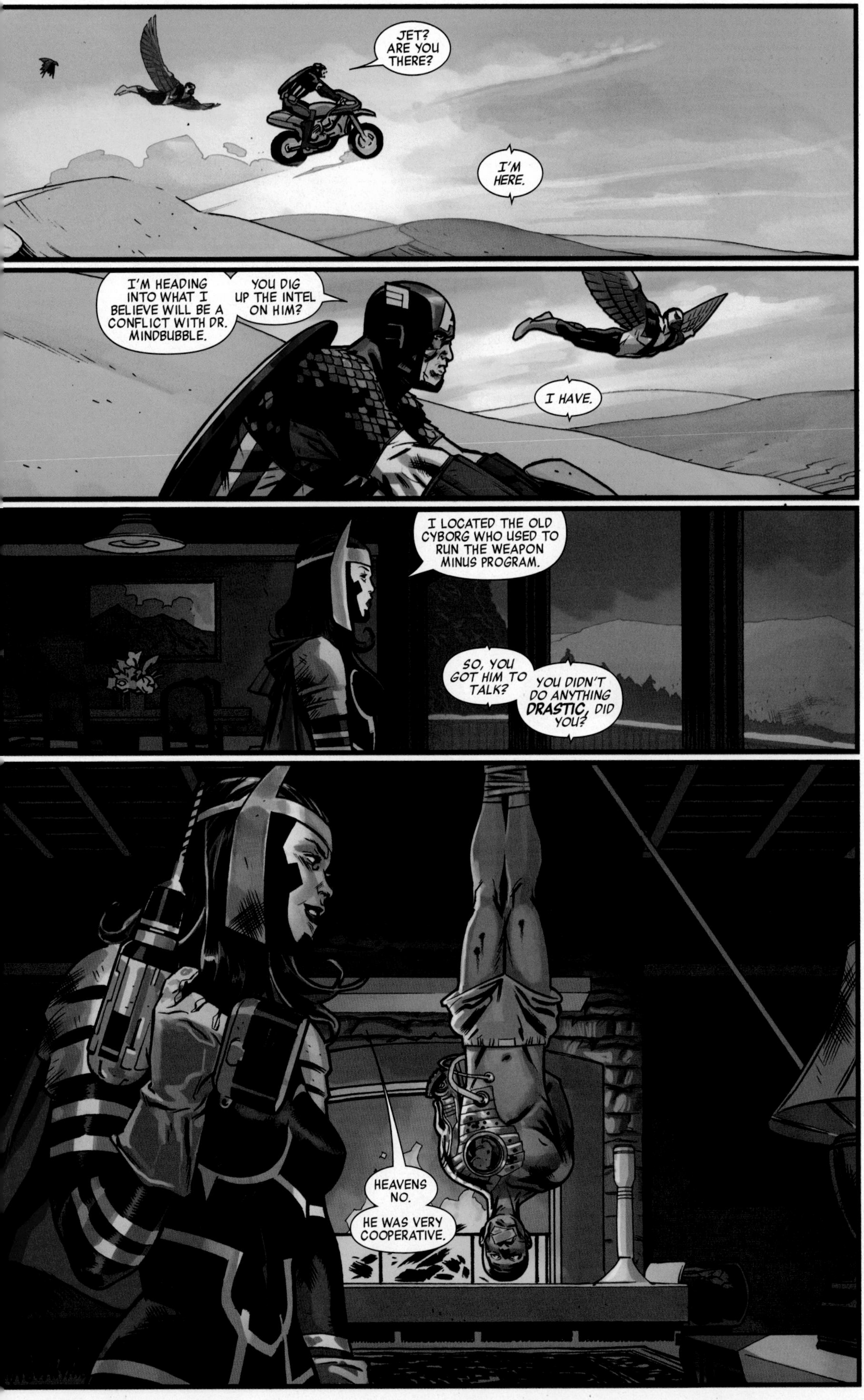
JET? ARE YOU THERE?
I'M HERE.
I'M HEADING INTO WHAT I BELIEVE WILL BE A CONFLICT WITH DR. MINDBUBBLE.
YOU DIG UP THE INTEL ON HIM?
I HAVE.
I LOCATED THE OLD CYBORG WHO USED TO RUN THE WEAPON MINUS PROGRAM.
SO, YOU GOT HIM TO TALK?
YOU DIDN'T DO ANYTHING DRASTIC, DID YOU?
HEAVENS NO.
HE WAS VERY COOPERATIVE.

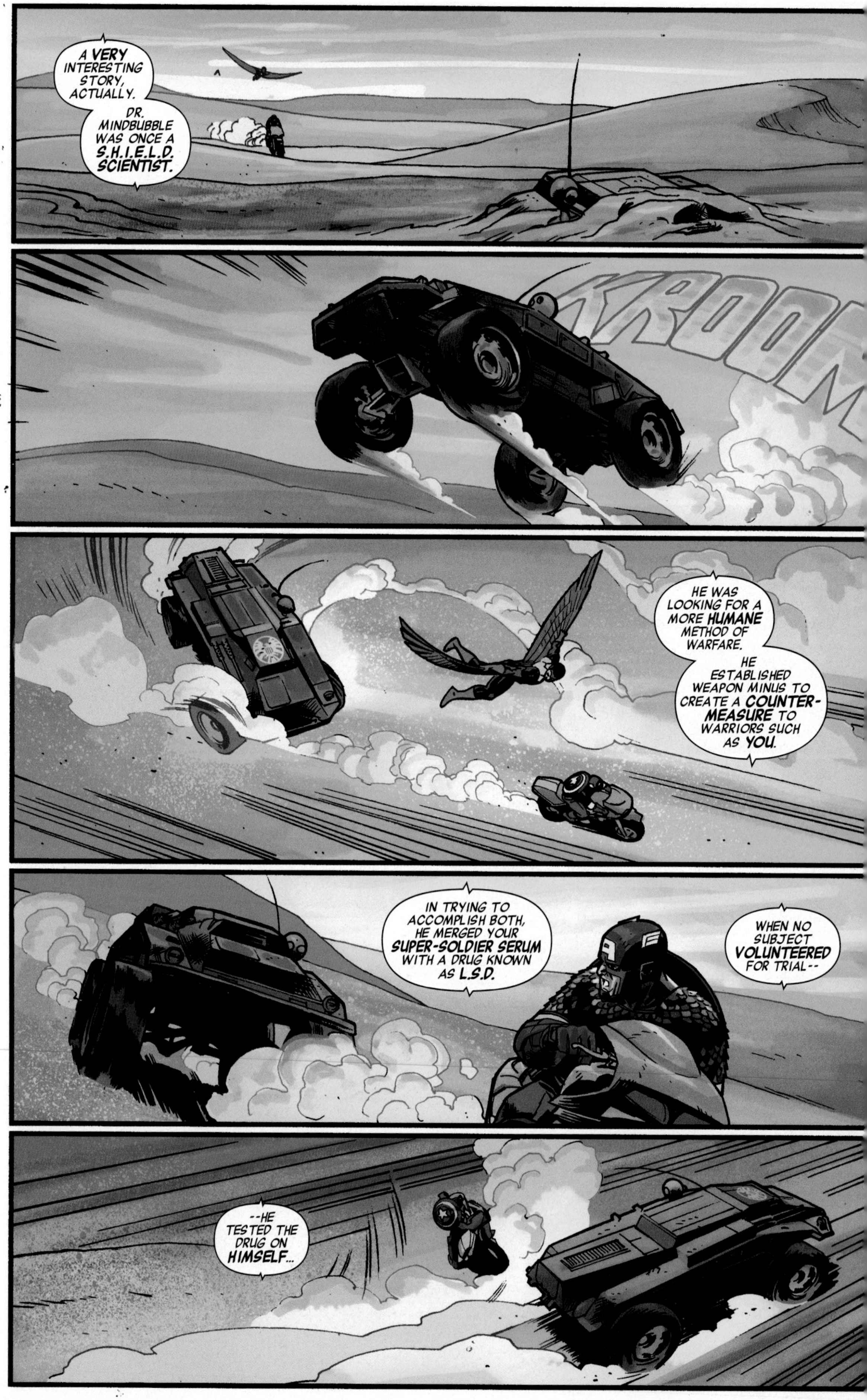
A VERY INTERESTING STORY, ACTUALLY.
DR. MINDBUBBLE WAS ONCE A S.H.I.E.L.D. SCIENTIST.
KROOM
HE WAS LOOKING FOR A MORE HUMANE METHOD OF WARFARE.
HE ESTABLISHED WEAPON MINUS TO CREATE A COUNTER-MEASURE TO WARRIORS SUCH AS YOU.
IN TRYING TO ACCOMPLISH BOTH, HE MERGED YOUR SUPER-SOLDIER SERUM WITH A DRUG KNOWN AS L.S.D.
WHEN NO SUBJECT VOLUNTEERED FOR TRIAL--
--HE TESTED THE DRUG ON HIMSELF...

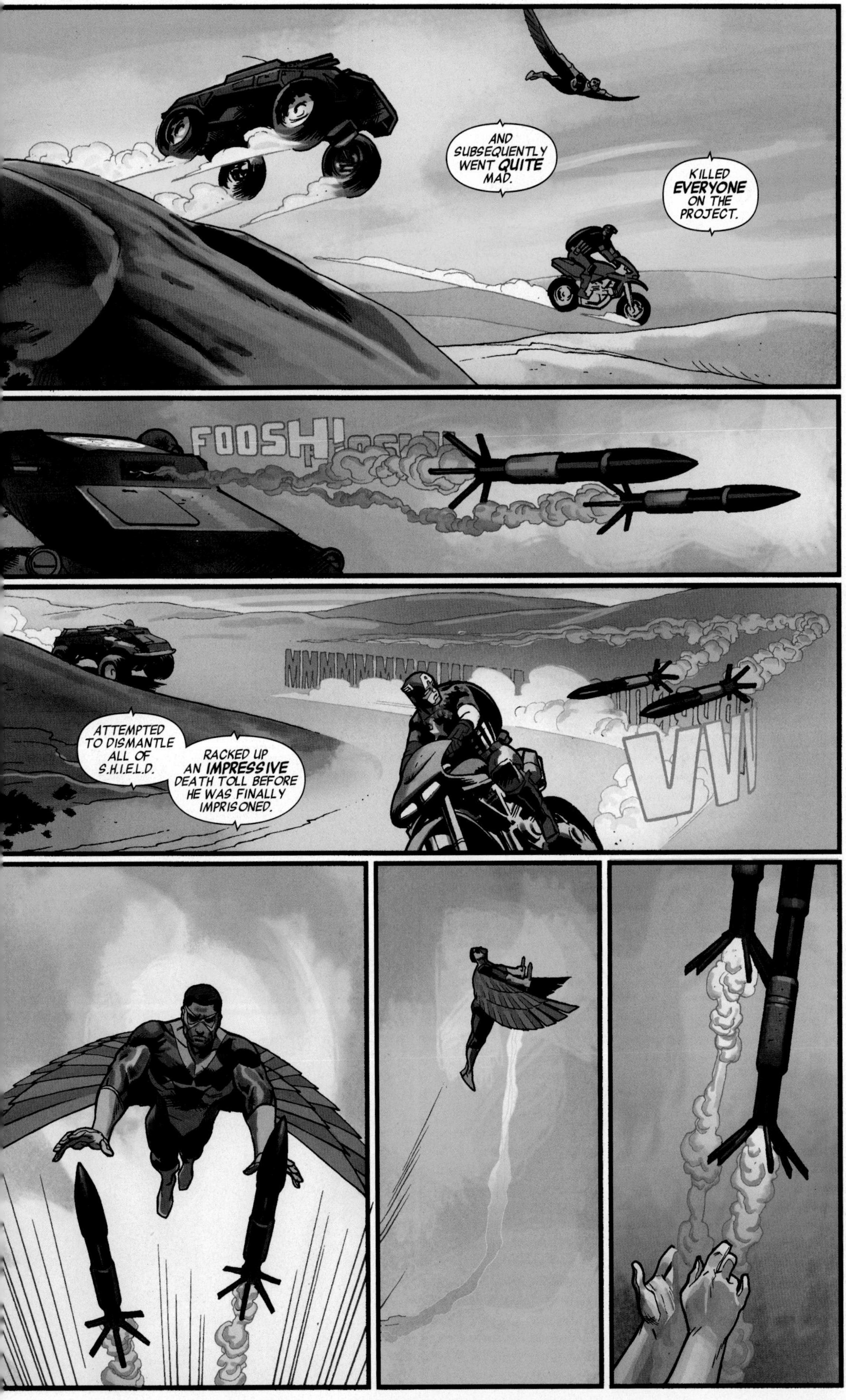
AND SUBSEQUENTLY WENT QUITE MAD.
KILLED EVERYONE ON THE PROJECT.
FOOSH!
ATTEMPTED TO DISMANTLE ALL OF S.H.I.E.L.D.
RACKED UP AN IMPRESSIVE DEATH TOLL BEFORE HE WAS FINALLY IMPRISONED.

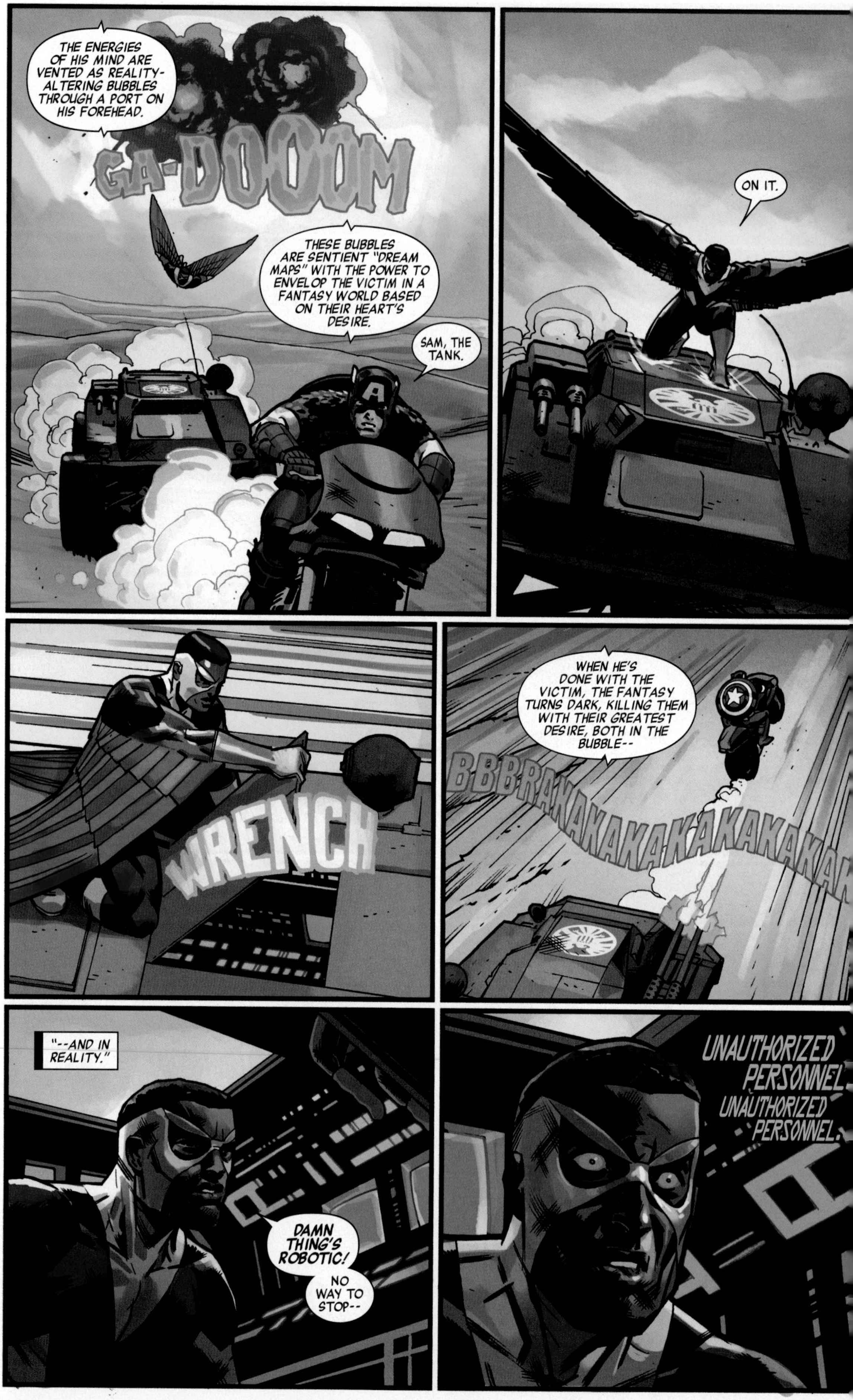
THE ENERGIES OF HIS MIND ARE VENTED AS REALITY-ALTERING BUBBLES THROUGH A PORT ON HIS FOREHEAD.
GA-DOOOM
THESE BUBBLES ARE SENTIENT "DREAM MAPS" WITH THE POWER TO ENVELOP THE VICTIM IN A FANTASY WORLD BASED ON THEIR HEART'S DESIRE.
SAM, THE TANK.
ON IT.
WRENCH
WHEN HE'S DONE WITH THE VICTIM, THE FANTASY TURNS DARK, KILLING THEM WITH THEIR GREATEST DESIRE, BOTH IN THE BUBBLE--
BBBRAKAKAKAKAKAKAKAKAK
"--AND IN REALITY."
DAMN THING'S ROBOTIC!
NO WAY TO STOP--
UNAUTHORIZED PERSONNEL. UNAUTHORIZED PERSONNEL.

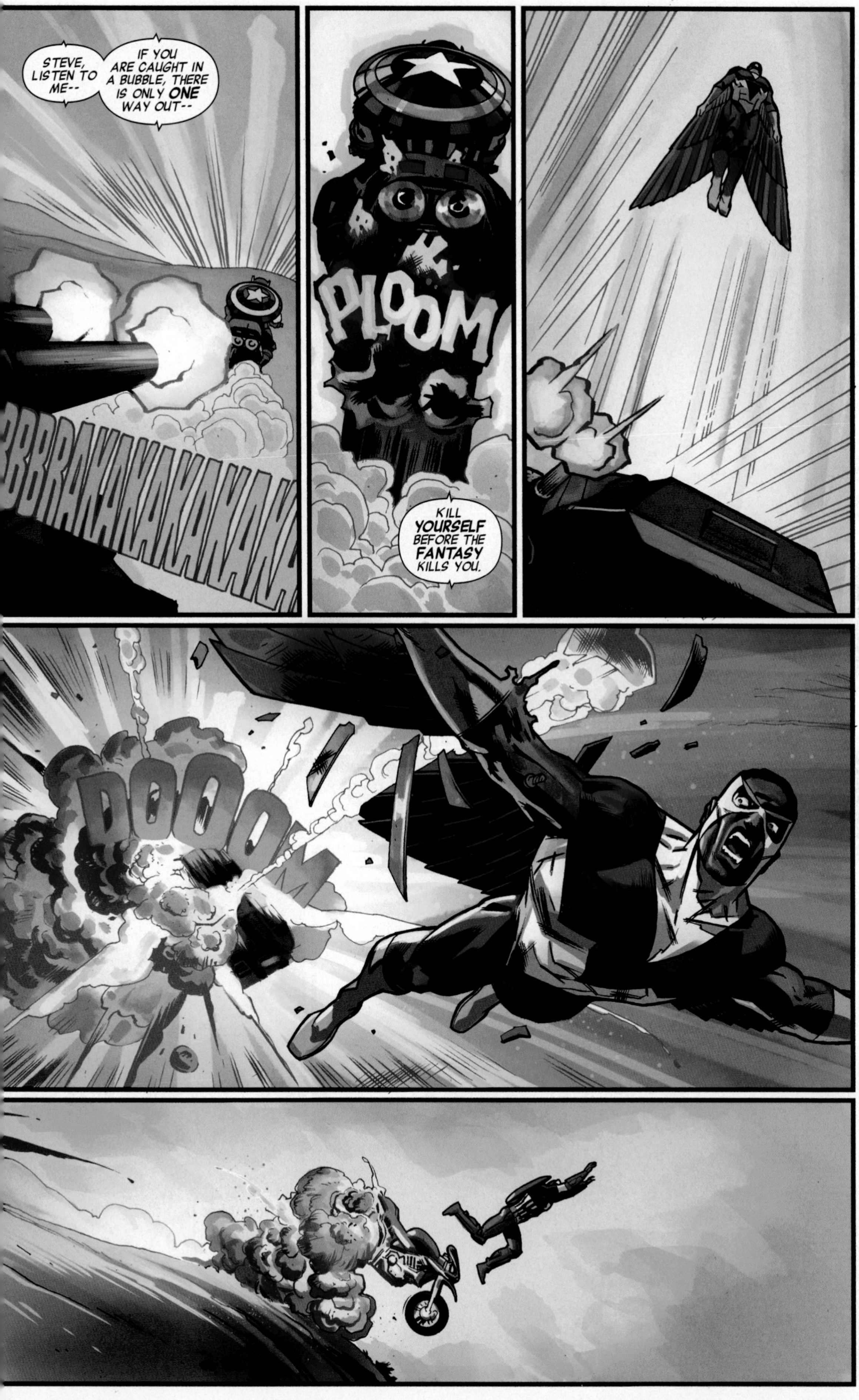
STEVE, LISTEN TO ME--
IF YOU ARE CAUGHT IN A BUBBLE, THERE IS ONLY ONE WAY OUT--
BBBRAKAKAKAKAKAK
PLOOM
KILL YOURSELF BEFORE THE FANTASY KILLS YOU.
DOOOM

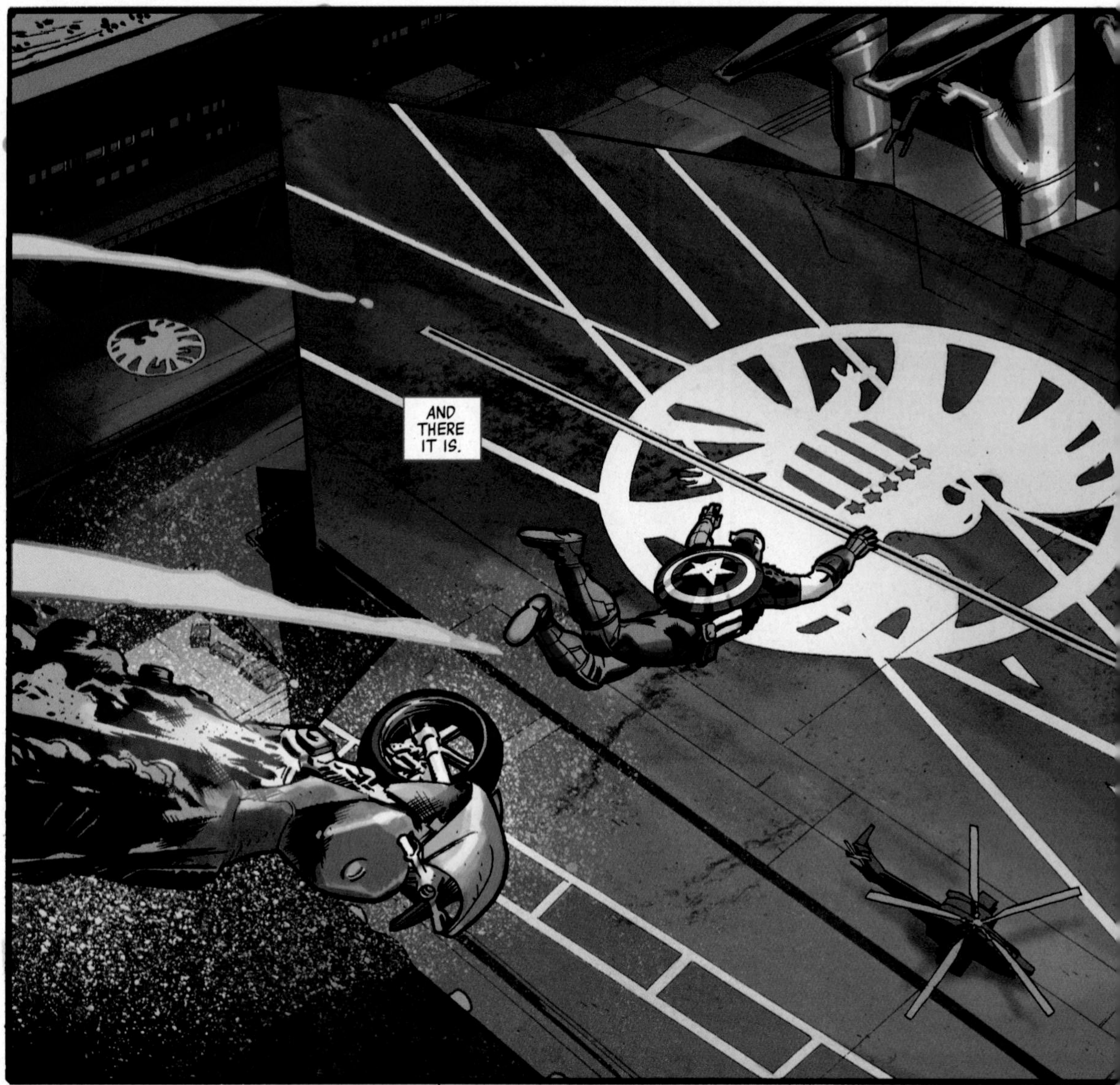
AND THERE IT IS.

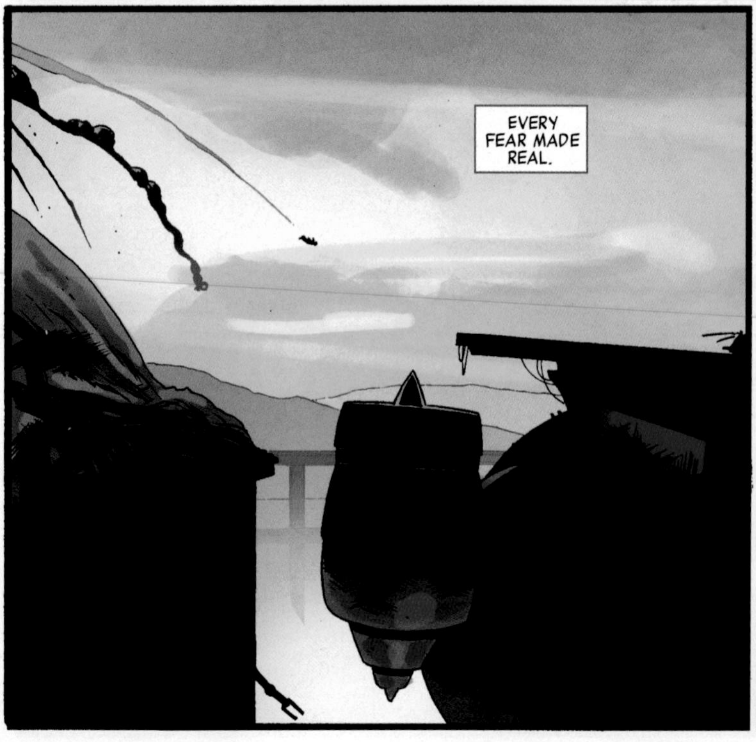
EVERY FEAR MADE REAL.

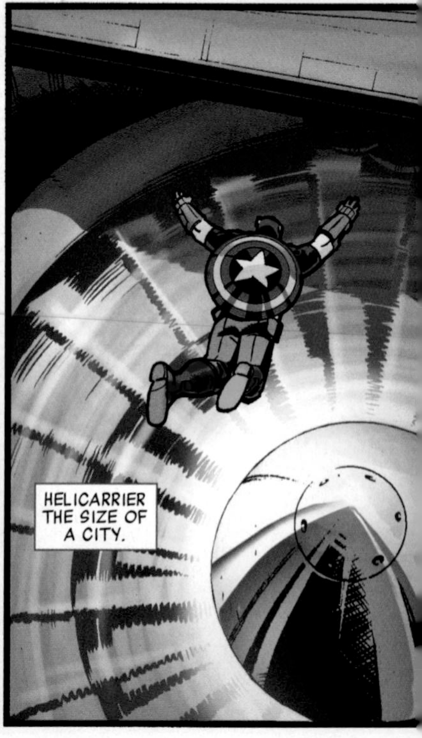
HELICARRIER THE SIZE OF A CITY.

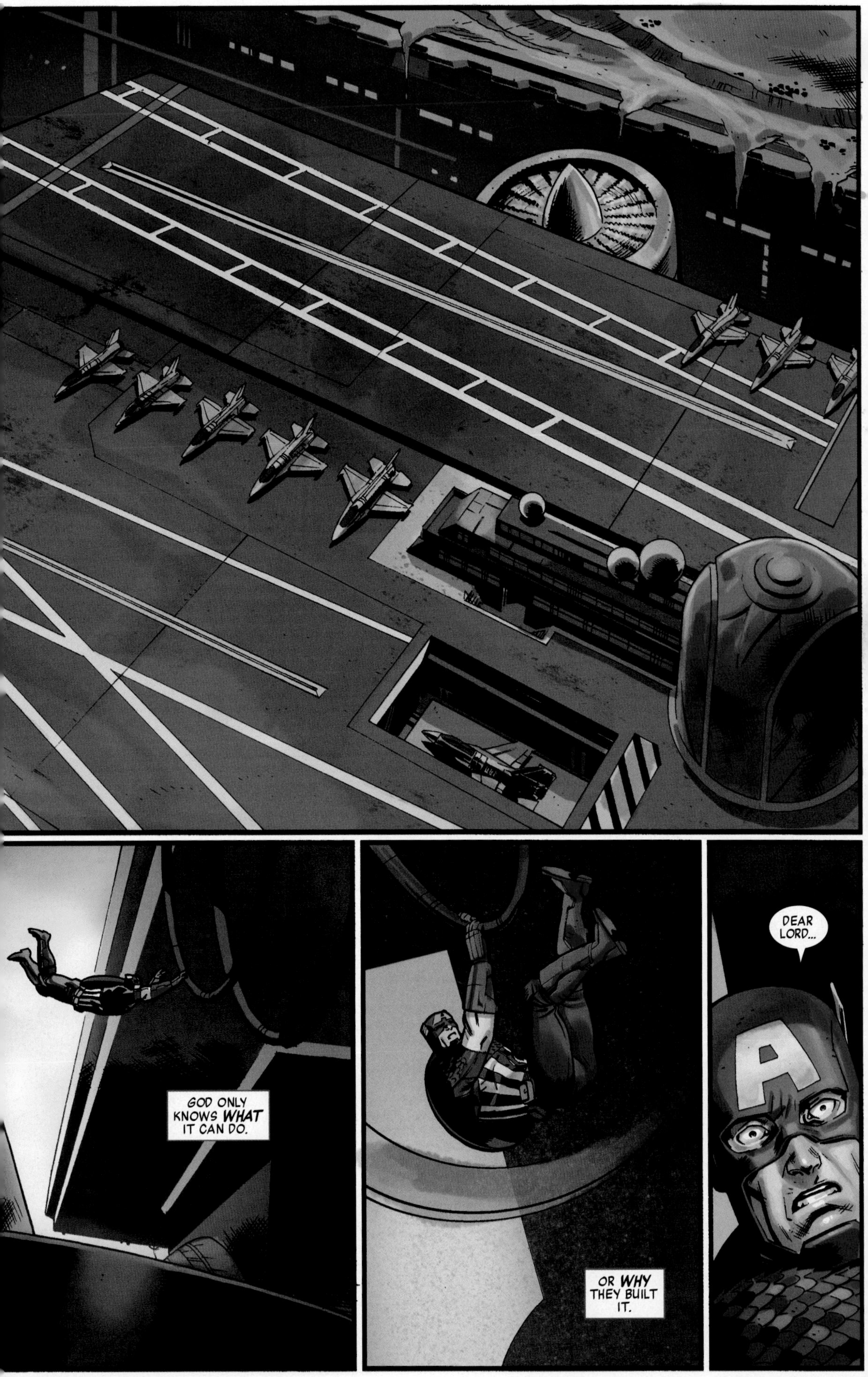
GOD ONLY KNOWS WHAT IT CAN DO.
OR WHY THEY BUILT IT.
DEAR LORD...

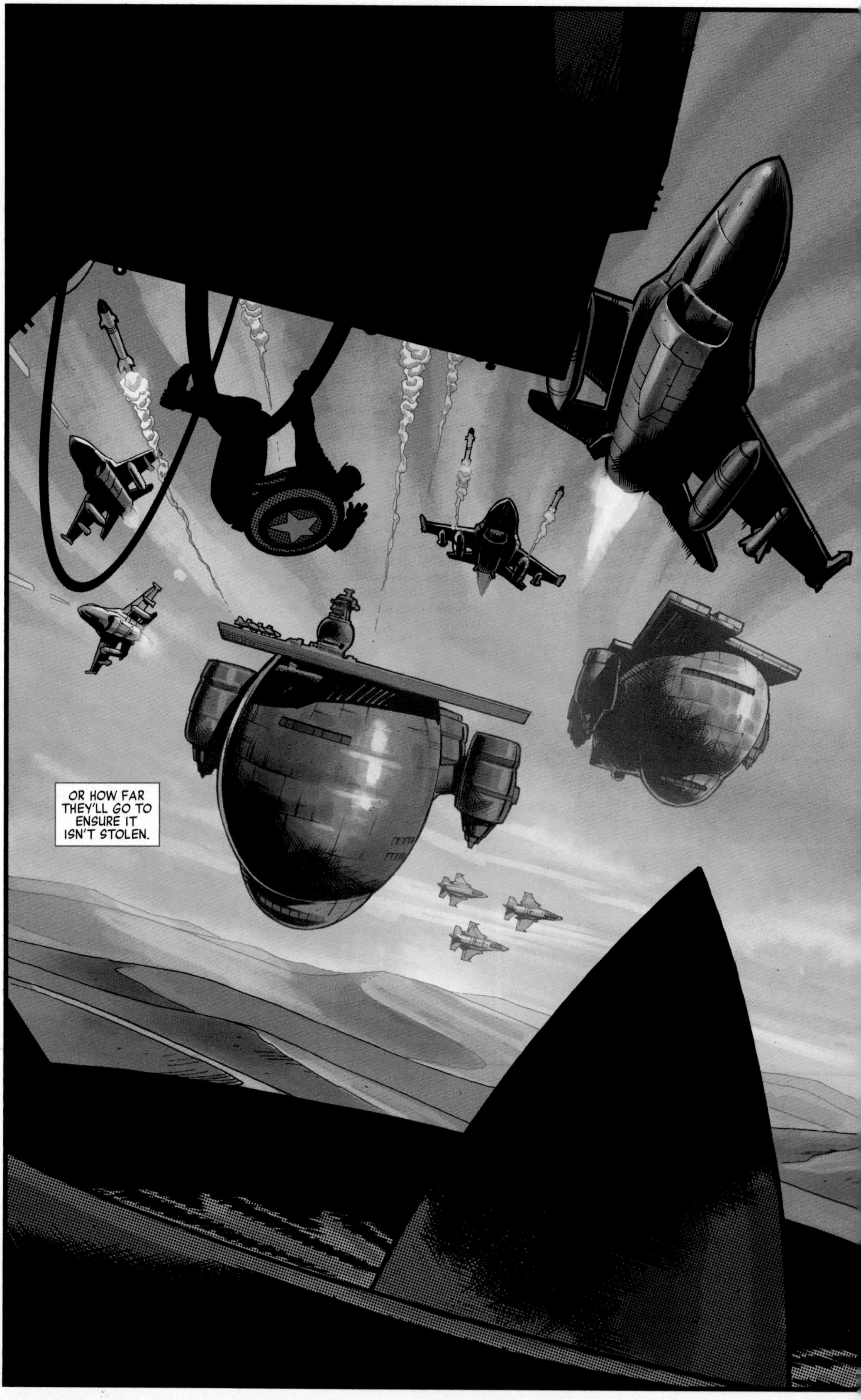
OR HOW FAR THEY'LL GO TO ENSURE IT ISN'T STOLEN.

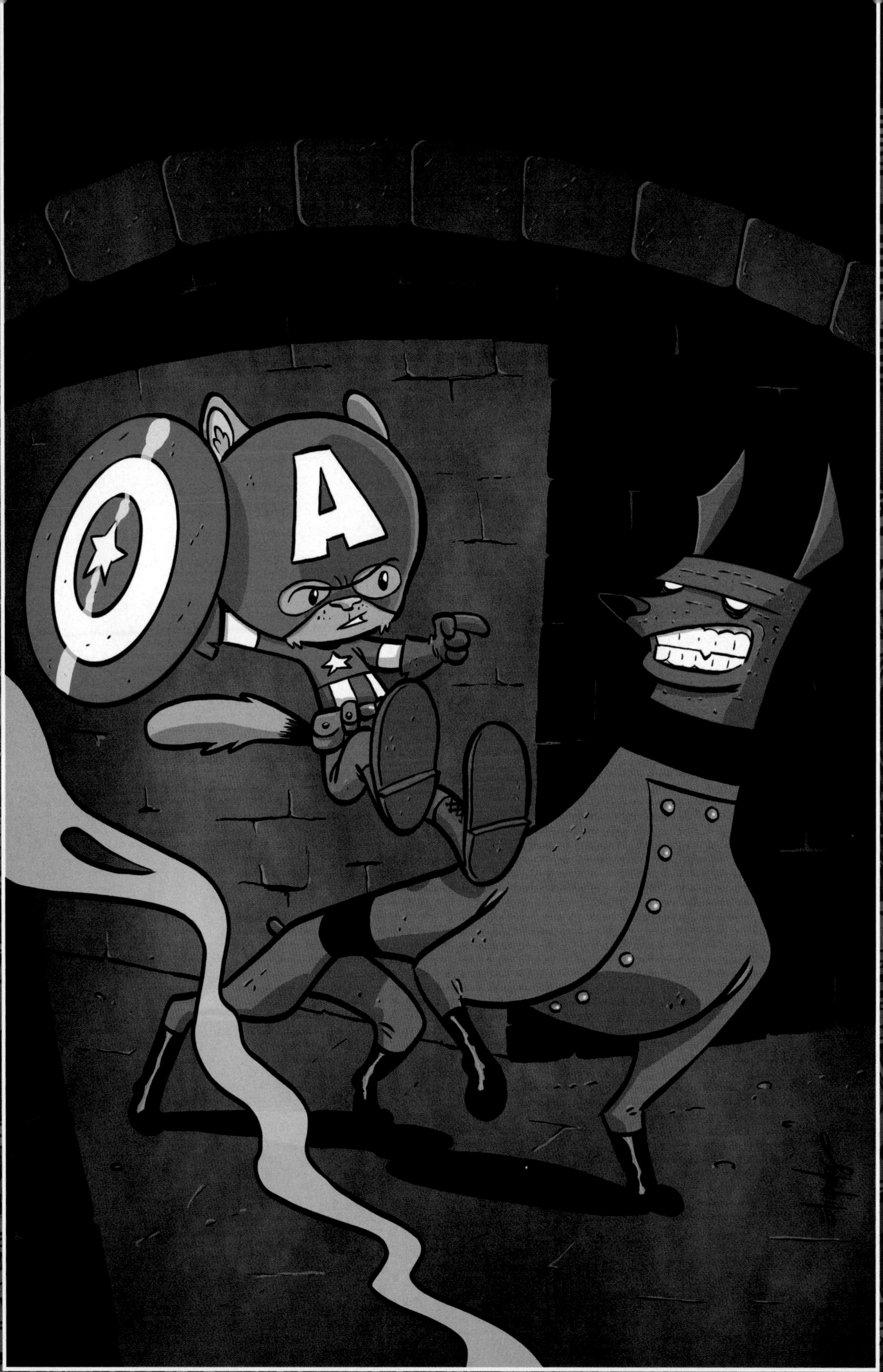

#16 ANIMAL VARIANT BY CHRIS ELIOPOULOS

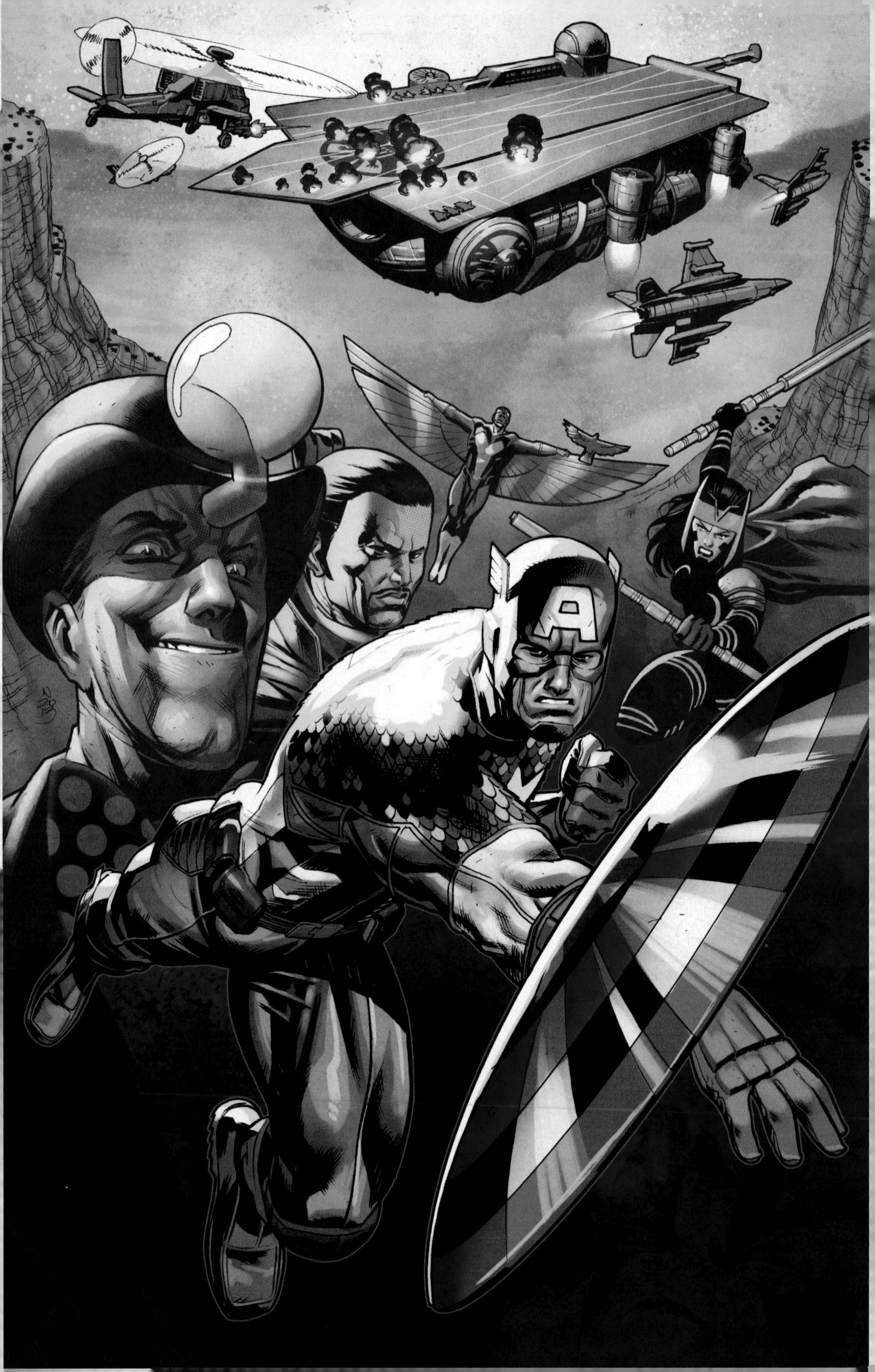

HOURS NOW PRAYING I WAS WRONG.

HOURS OF MY GUT TELLING ME THAT PRAYER IS A WASTE OF TIME.

DIDN'T LIKE MARIA HILL'S BEHAVIOR AT THE HUB.

SHE WAS HESITATING, CONSIDERING HER WORDS--

--LEARNED HER TELLS--

--SHE WAS *LYING*.

CONCEALING THIS *MISERABLE* SECRET.

A HELICARRIER UNLIKE *ANYTHING* I'VE EVER SEEN.

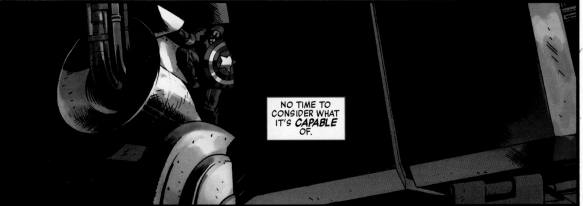

NO TIME TO CONSIDER WHAT IT'S *CAPABLE* OF.

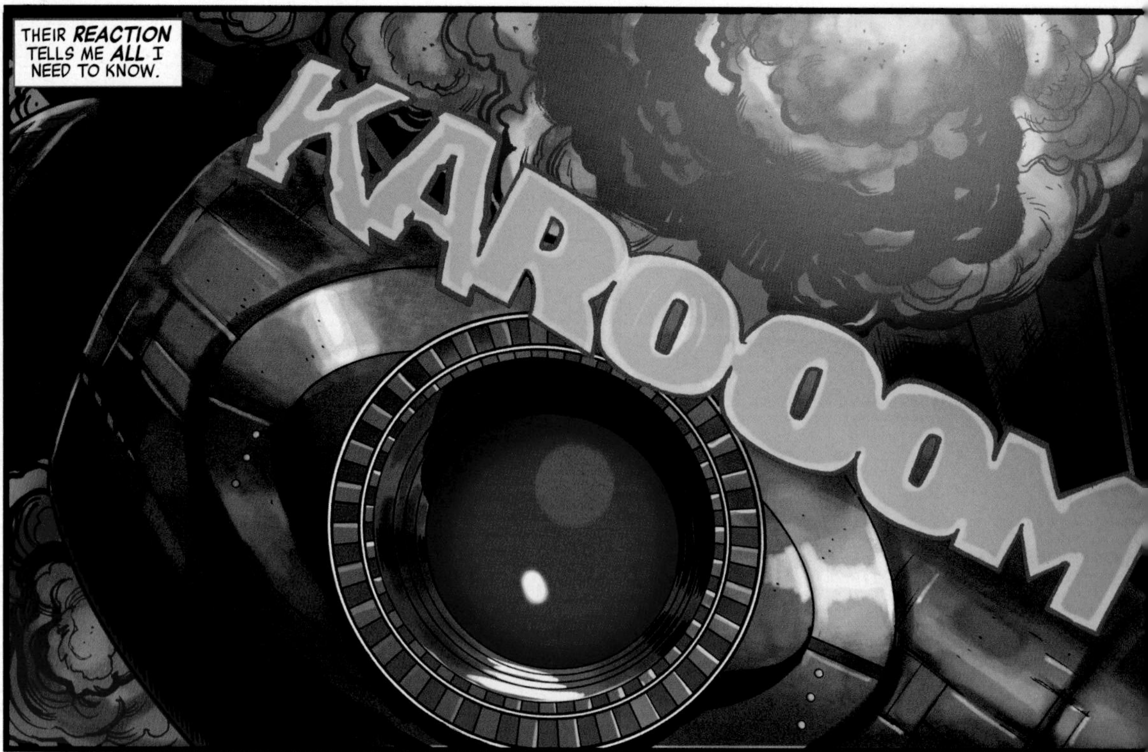
THEIR *REACTION* TELLS ME *ALL* I NEED TO KNOW.
KAROOOM

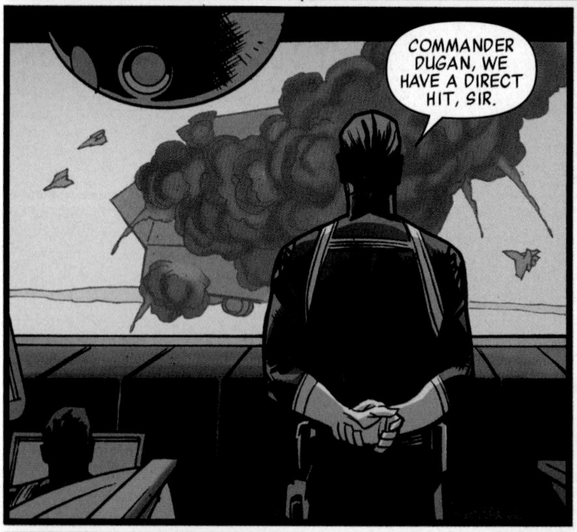
COMMANDER DUGAN, WE HAVE A DIRECT HIT, SIR.

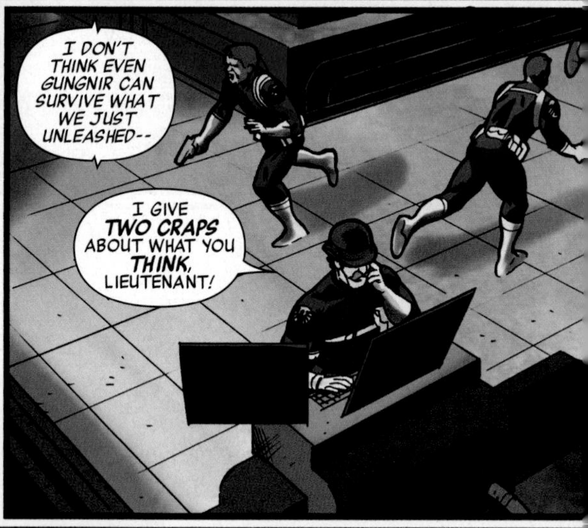
I DON'T THINK EVEN GUNGNIR CAN SURVIVE WHAT WE JUST UNLEASHED--
I GIVE *TWO CRAPS* ABOUT WHAT YOU *THINK*, LIEUTENANT!

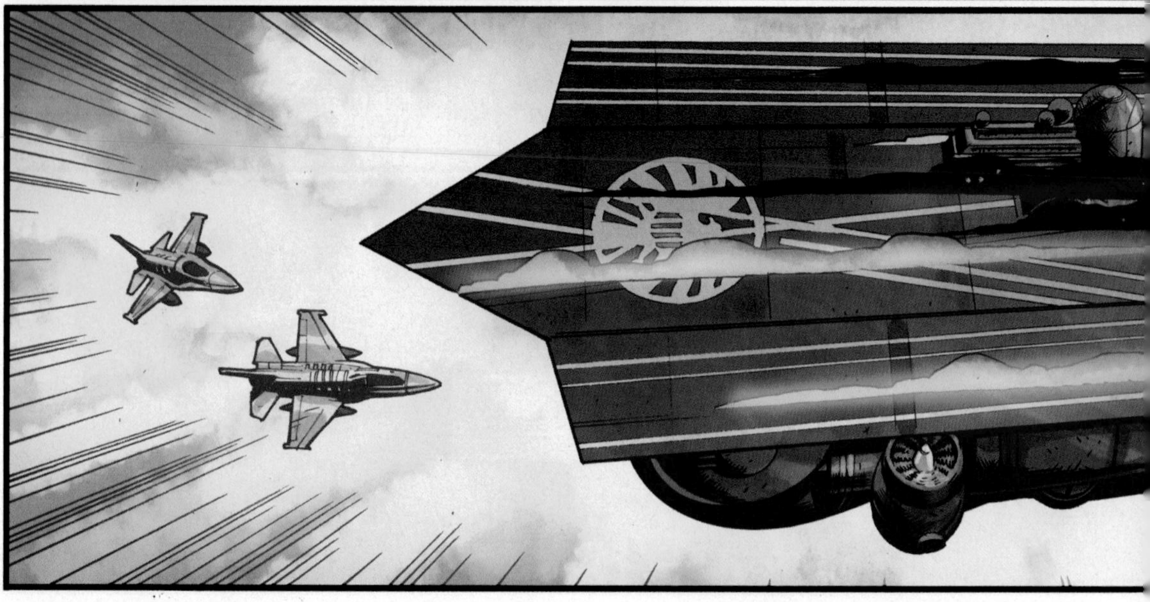

DOOOMM

I WANT **VISUAL CONFIRMATION** THAT MONSTER IS GOING **DOWN!**

WE HIT IT WITH A FULL BARRAGE FROM TWO HELICARRIERS AND THREE ATTACK VIPERS, SIR.

THERE IS **NO WAY** ON **GOD'S GREEN EARTH...**

...IT SURVIVED.

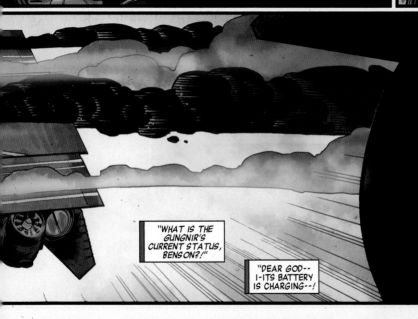

"WHAT IS THE **GUNGNIR'S** CURRENT STATUS, BENSON?!"

"DEAR GOD-- I-ITS BATTERY IS CHARGING--!"

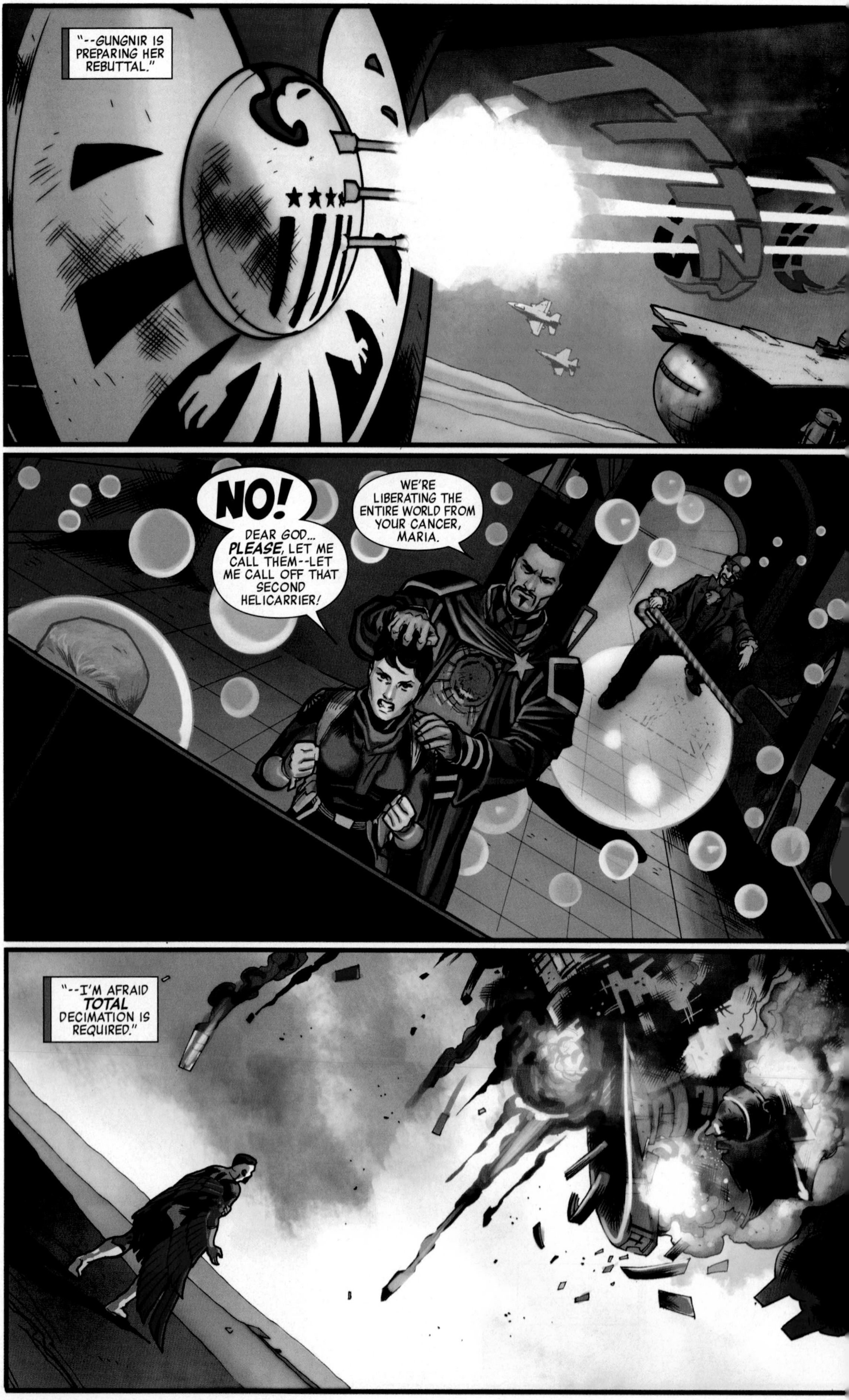
"--GUNGNIR IS PREPARING HER REBUTTAL."
NO!
DEAR GOD... PLEASE, LET ME CALL THEM--LET ME CALL OFF THAT SECOND HELICARRIER!
WE'RE LIBERATING THE ENTIRE WORLD FROM YOUR CANCER, MARIA.
"--I'M AFRAID TOTAL DECIMATION IS REQUIRED."

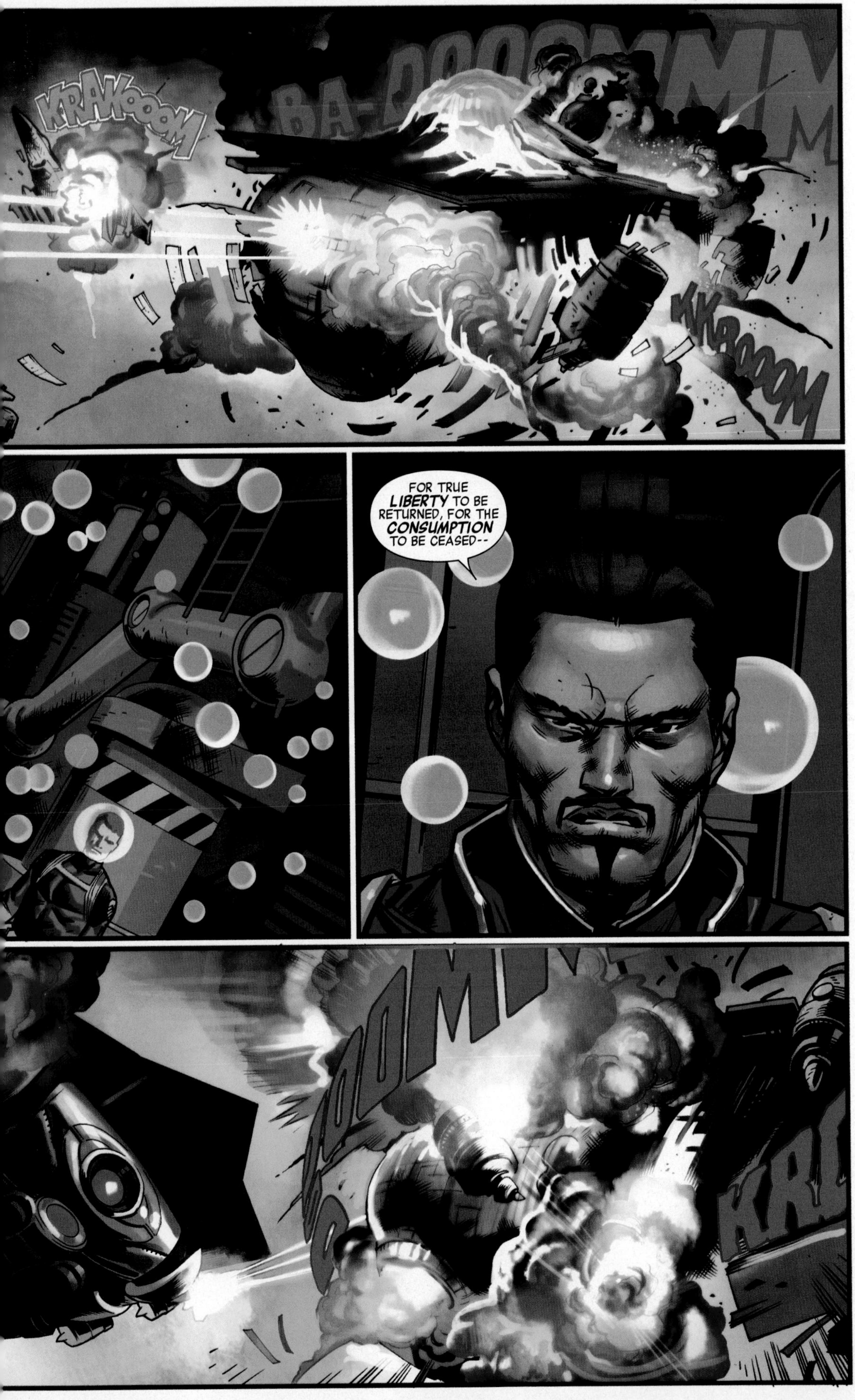
KRAKOOOM
FOR TRUE LIBERTY TO BE RETURNED, FOR THE CONSUMPTION TO BE CEASED--

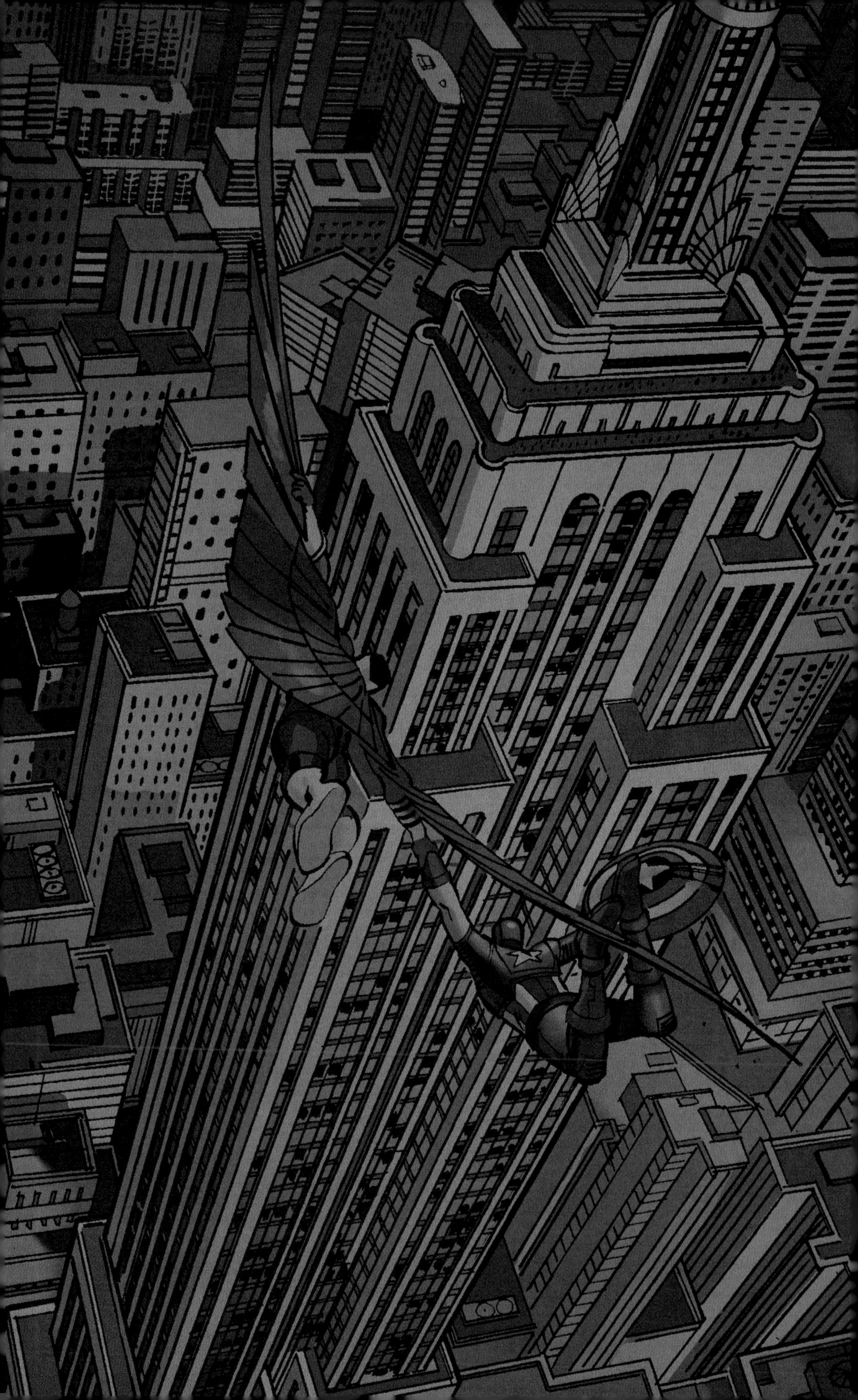

THERE NOW. IT'S DONE.

PAINFUL, BUT *NECESSARY.*

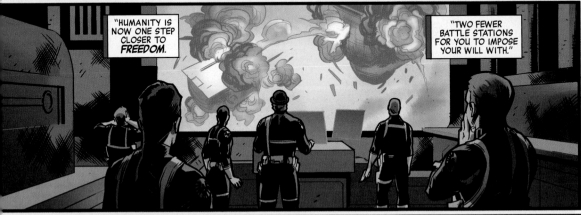

"HUMANITY IS NOW ONE STEP CLOSER TO *FREEDOM.*

"TWO FEWER BATTLE STATIONS FOR YOU TO IMPOSE YOUR WILL WITH."

MOTHER OF GOD.

WAR REVEALS MANY UGLY TRUTHS TO A SOLDIER.

PRIMARY AMONG THEM IS HOW *QUICKLY* LIFE CAN BE SNUFFED OUT IN *VAST* QUANTITY.

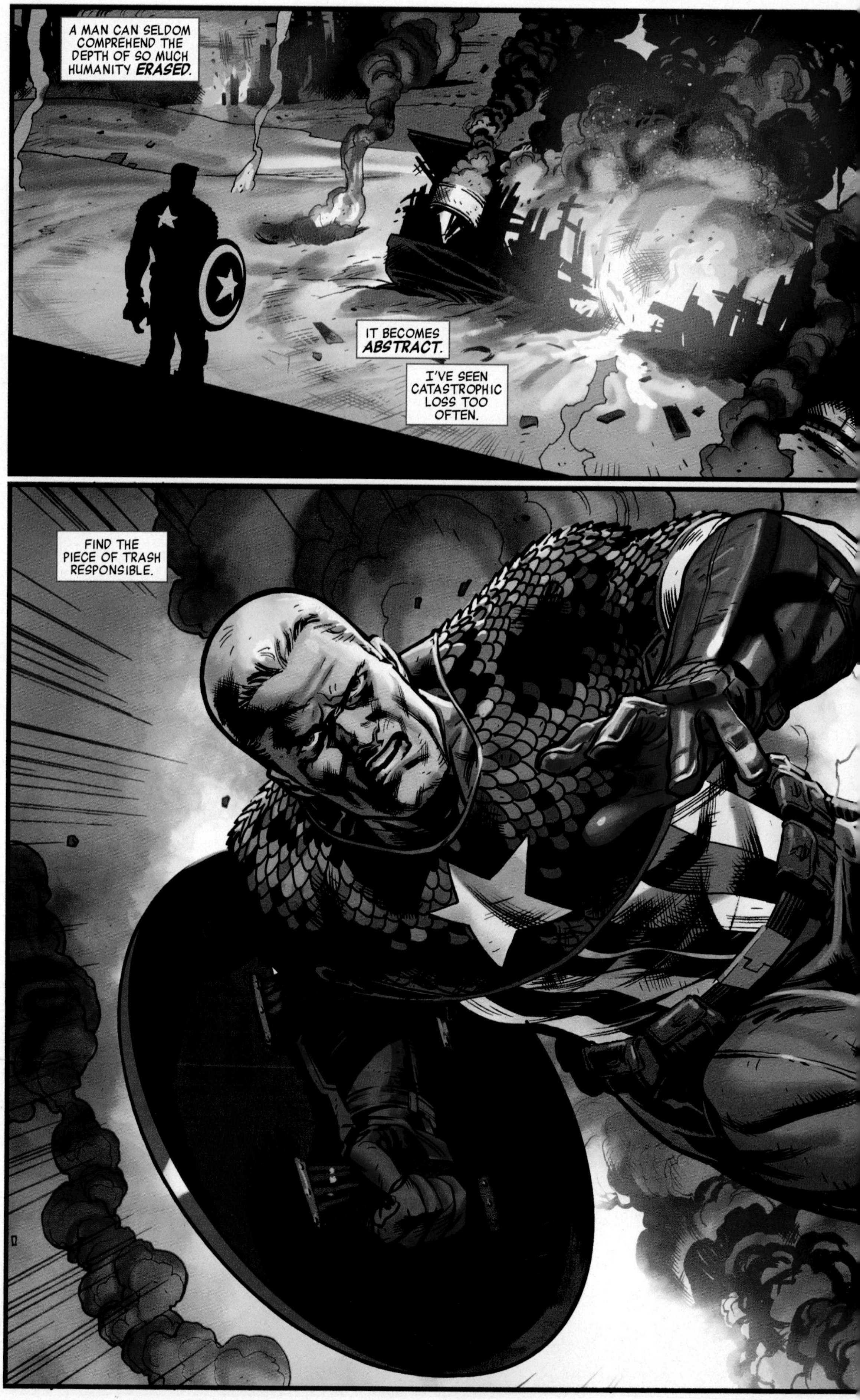
A MAN CAN SELDOM COMPREHEND THE DEPTH OF SO MUCH HUMANITY ERASED.
IT BECOMES ABSTRACT.
I'VE SEEN CATASTROPHIC LOSS TOO OFTEN.
FIND THE PIECE OF TRASH RESPONSIBLE.

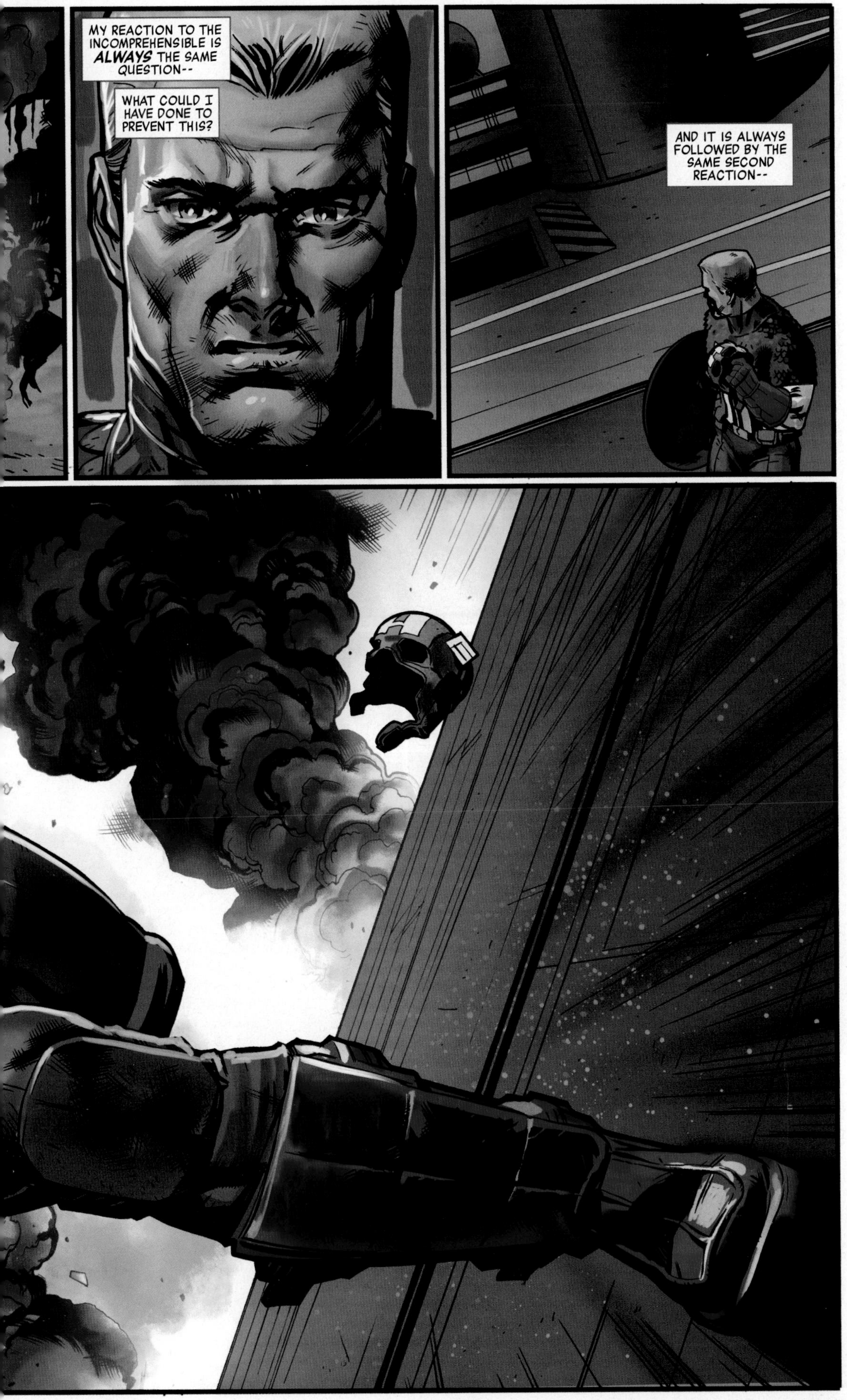

MY REACTION TO THE INCOMPREHENSIBLE IS ALWAYS THE SAME QUESTION--
WHAT COULD I HAVE DONE TO PREVENT THIS?
AND IT IS ALWAYS FOLLOWED BY THE SAME SECOND REACTION--

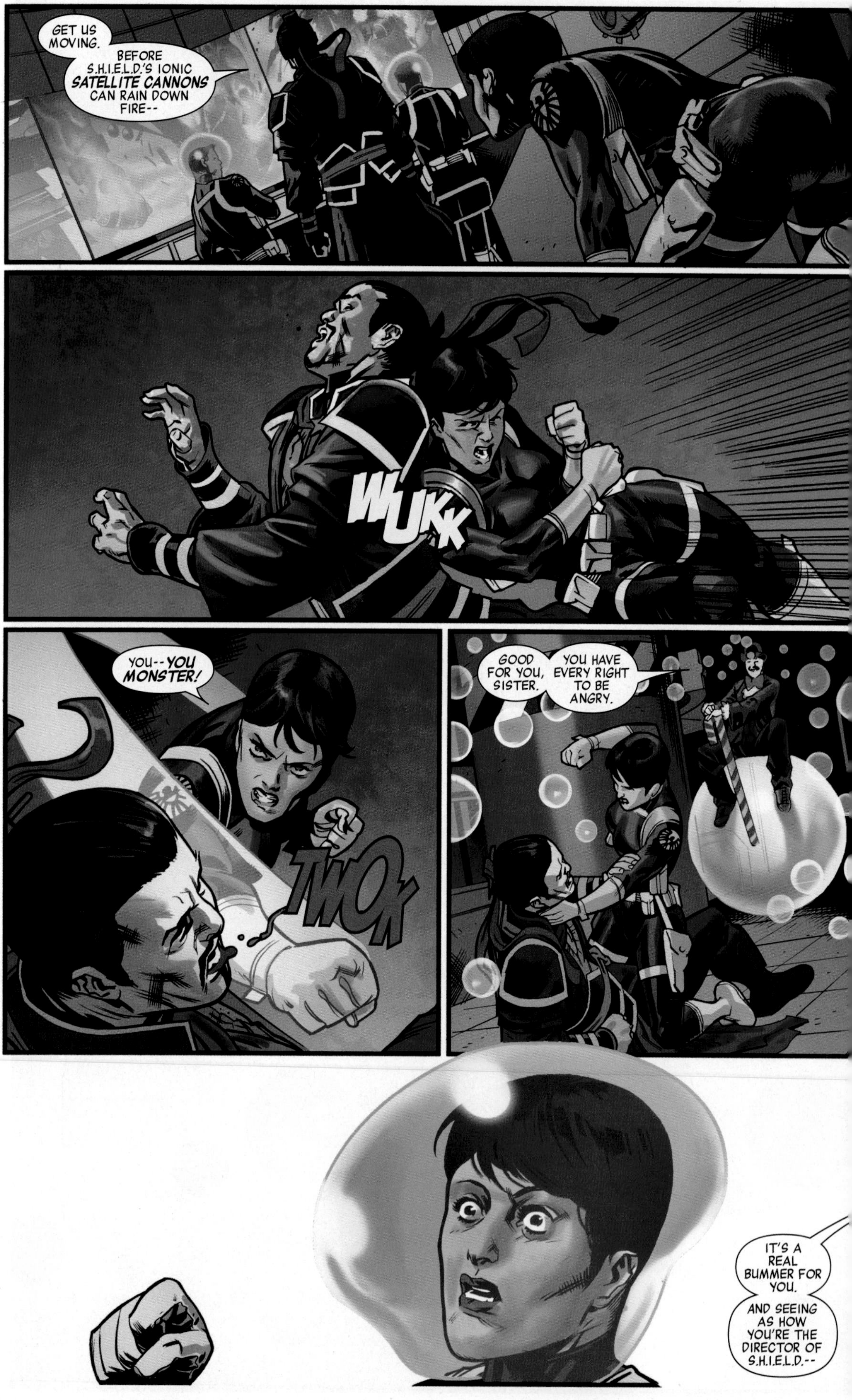
GET US MOVING.
BEFORE S.H.I.E.L.D.'S IONIC SATELLITE CANNONS CAN RAIN DOWN FIRE--
WUKK
YOU--YOU MONSTER!
TWOK
GOOD FOR YOU, SISTER.
YOU HAVE EVERY RIGHT TO BE ANGRY.
IT'S A REAL BUMMER FOR YOU.
AND SEEING AS HOW YOU'RE THE DIRECTOR OF S.H.I.E.L.D.--

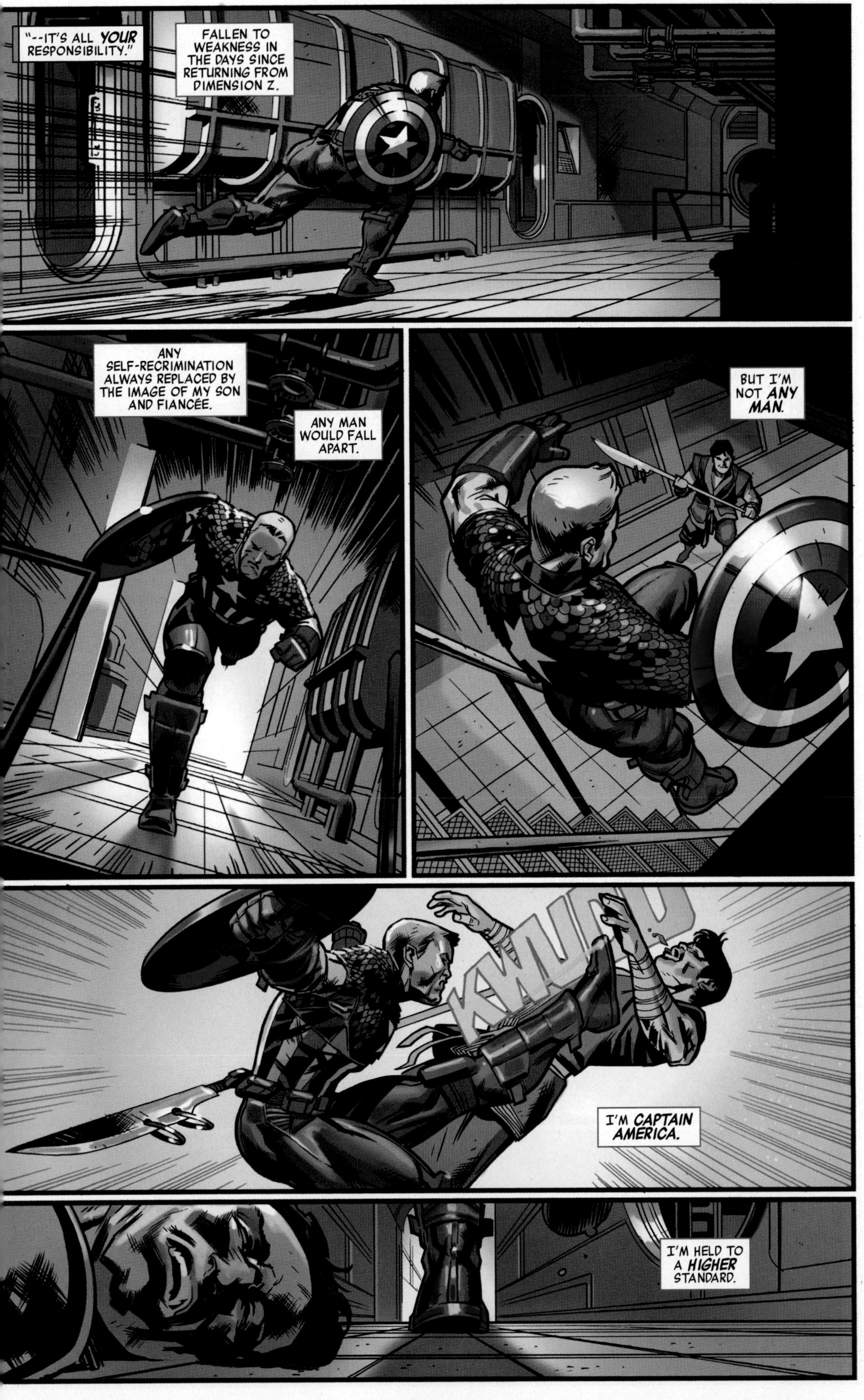
"--IT'S ALL *YOUR* RESPONSIBILITY."
FALLEN TO WEAKNESS IN THE DAYS SINCE RETURNING FROM DIMENSION Z.
ANY SELF-RECRIMINATION ALWAYS REPLACED BY THE IMAGE OF MY SON AND FIANCÉE.
ANY MAN WOULD FALL APART.
BUT I'M NOT *ANY MAN*.
KWUDD
I'M *CAPTAIN AMERICA*.
I'M HELD TO A *HIGHER* STANDARD.

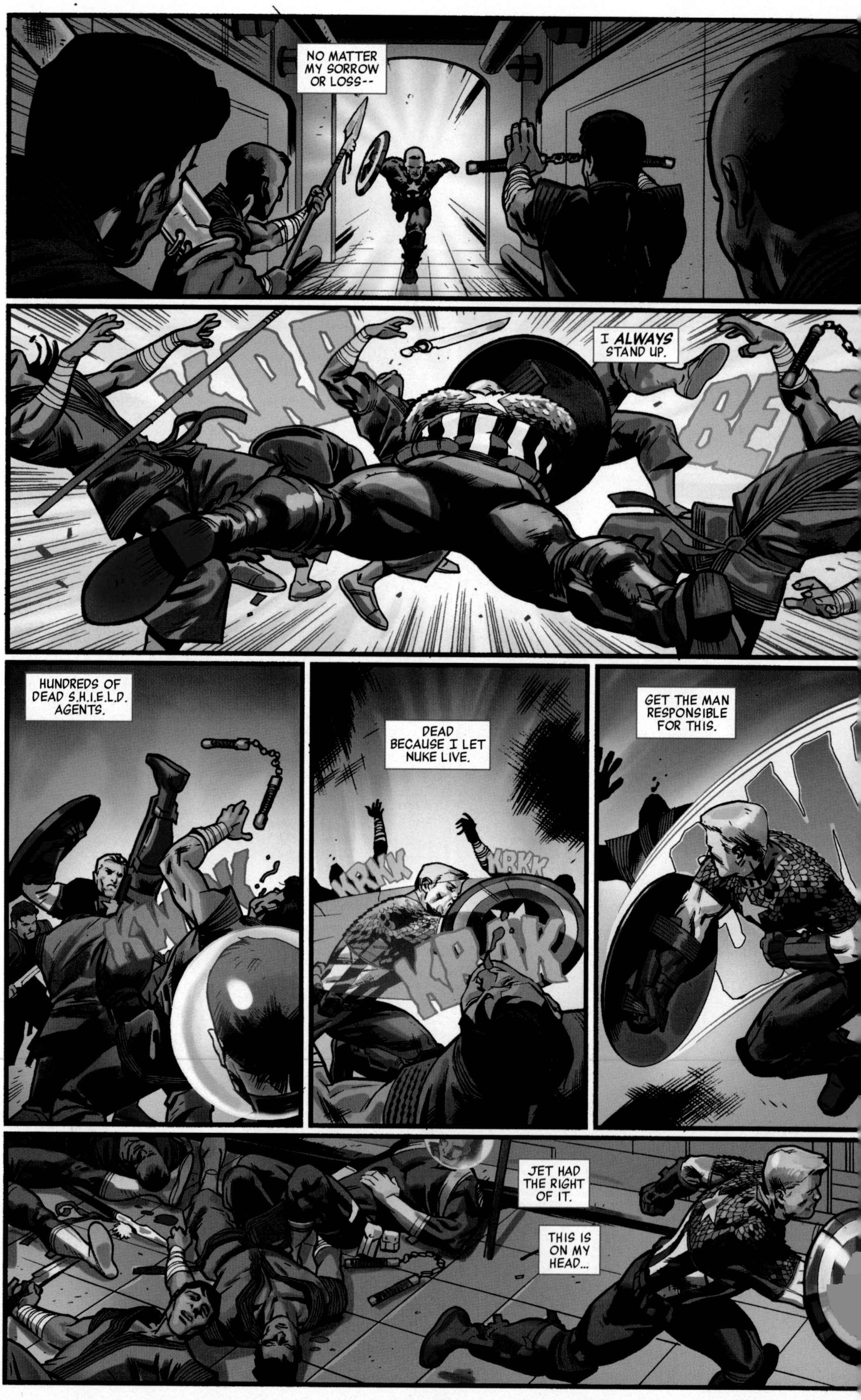
NO MATTER MY SORROW OR LOSS--
I ALWAYS STAND UP.
HUNDREDS OF DEAD S.H.I.E.L.D. AGENTS.
DEAD BECAUSE I LET NUKE LIVE.
KRKK
KRKK
KRAK
GET THE MAN RESPONSIBLE FOR THIS.
JET HAD THE RIGHT OF IT.
THIS IS ON MY HEAD...

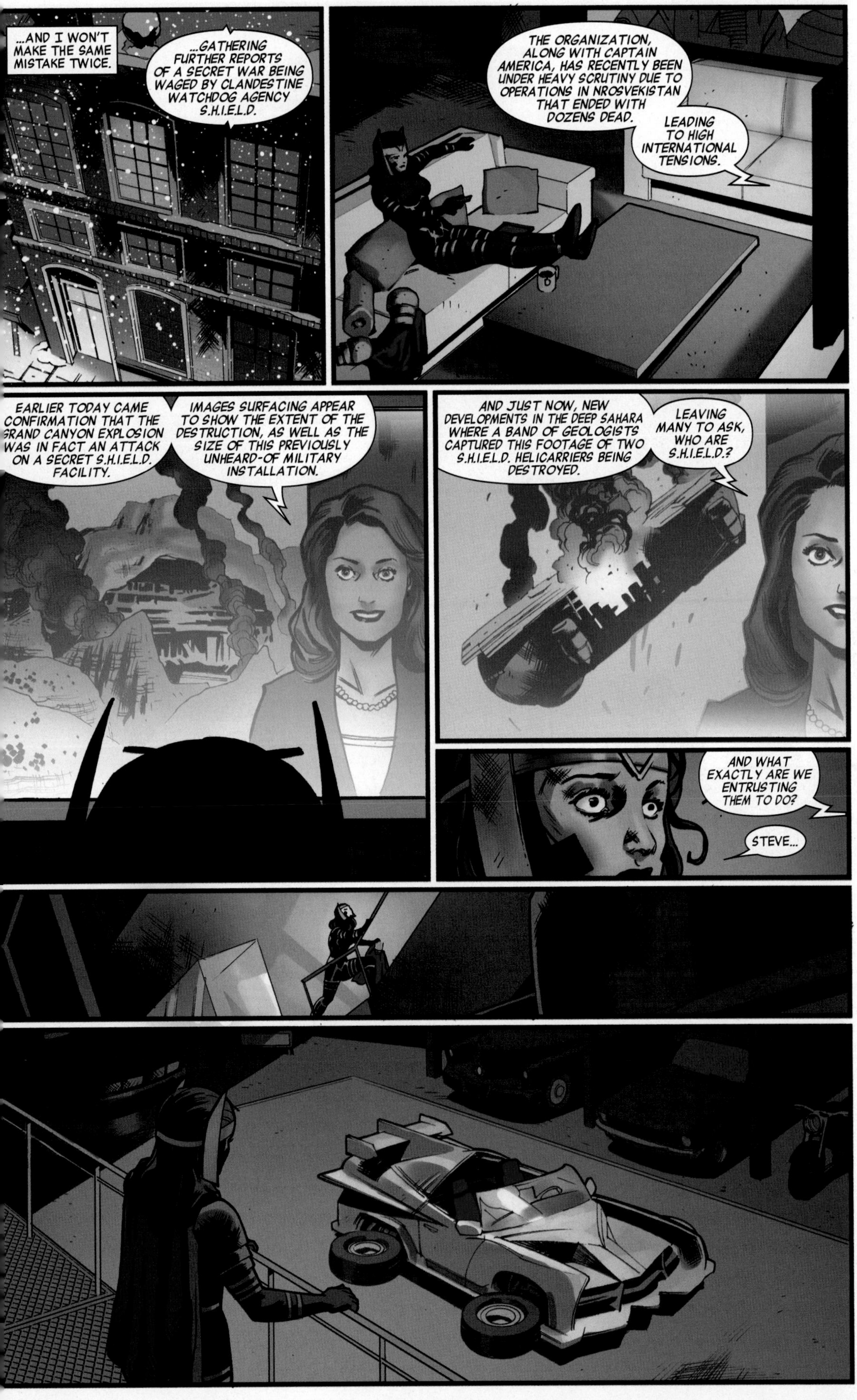
...AND I WON'T MAKE THE SAME MISTAKE TWICE.
...GATHERING FURTHER REPORTS OF A SECRET WAR BEING WAGED BY CLANDESTINE WATCHDOG AGENCY S.H.I.E.L.D.
THE ORGANIZATION, ALONG WITH CAPTAIN AMERICA, HAS RECENTLY BEEN UNDER HEAVY SCRUTINY DUE TO OPERATIONS IN NROSVEKISTAN THAT ENDED WITH DOZENS DEAD.
LEADING TO HIGH INTERNATIONAL TENSIONS.
EARLIER TODAY CAME CONFIRMATION THAT THE GRAND CANYON EXPLOSION WAS IN FACT AN ATTACK ON A SECRET S.H.I.E.L.D. FACILITY.
IMAGES SURFACING APPEAR TO SHOW THE EXTENT OF THE DESTRUCTION, AS WELL AS THE SIZE OF THIS PREVIOUSLY UNHEARD-OF MILITARY INSTALLATION.
AND JUST NOW, NEW DEVELOPMENTS IN THE DEEP SAHARA WHERE A BAND OF GEOLOGISTS CAPTURED THIS FOOTAGE OF TWO S.H.I.E.L.D. HELICARRIERS BEING DESTROYED.
LEAVING MANY TO ASK, WHO ARE S.H.I.E.L.D.?
AND WHAT EXACTLY ARE WE ENTRUSTING THEM TO DO?
STEVE...

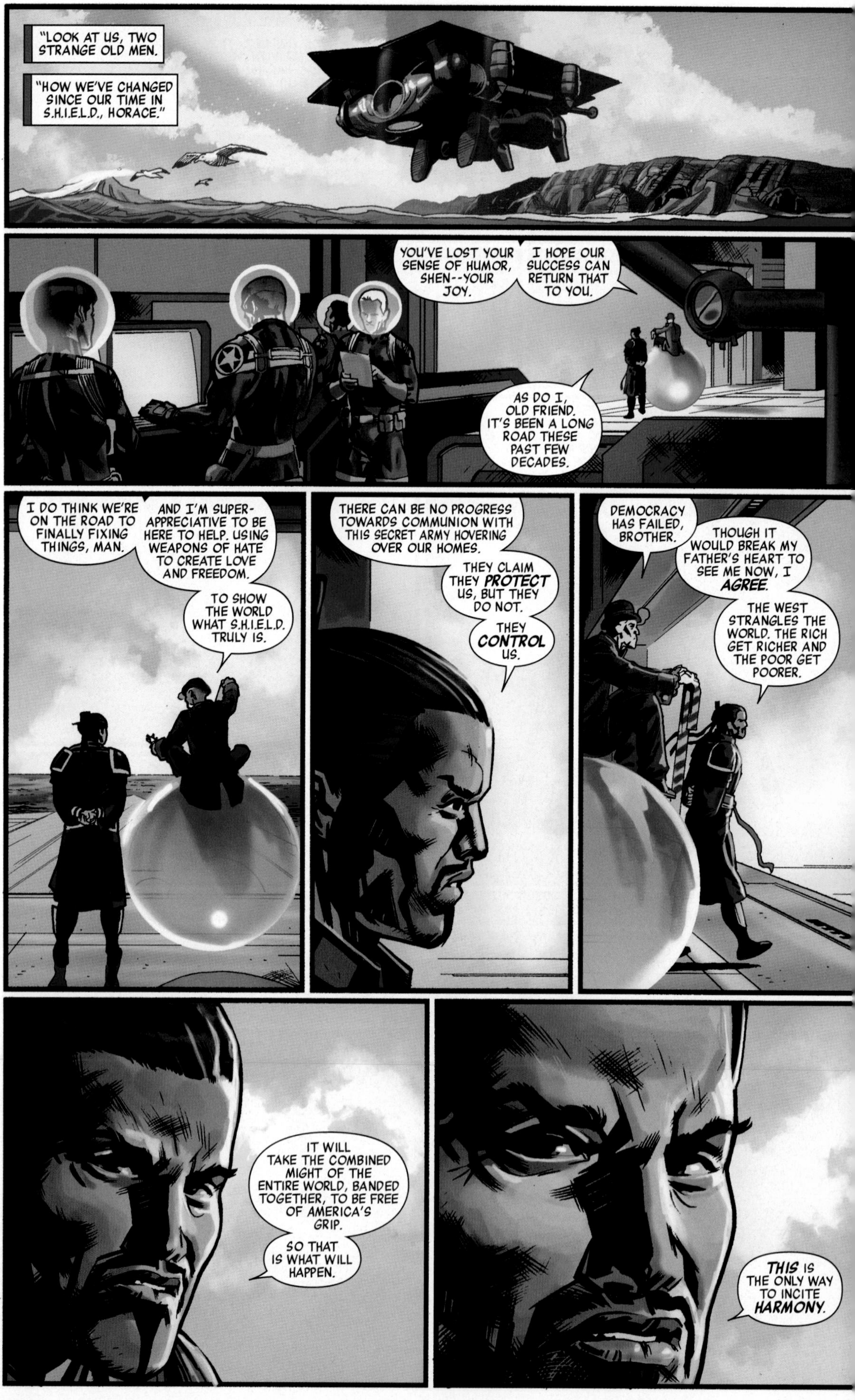
"LOOK AT US, TWO STRANGE OLD MEN.
"HOW WE'VE CHANGED SINCE OUR TIME IN S.H.I.E.L.D., HORACE."
YOU'VE LOST YOUR SENSE OF HUMOR, SHEN--YOUR JOY.
I HOPE OUR SUCCESS CAN RETURN THAT TO YOU.
AS DO I, OLD FRIEND. IT'S BEEN A LONG ROAD THESE PAST FEW DECADES.
I DO THINK WE'RE ON THE ROAD TO FINALLY FIXING THINGS, MAN.
AND I'M SUPER-APPRECIATIVE TO BE HERE TO HELP. USING WEAPONS OF HATE TO CREATE LOVE AND FREEDOM.
TO SHOW THE WORLD WHAT S.H.I.E.L.D. TRULY IS.
THERE CAN BE NO PROGRESS TOWARDS COMMUNION WITH THIS SECRET ARMY HOVERING OVER OUR HOMES.
THEY CLAIM THEY PROTECT US, BUT THEY DO NOT.
THEY CONTROL US.
DEMOCRACY HAS FAILED, BROTHER.
THOUGH IT WOULD BREAK MY FATHER'S HEART TO SEE ME NOW, I AGREE.
THE WEST STRANGLES THE WORLD. THE RICH GET RICHER AND THE POOR GET POORER.
IT WILL TAKE THE COMBINED MIGHT OF THE ENTIRE WORLD, BANDED TOGETHER, TO BE FREE OF AMERICA'S GRIP.
SO THAT IS WHAT WILL HAPPEN.
THIS IS THE ONLY WAY TO INCITE HARMONY.

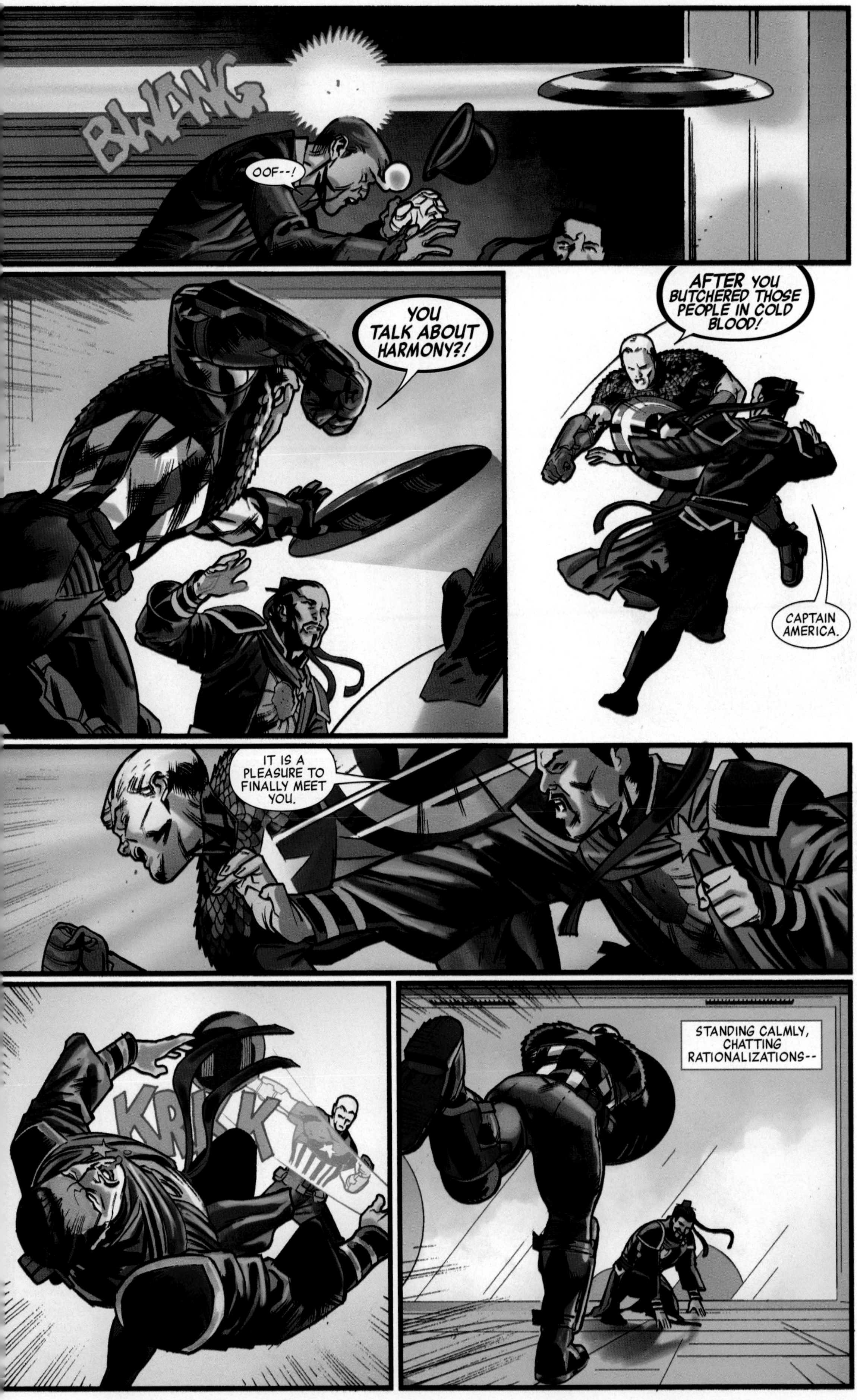
BWANG
OOF--!
YOU TALK ABOUT HARMONY?!
AFTER YOU BUTCHERED THOSE PEOPLE IN COLD BLOOD!
CAPTAIN AMERICA.
IT IS A PLEASURE TO FINALLY MEET YOU.
KRAK
STANDING CALMLY, CHATTING RATIONALIZATIONS--

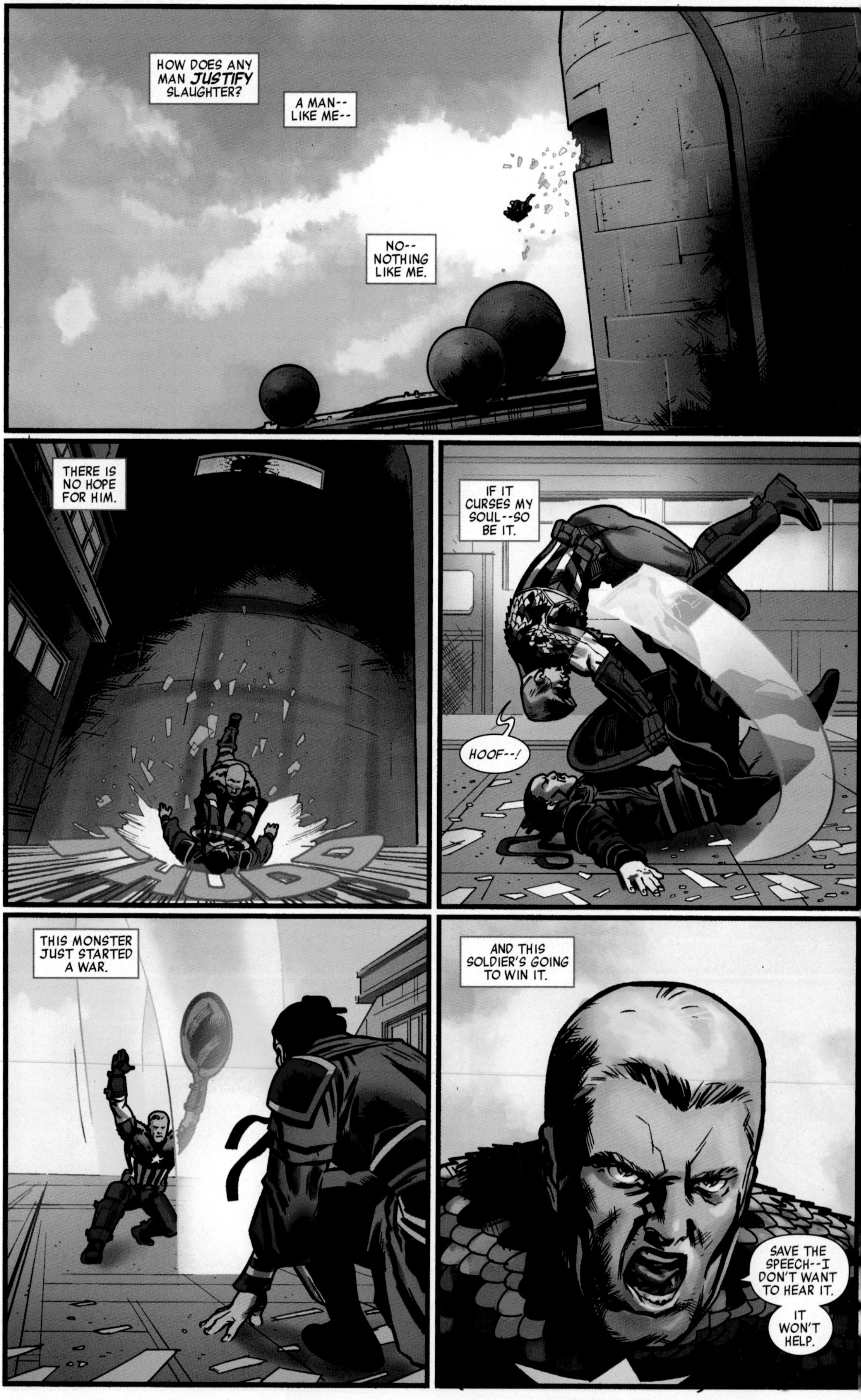

HOW DOES ANY MAN JUSTIFY SLAUGHTER?
A MAN-- LIKE ME--
NO-- NOTHING LIKE ME.
THERE IS NO HOPE FOR HIM.
IF IT CURSES MY SOUL--SO BE IT.
HOOF--!
THIS MONSTER JUST STARTED A WAR.
AND THIS SOLDIER'S GOING TO WIN IT.
SAVE THE SPEECH--I DON'T WANT TO HEAR IT.
IT WON'T HELP.

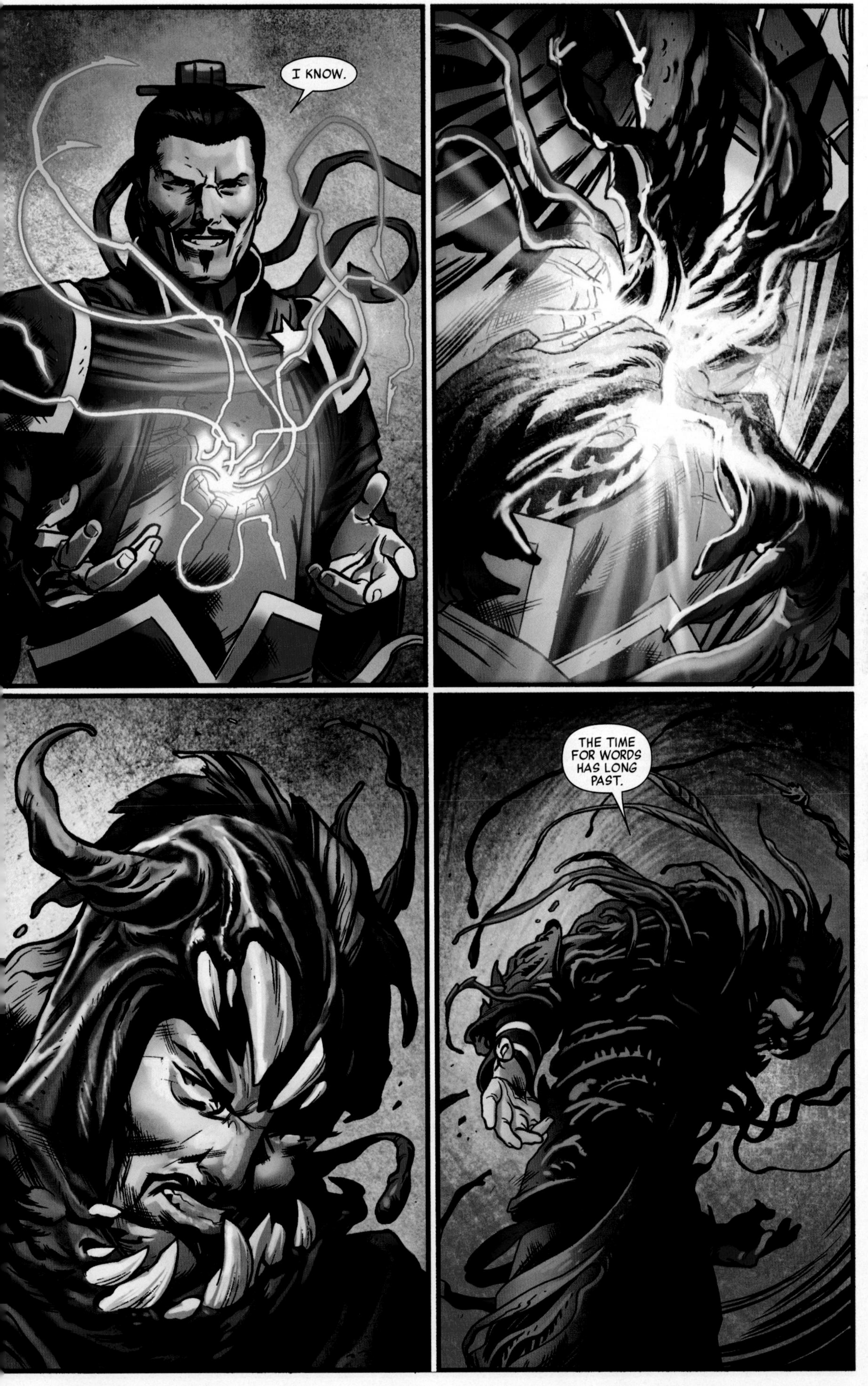
I KNOW.
THE TIME FOR WORDS HAS LONG PAST.

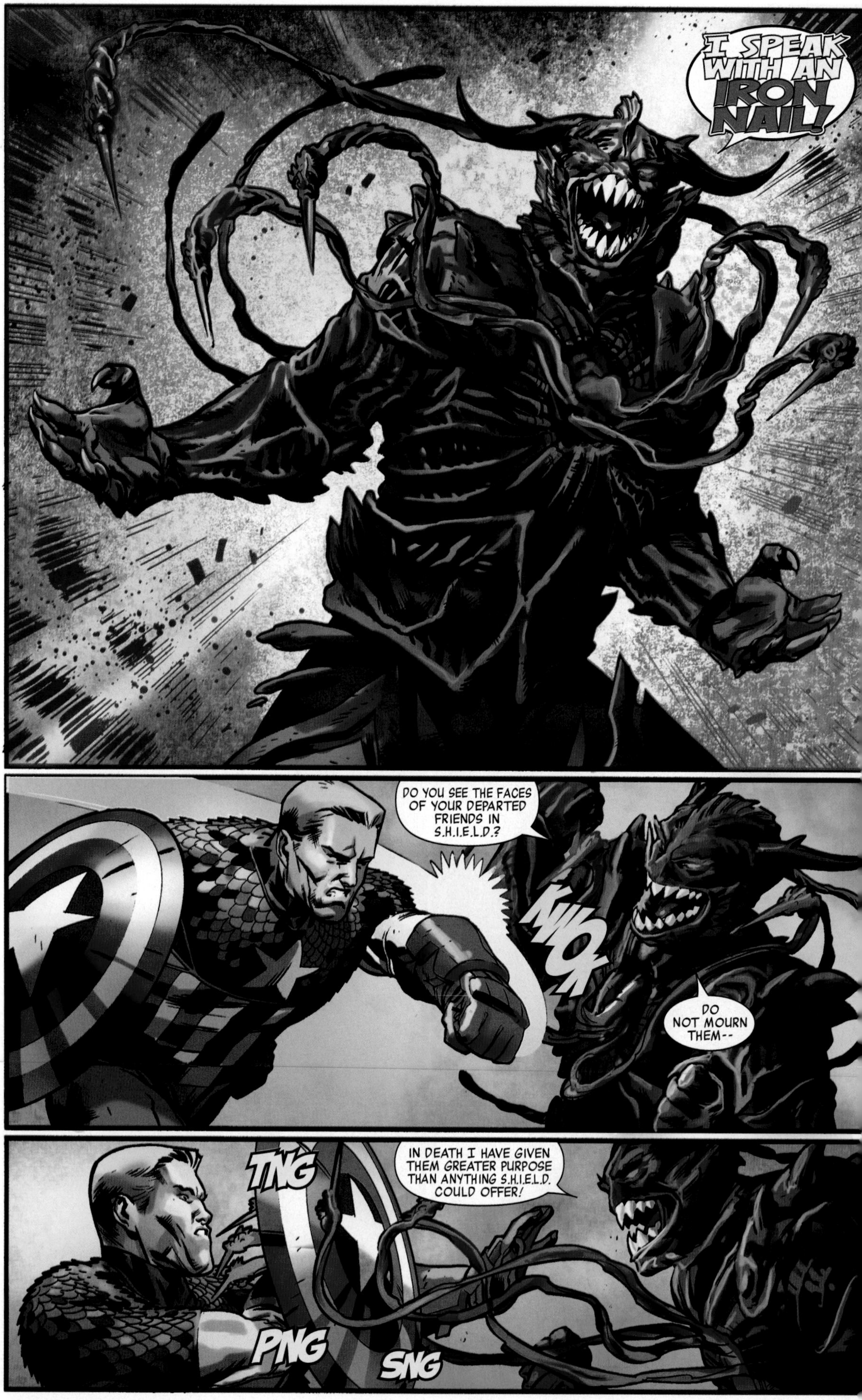
I SPEAK WITH AN IRON NAIL!
DO YOU SEE THE FACES OF YOUR DEPARTED FRIENDS IN S.H.I.E.L.D.?
KWOK
DO NOT MOURN THEM--
TNG
IN DEATH I HAVE GIVEN THEM GREATER PURPOSE THAN ANYTHING S.H.I.E.L.D. COULD OFFER!
PNG
SNG

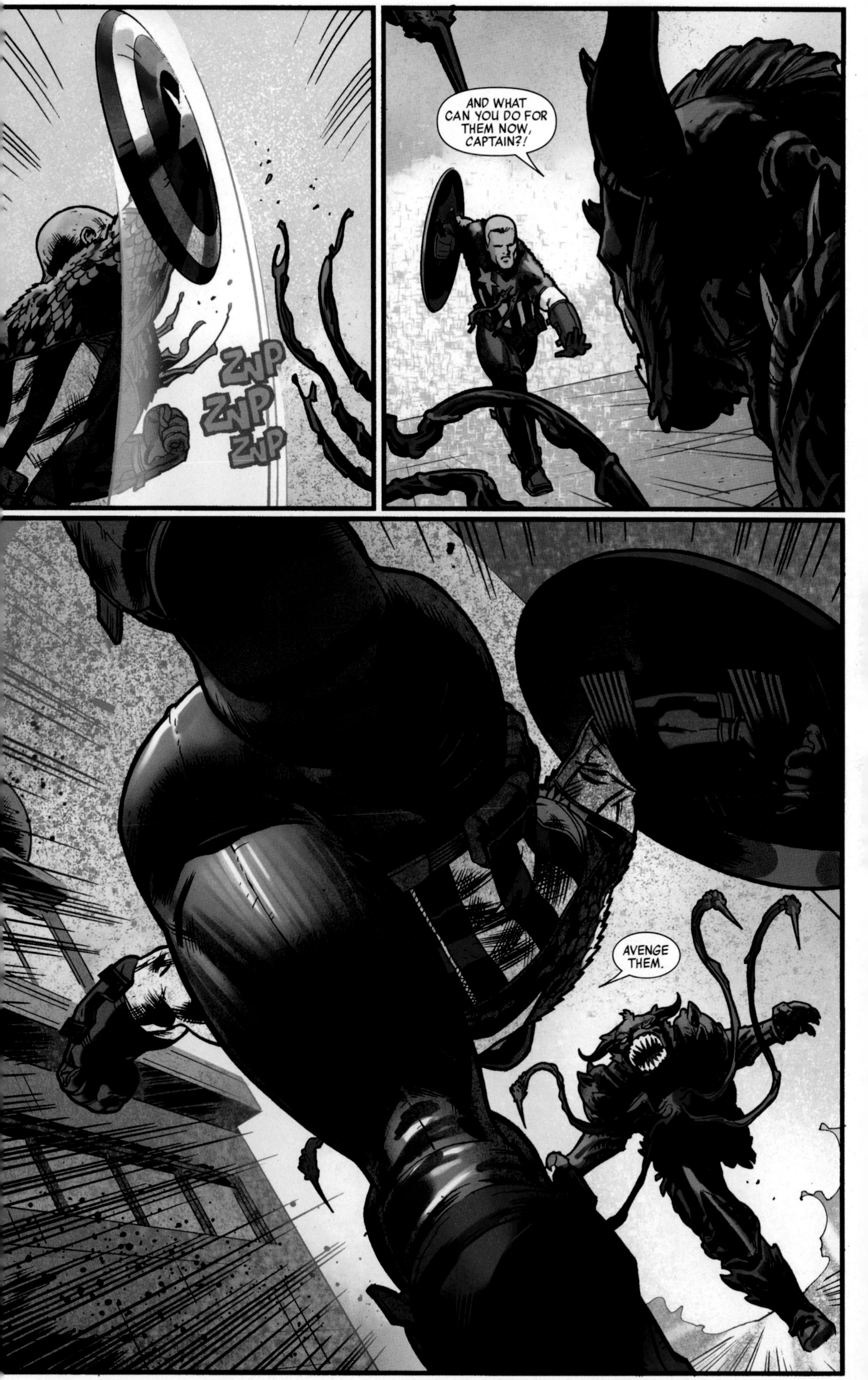
ZNP
ZNP
ZNP
AND WHAT CAN YOU DO FOR THEM NOW, CAPTAIN?!
AVENGE THEM.

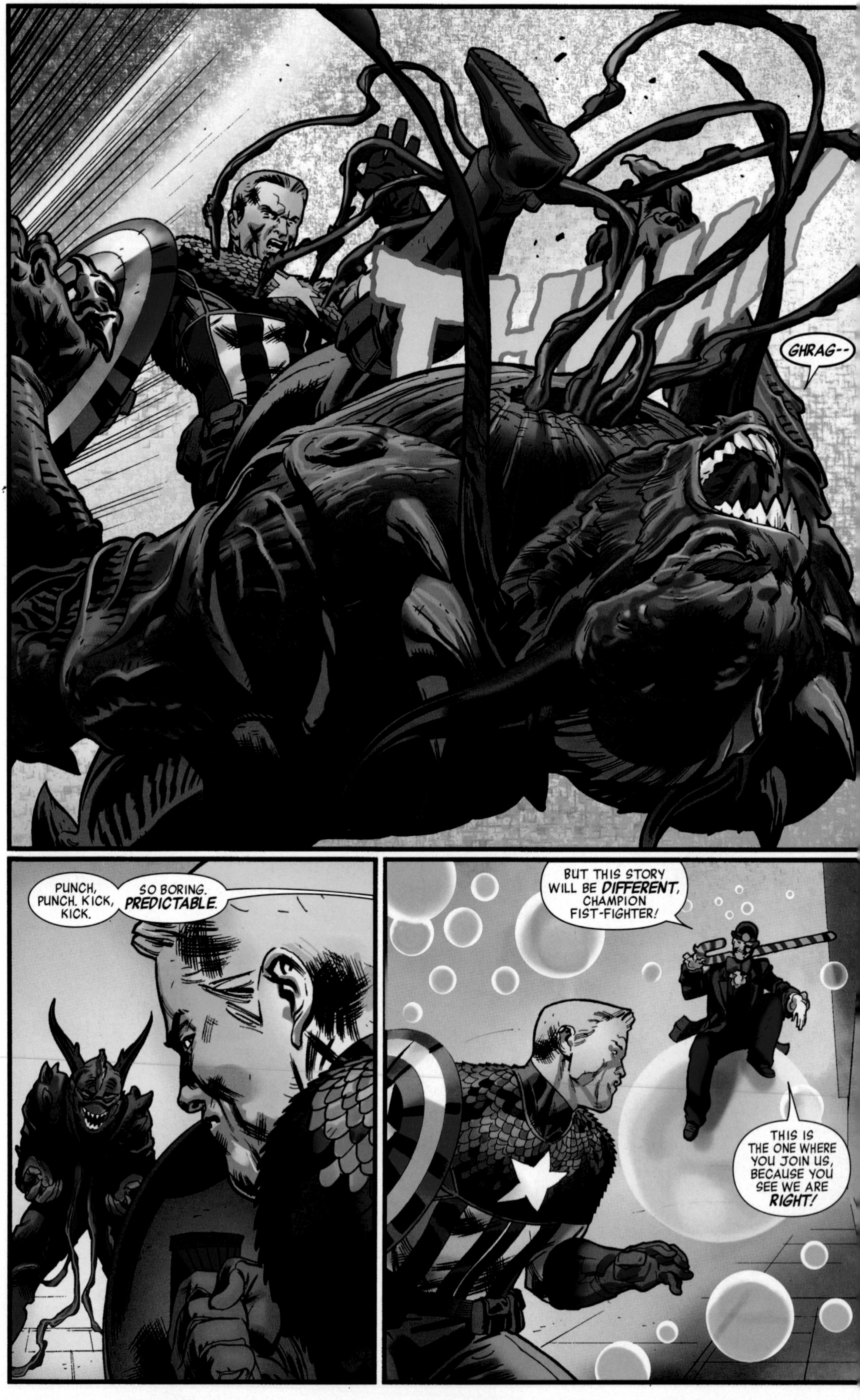
THWAM
GHRAG--
PUNCH, PUNCH. KICK, KICK.
SO BORING. PREDICTABLE.
BUT THIS STORY WILL BE DIFFERENT, CHAMPION FIST-FIGHTER!
THIS IS THE ONE WHERE YOU JOIN US, BECAUSE YOU SEE WE ARE RIGHT!

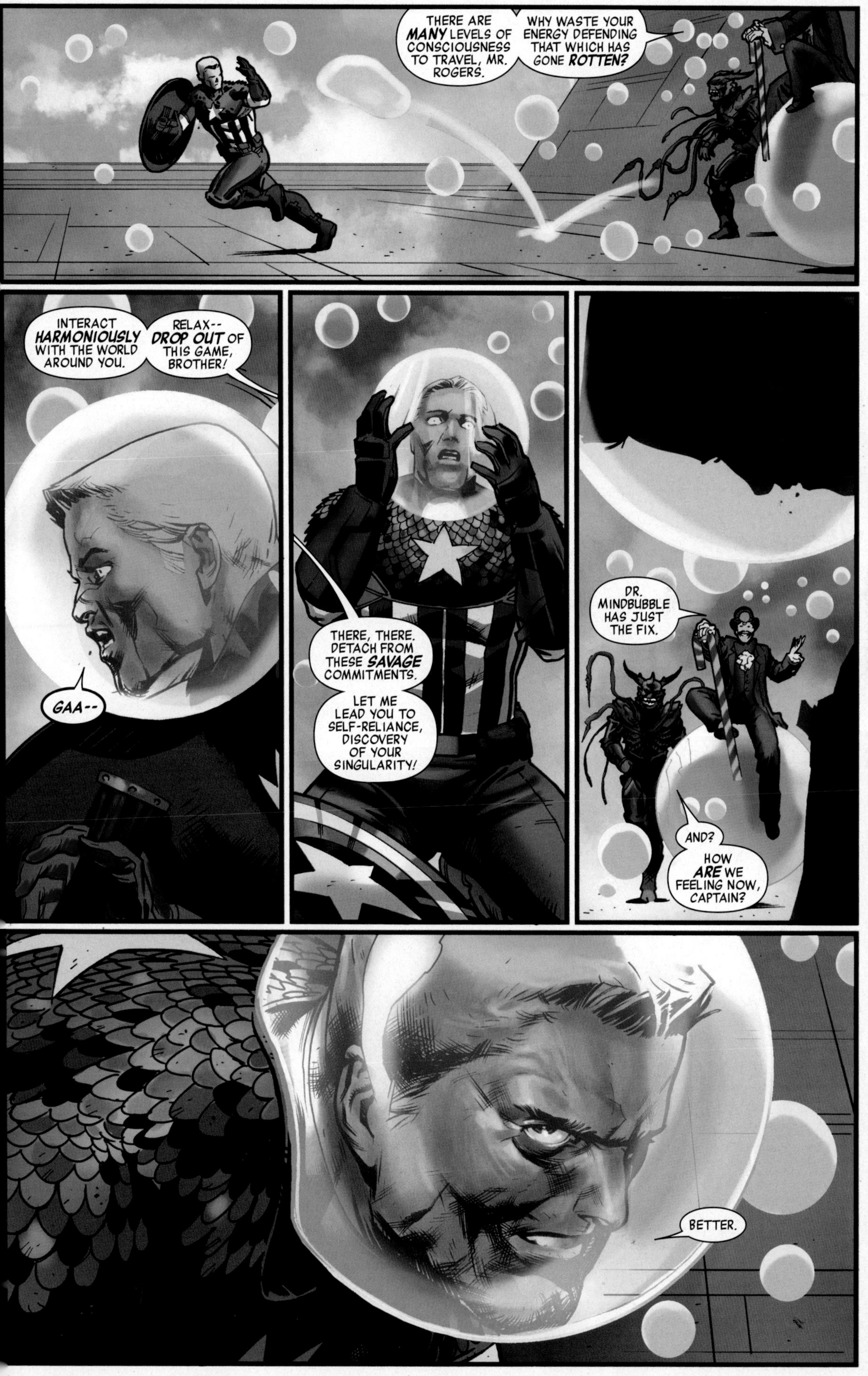
THERE ARE MANY LEVELS OF CONSCIOUSNESS TO TRAVEL, MR. ROGERS.
WHY WASTE YOUR ENERGY DEFENDING THAT WHICH HAS GONE ROTTEN?
INTERACT HARMONIOUSLY WITH THE WORLD AROUND YOU.
RELAX-- DROP OUT OF THIS GAME, BROTHER!
GAA--
THERE, THERE. DETACH FROM THESE SAVAGE COMMITMENTS.
LET ME LEAD YOU TO SELF-RELIANCE, DISCOVERY OF YOUR SINGULARITY!
DR. MINDBUBBLE HAS JUST THE FIX.
AND?
HOW ARE WE FEELING NOW, CAPTAIN?
BETTER.

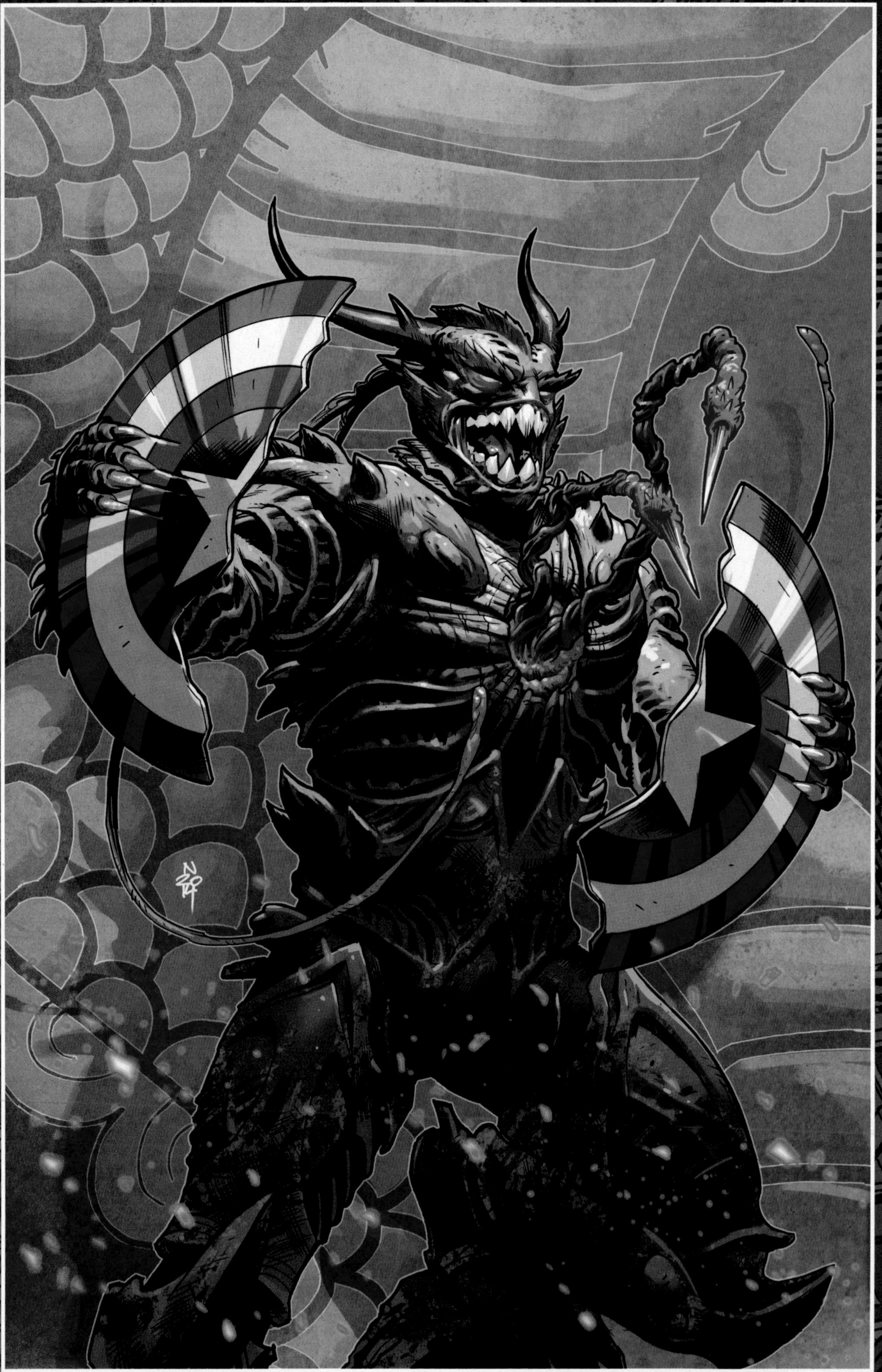

TWENTY

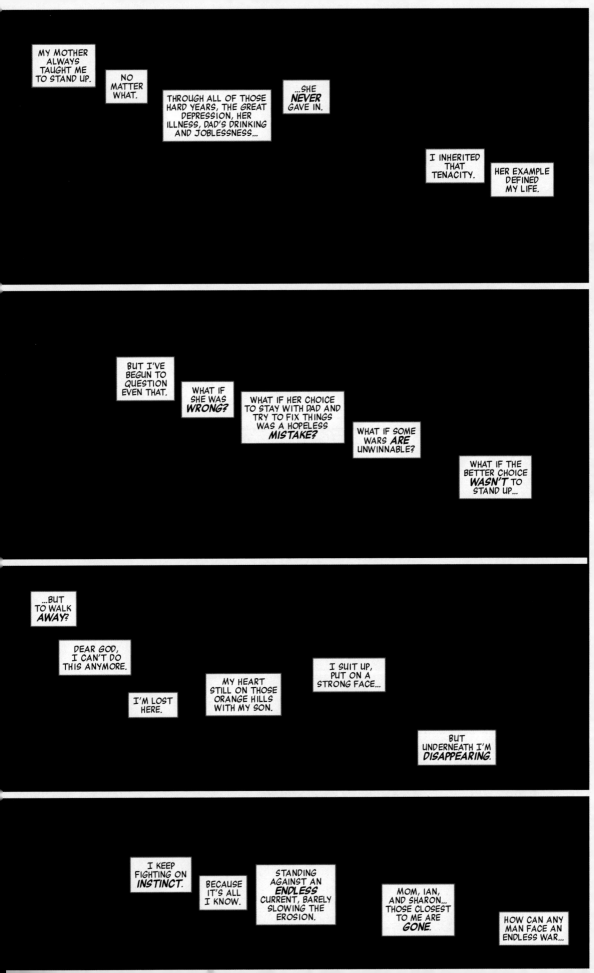

MY MOTHER ALWAYS TAUGHT ME TO STAND UP.

NO MATTER WHAT.

THROUGH ALL OF THOSE HARD YEARS, THE GREAT DEPRESSION, HER ILLNESS, DAD'S DRINKING AND JOBLESSNESS...

...SHE *NEVER* GAVE IN.

I INHERITED THAT TENACITY.

HER EXAMPLE DEFINED MY LIFE.

BUT I'VE BEGUN TO QUESTION EVEN THAT.

WHAT IF SHE WAS *WRONG?*

WHAT IF HER CHOICE TO STAY WITH DAD AND TRY TO FIX THINGS WAS A HOPELESS *MISTAKE?*

WHAT IF SOME WARS *ARE* UNWINNABLE?

WHAT IF THE BETTER CHOICE *WASN'T* TO STAND UP...

...BUT TO WALK *AWAY?*

DEAR GOD, I CAN'T DO THIS ANYMORE.

I'M LOST HERE.

MY HEART STILL ON THOSE ORANGE HILLS WITH MY SON.

I SUIT UP, PUT ON A STRONG FACE...

BUT UNDERNEATH I'M *DISAPPEARING.*

I KEEP FIGHTING ON *INSTINCT.*

BECAUSE IT'S ALL I KNOW.

STANDING AGAINST AN *ENDLESS* CURRENT, BARELY SLOWING THE EROSION.

MOM, IAN, AND SHARON... THOSE CLOSEST TO ME ARE *GONE.*

HOW CAN ANY MAN FACE AN ENDLESS WAR...

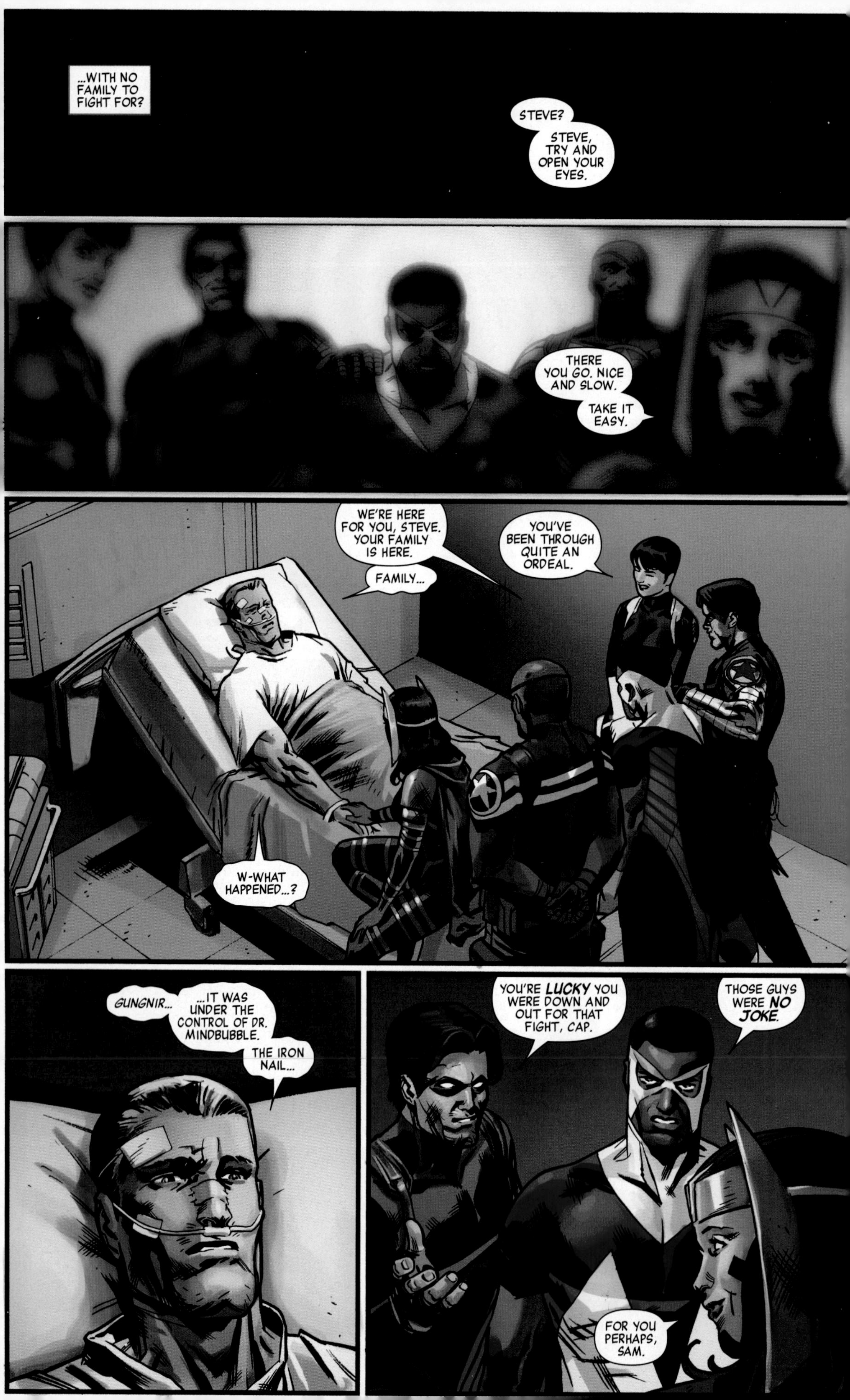
...WITH NO FAMILY TO FIGHT FOR?
STEVE?
STEVE, TRY AND OPEN YOUR EYES.
THERE YOU GO. NICE AND SLOW.
TAKE IT EASY.
WE'RE HERE FOR YOU, STEVE. YOUR FAMILY IS HERE.
FAMILY...
YOU'VE BEEN THROUGH QUITE AN ORDEAL.
W-WHAT HAPPENED...?
GUNGNIR...
...IT WAS UNDER THE CONTROL OF DR. MINDBUBBLE.
THE IRON NAIL...
YOU'RE LUCKY YOU WERE DOWN AND OUT FOR THAT FIGHT, CAP.
THOSE GUYS WERE NO JOKE.
FOR YOU PERHAPS, SAM.

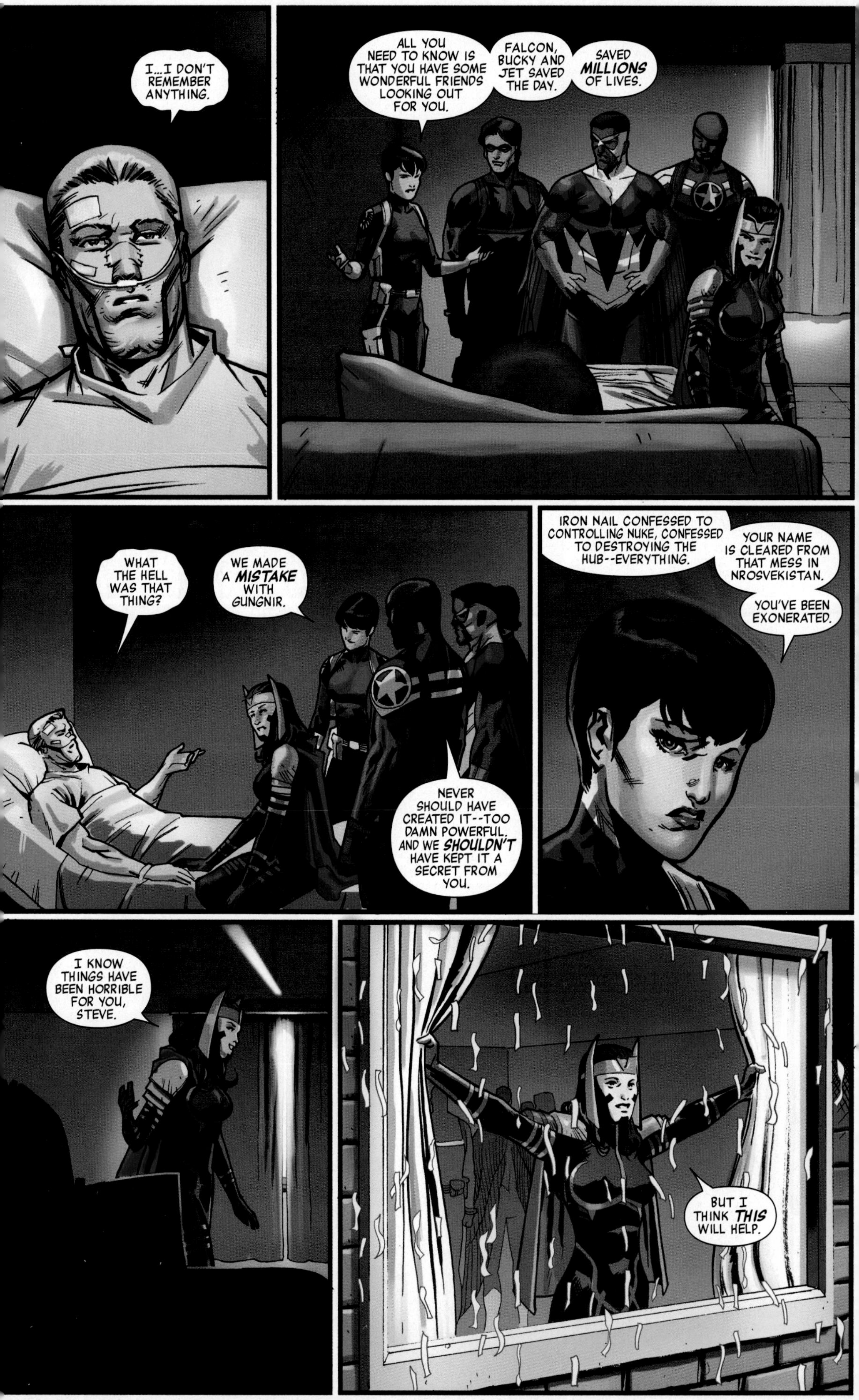
I...I DON'T REMEMBER ANYTHING.
ALL YOU NEED TO KNOW IS THAT YOU HAVE SOME WONDERFUL FRIENDS LOOKING OUT FOR YOU.
FALCON, BUCKY AND JET SAVED THE DAY.
SAVED MILLIONS OF LIVES.
WHAT THE HELL WAS THAT THING?
WE MADE A MISTAKE WITH GUNGNIR.
NEVER SHOULD HAVE CREATED IT--TOO DAMN POWERFUL, AND WE SHOULDN'T HAVE KEPT IT A SECRET FROM YOU.
IRON NAIL CONFESSED TO CONTROLLING NUKE, CONFESSED TO DESTROYING THE HUB--EVERYTHING.
YOUR NAME IS CLEARED FROM THAT MESS IN NROSVEKISTAN.
YOU'VE BEEN EXONERATED.
I KNOW THINGS HAVE BEEN HORRIBLE FOR YOU, STEVE.
BUT I THINK THIS WILL HELP.

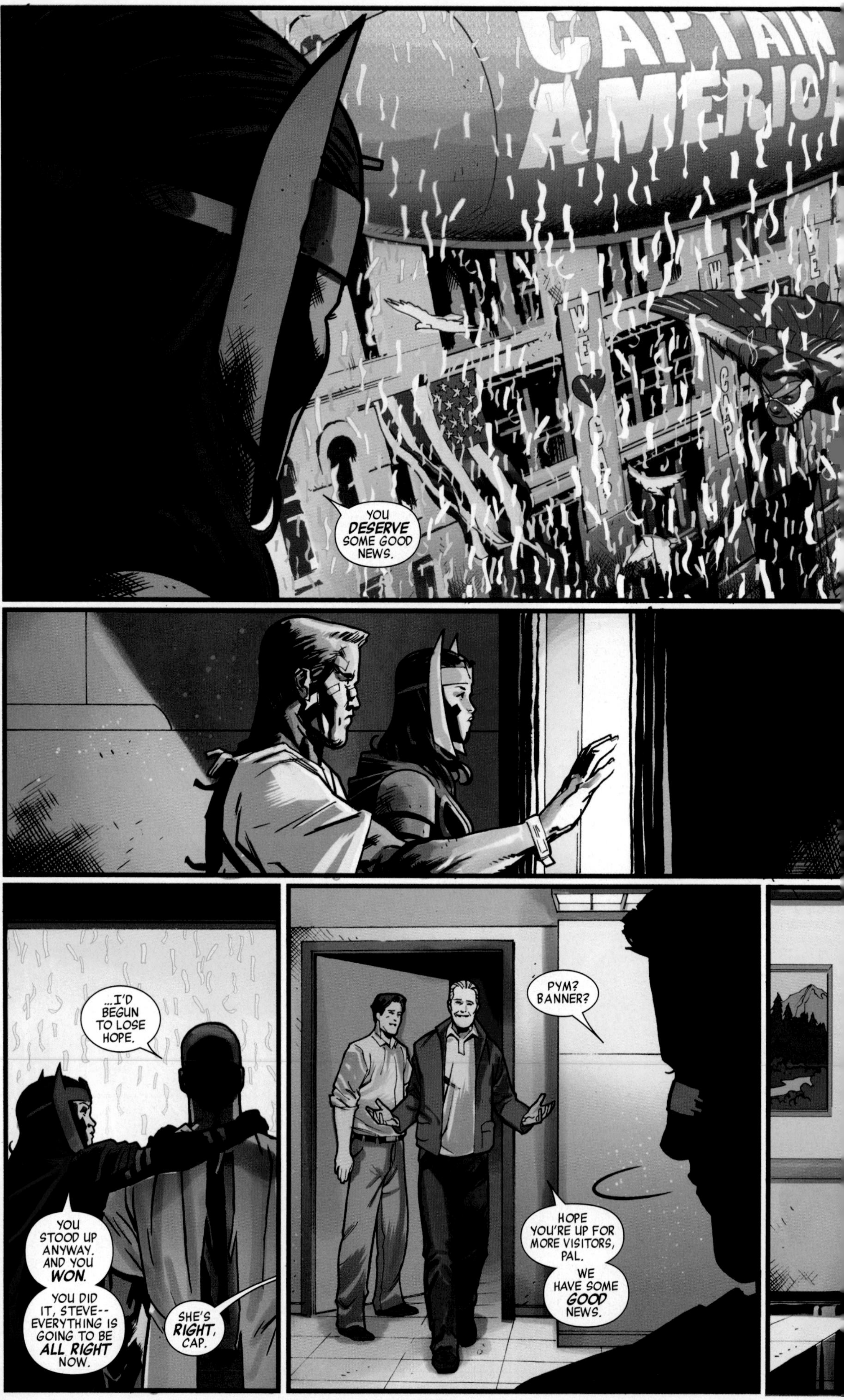
CAPTAIN AMERICA
YOU DESERVE SOME GOOD NEWS.
...I'D BEGUN TO LOSE HOPE.
YOU STOOD UP ANYWAY. AND YOU WON.
YOU DID IT, STEVE-- EVERYTHING IS GOING TO BE ALL RIGHT NOW.
SHE'S RIGHT, CAP.
PYM? BANNER?
HOPE YOU'RE UP FOR MORE VISITORS, PAL.
WE HAVE SOME GOOD NEWS.

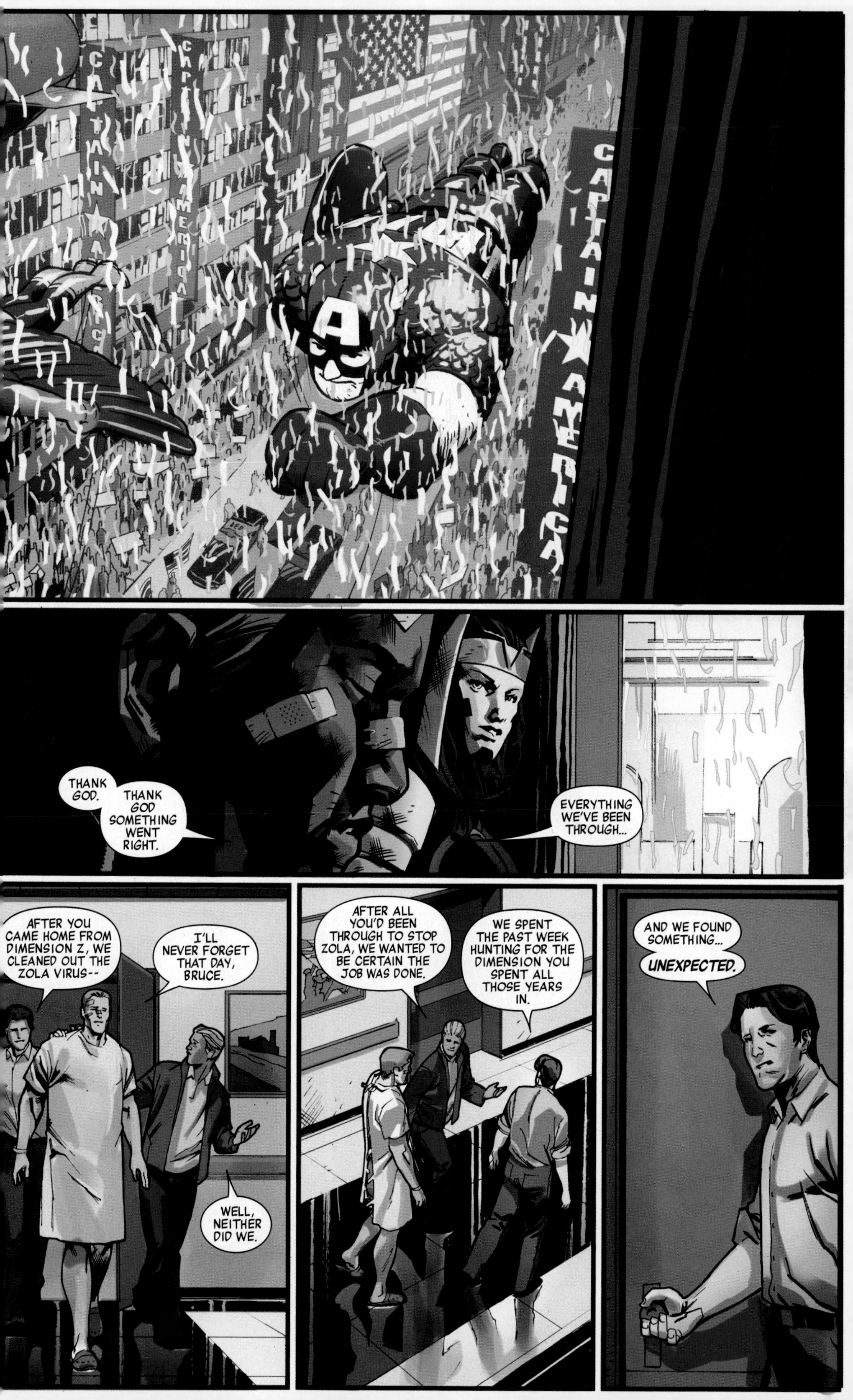

CAPTAIN AMERICA
CAPTAIN AMERICA
CAPTAIN ★ AMERICA
THANK GOD.
THANK GOD SOMETHING WENT RIGHT.
EVERYTHING WE'VE BEEN THROUGH...
AFTER YOU CAME HOME FROM DIMENSION Z, WE CLEANED OUT THE ZOLA VIRUS--
I'LL NEVER FORGET THAT DAY, BRUCE.
WELL, NEITHER DID WE.
AFTER ALL YOU'D BEEN THROUGH TO STOP ZOLA, WE WANTED TO BE CERTAIN THE JOB WAS DONE.
WE SPENT THE PAST WEEK HUNTING FOR THE DIMENSION YOU SPENT ALL THOSE YEARS IN.
AND WE FOUND SOMETHING... ***UNEXPECTED.***

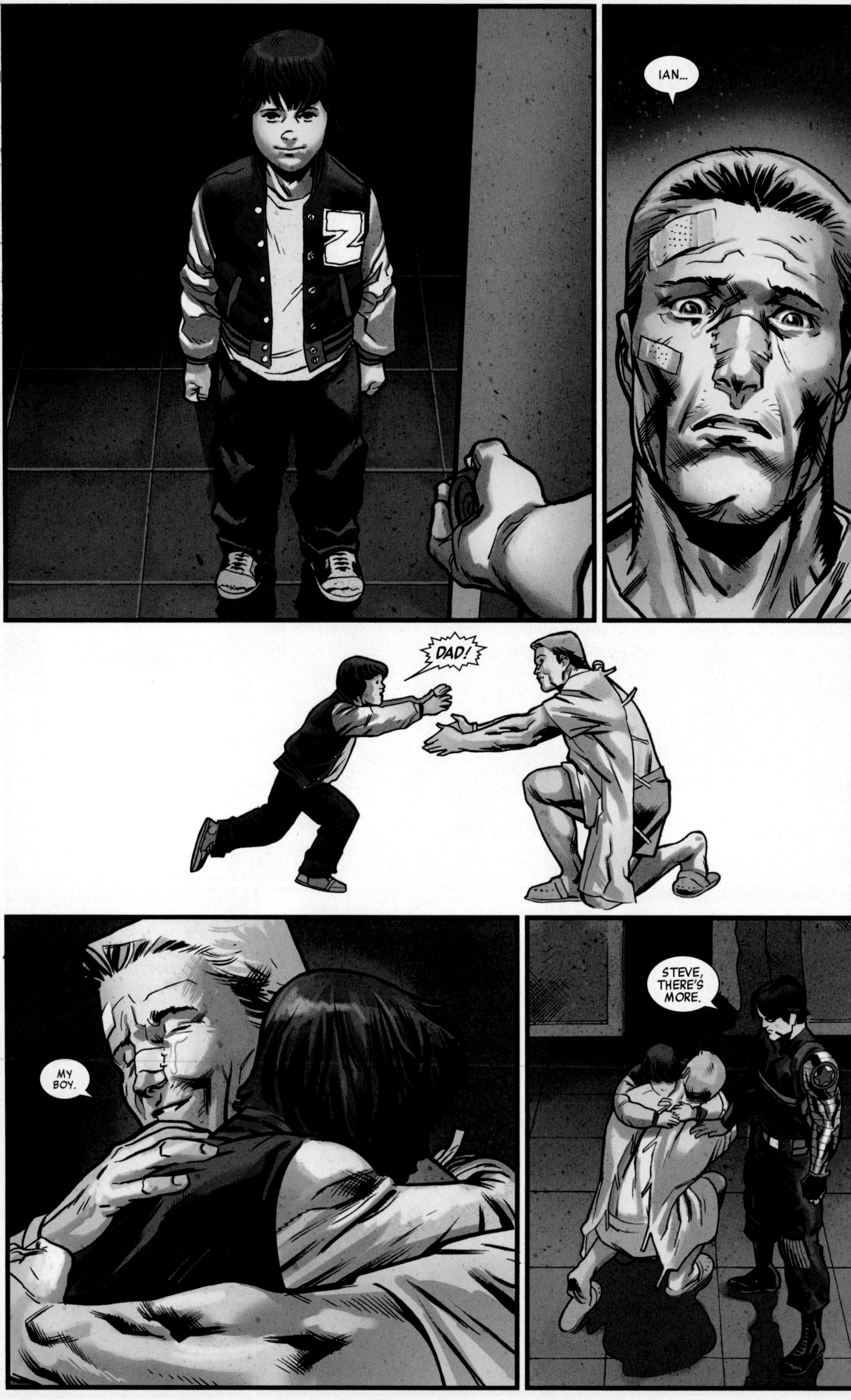
IAN...
DAD!
MY BOY.
STEVE, THERE'S MORE.

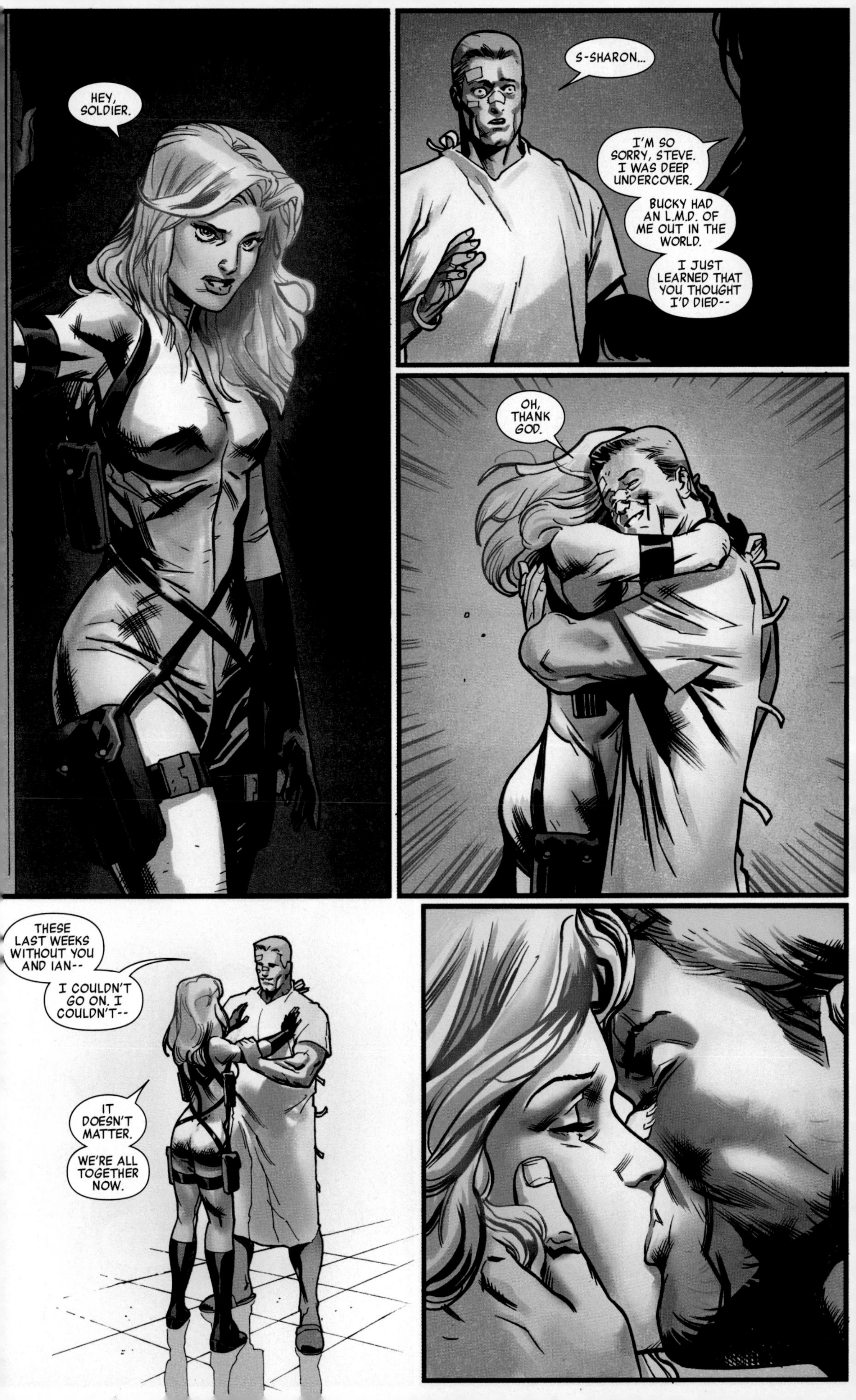
HEY, SOLDIER.
S-SHARON...
I'M SO SORRY, STEVE. I WAS DEEP UNDERCOVER.
BUCKY HAD AN L.M.D. OF ME OUT IN THE WORLD.
I JUST LEARNED THAT YOU THOUGHT I'D DIED--
OH, THANK GOD.
THESE LAST WEEKS WITHOUT YOU AND IAN--
I COULDN'T GO ON. I COULDN'T--
IT DOESN'T MATTER.
WE'RE ALL TOGETHER NOW.

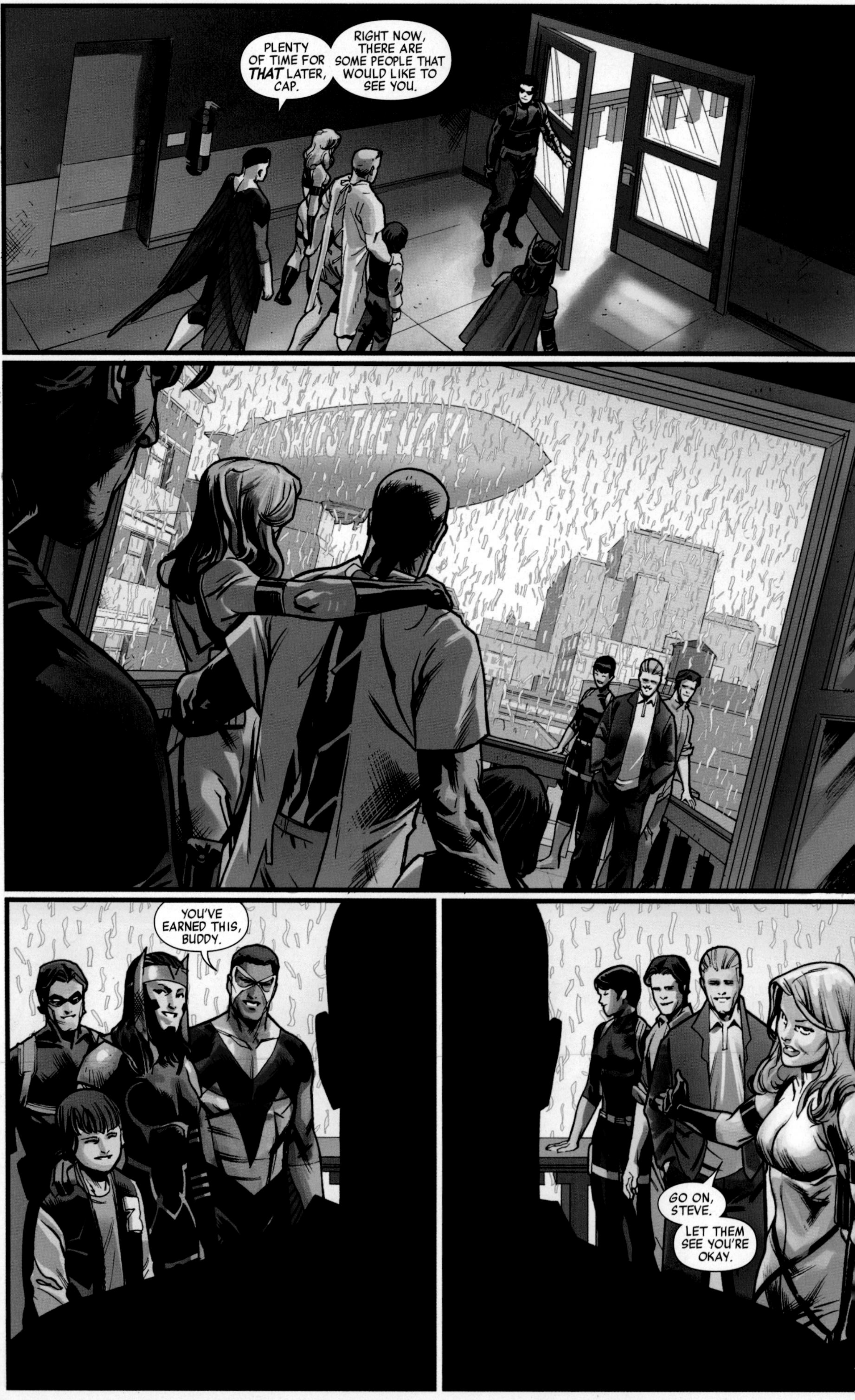
PLENTY OF TIME FOR THAT LATER, CAP.
RIGHT NOW, THERE ARE SOME PEOPLE THAT WOULD LIKE TO SEE YOU.
YOU'VE EARNED THIS, BUDDY.
GO ON, STEVE.
LET THEM SEE YOU'RE OKAY.

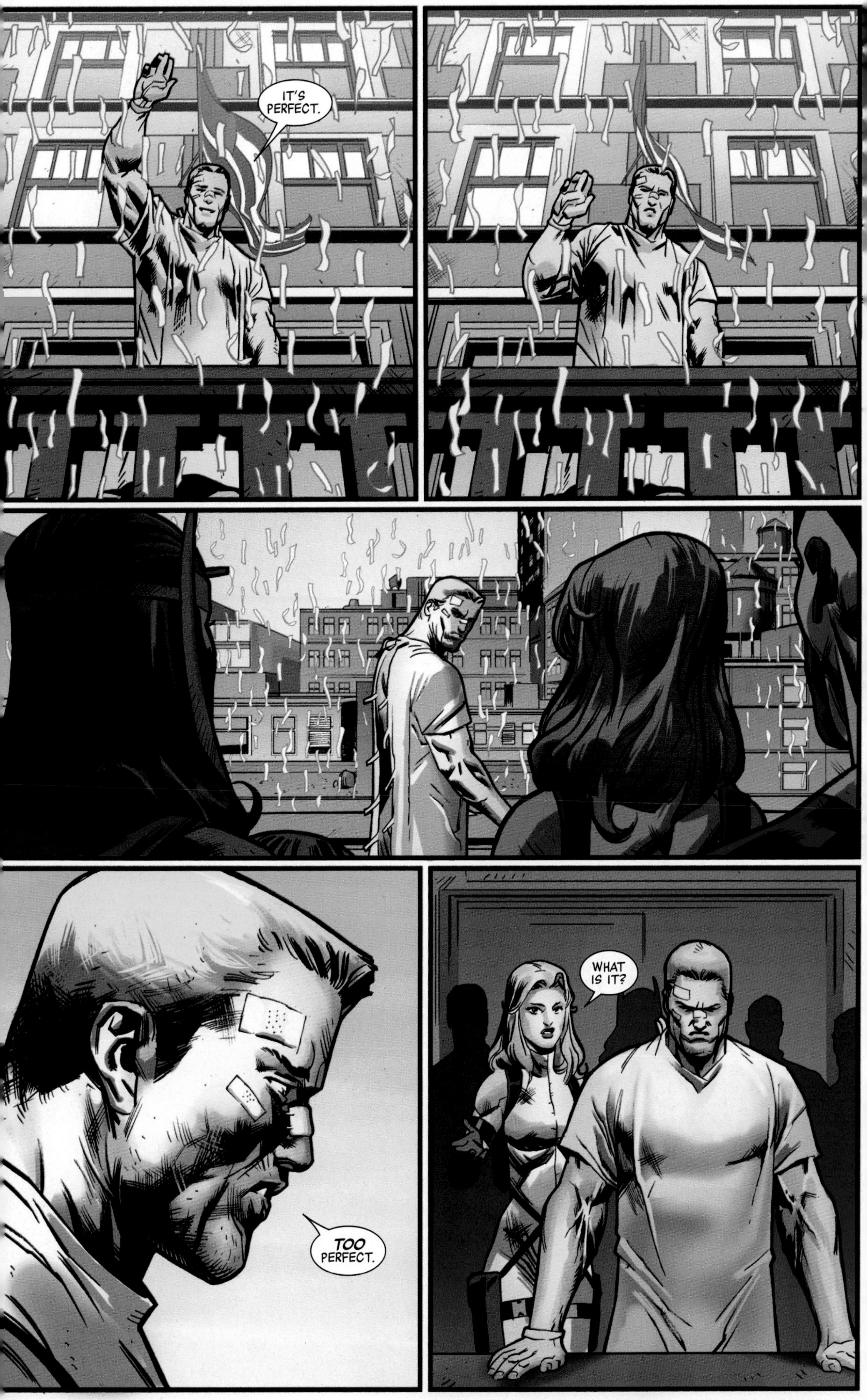
IT'S PERFECT.
WHAT IS IT?
TOO PERFECT.

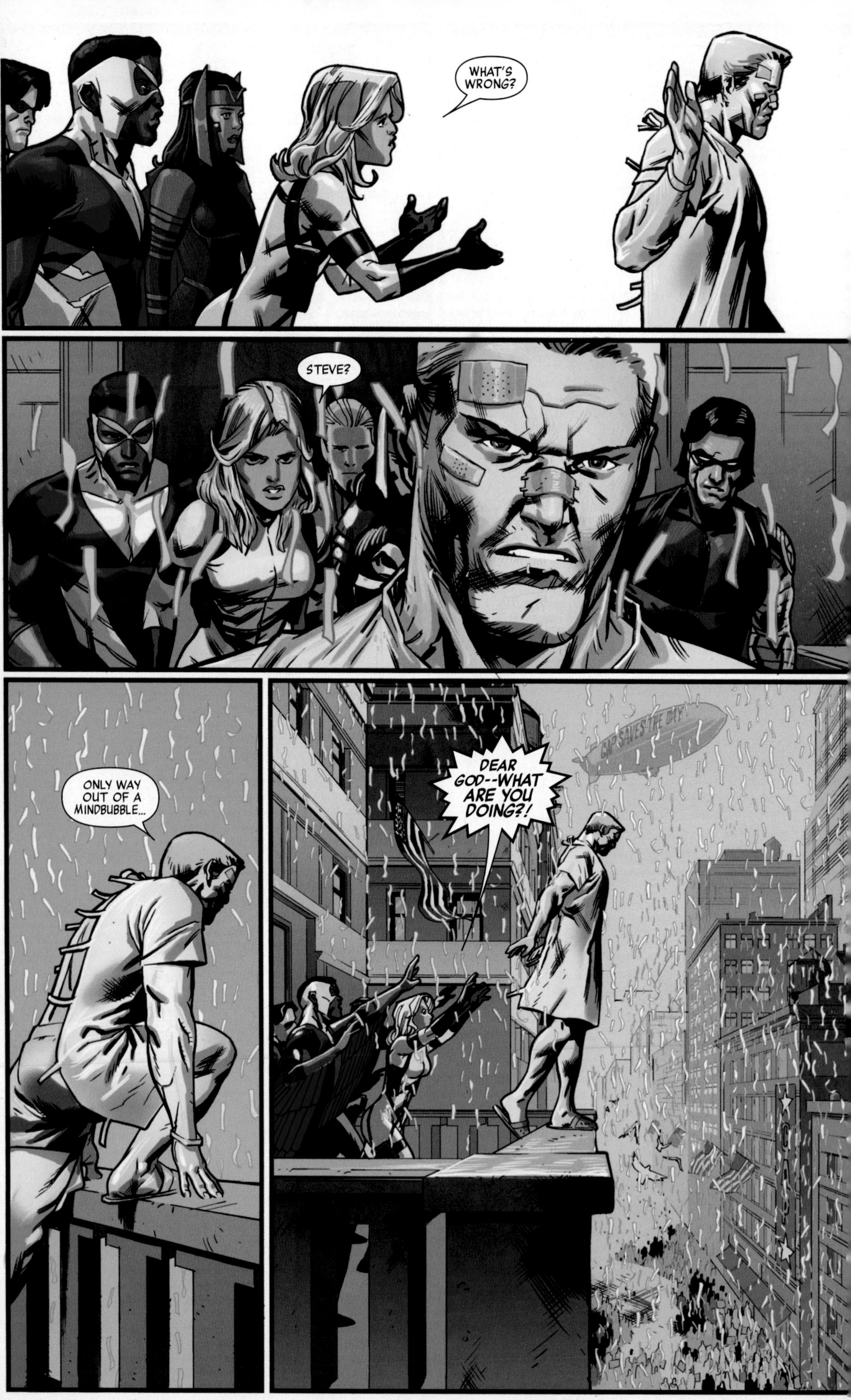
WHAT'S WRONG?
STEVE?
ONLY WAY OUT OF A MINDBUBBLE...
DEAR GOD--WHAT ARE YOU DOING?!
CAP SAVES THE DAY!

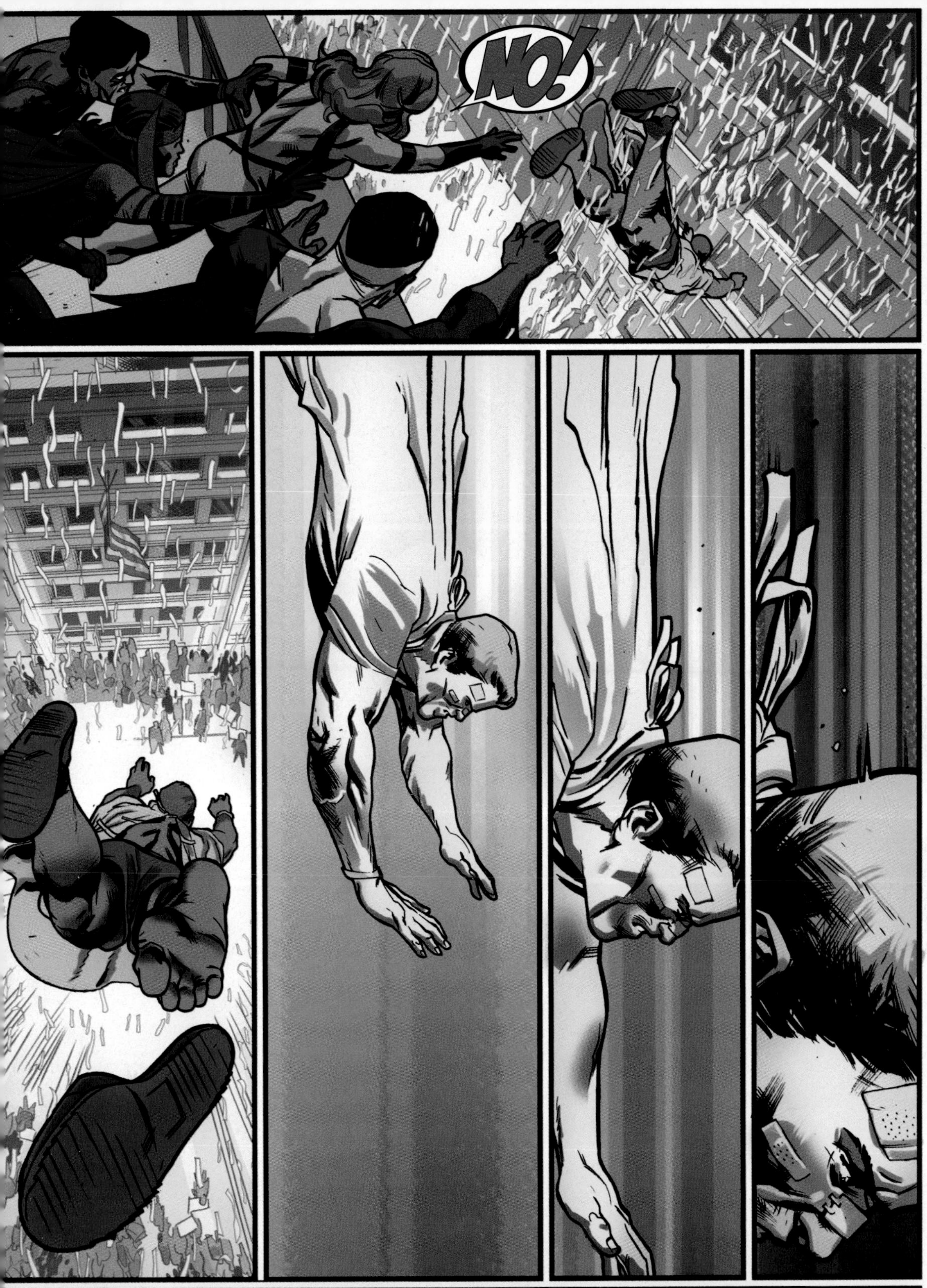
NO!

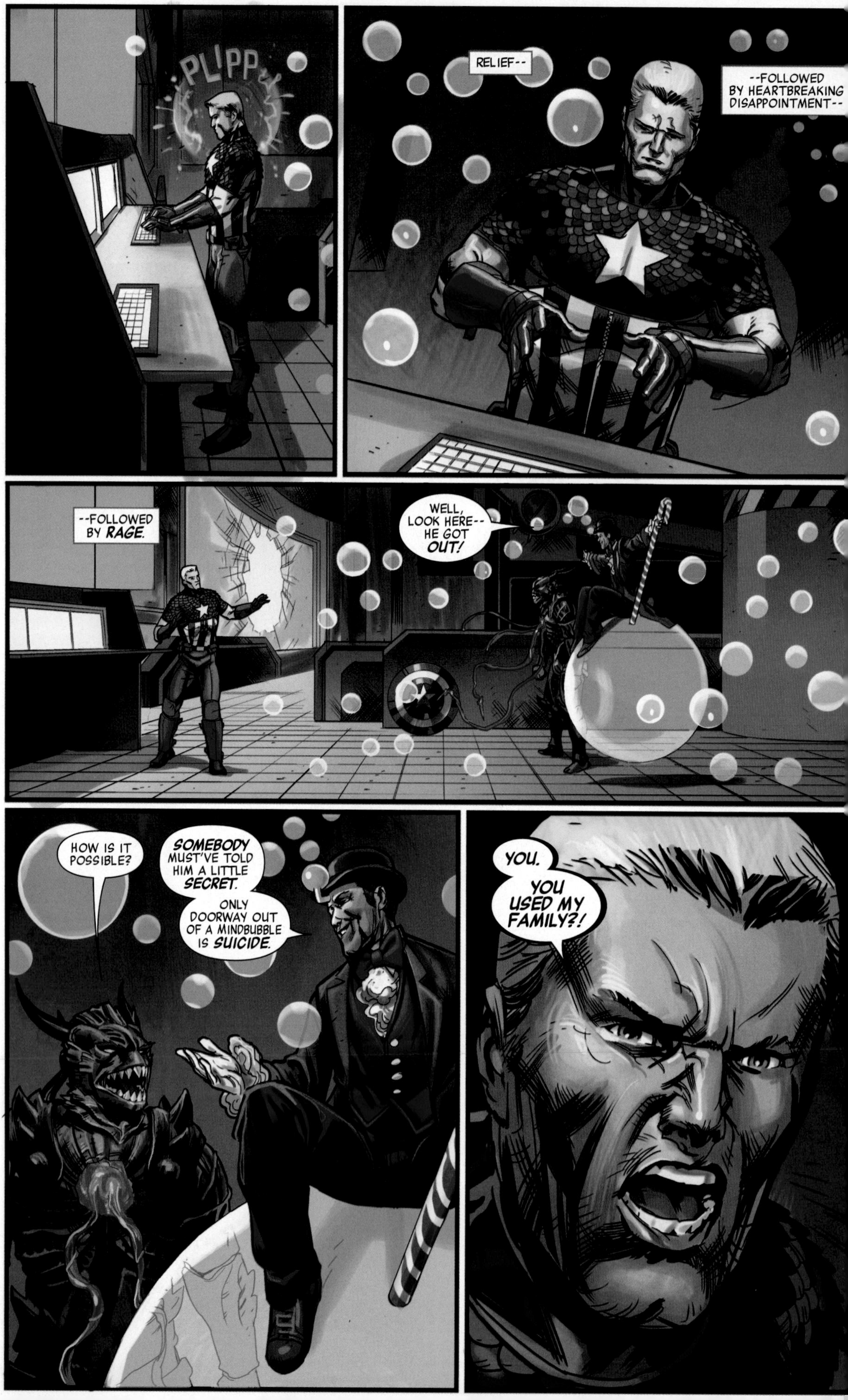
PLIPP
RELIEF--
--FOLLOWED BY HEARTBREAKING DISAPPOINTMENT--
--FOLLOWED BY RAGE.
WELL, LOOK HERE--HE GOT OUT!
HOW IS IT POSSIBLE?
SOMEBODY MUST'VE TOLD HIM A LITTLE SECRET.
ONLY DOORWAY OUT OF A MINDBUBBLE IS SUICIDE.
YOU.
YOU USED MY FAMILY?!

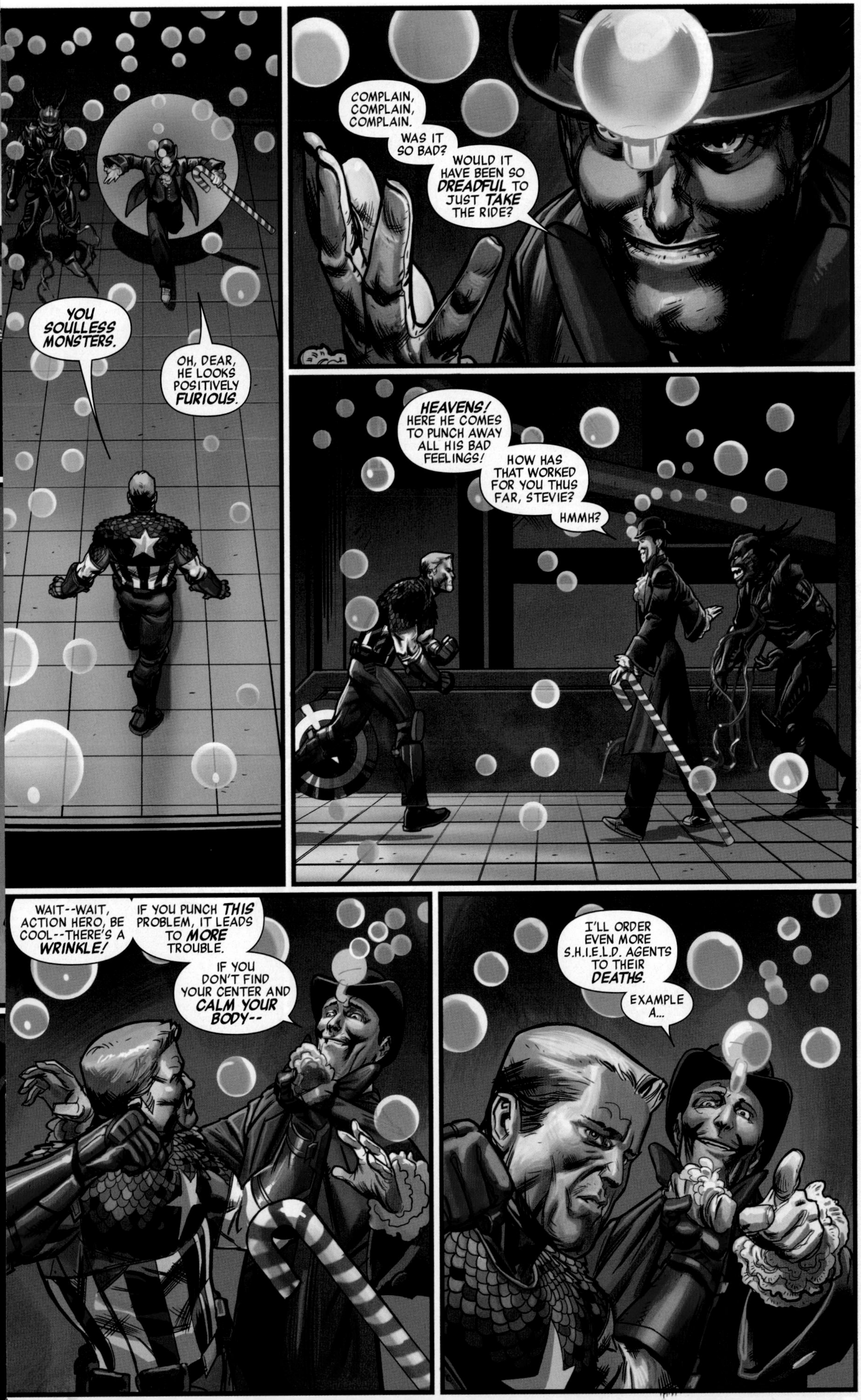
YOU SOULLESS MONSTERS.
OH, DEAR, HE LOOKS POSITIVELY FURIOUS.
COMPLAIN, COMPLAIN, COMPLAIN.
WAS IT SO BAD?
WOULD IT HAVE BEEN SO DREADFUL TO JUST TAKE THE RIDE?
HEAVENS! HERE HE COMES TO PUNCH AWAY ALL HIS BAD FEELINGS!
HOW HAS THAT WORKED FOR YOU THUS FAR, STEVIE?
HMMH?
WAIT--WAIT, ACTION HERO, BE COOL--THERE'S A WRINKLE!
IF YOU PUNCH THIS PROBLEM, IT LEADS TO MORE TROUBLE.
IF YOU DON'T FIND YOUR CENTER AND CALM YOUR BODY--
I'LL ORDER EVEN MORE S.H.I.E.L.D. AGENTS TO THEIR DEATHS.
EXAMPLE A...

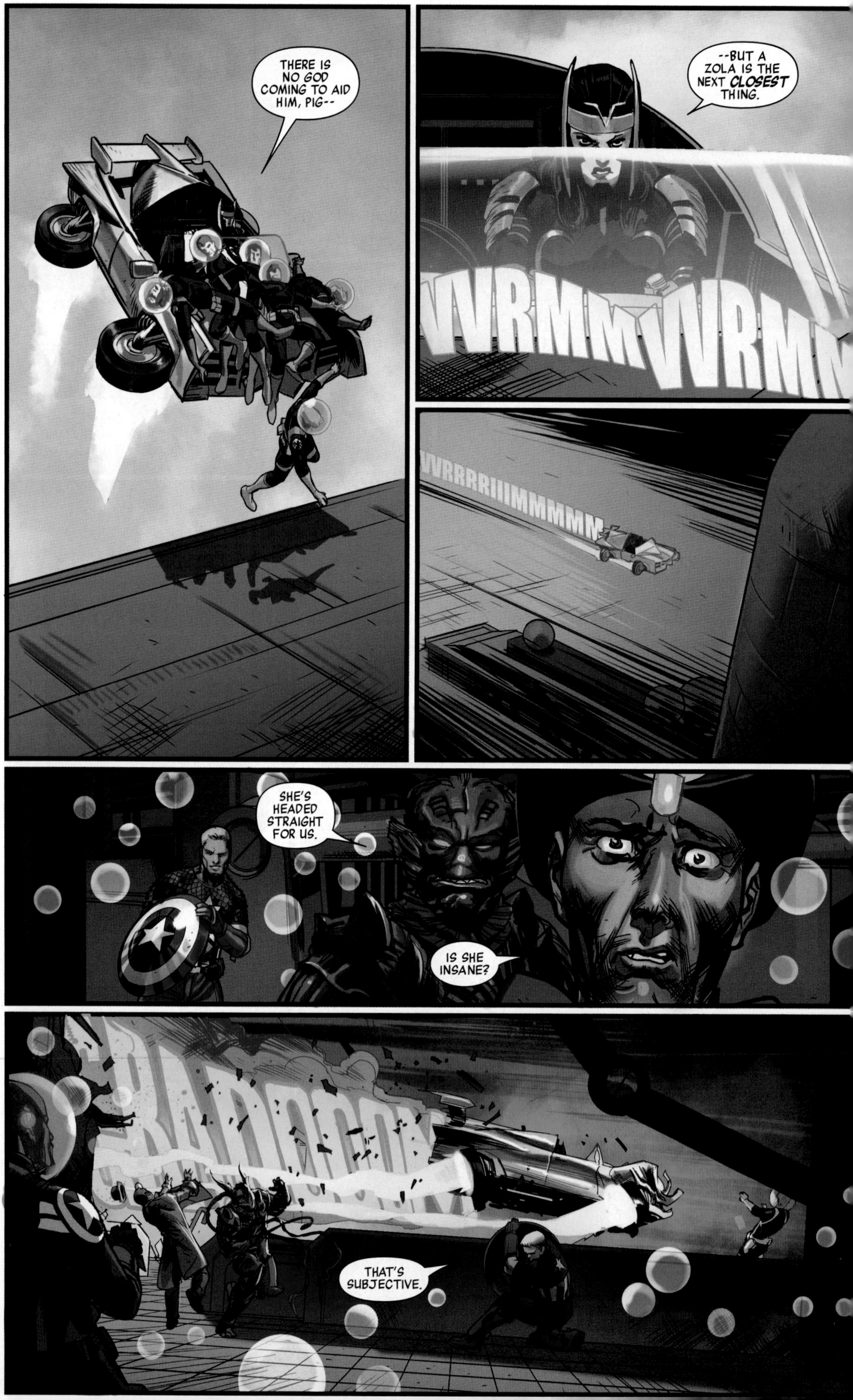
THERE IS NO GOD COMING TO AID HIM, PIG--
--BUT A ZOLA IS THE NEXT CLOSEST THING.
VVRMM VVRMM
VVRRRRIIIMMMMM
SHE'S HEADED STRAIGHT FOR US.
IS SHE INSANE?
THAT'S SUBJECTIVE.

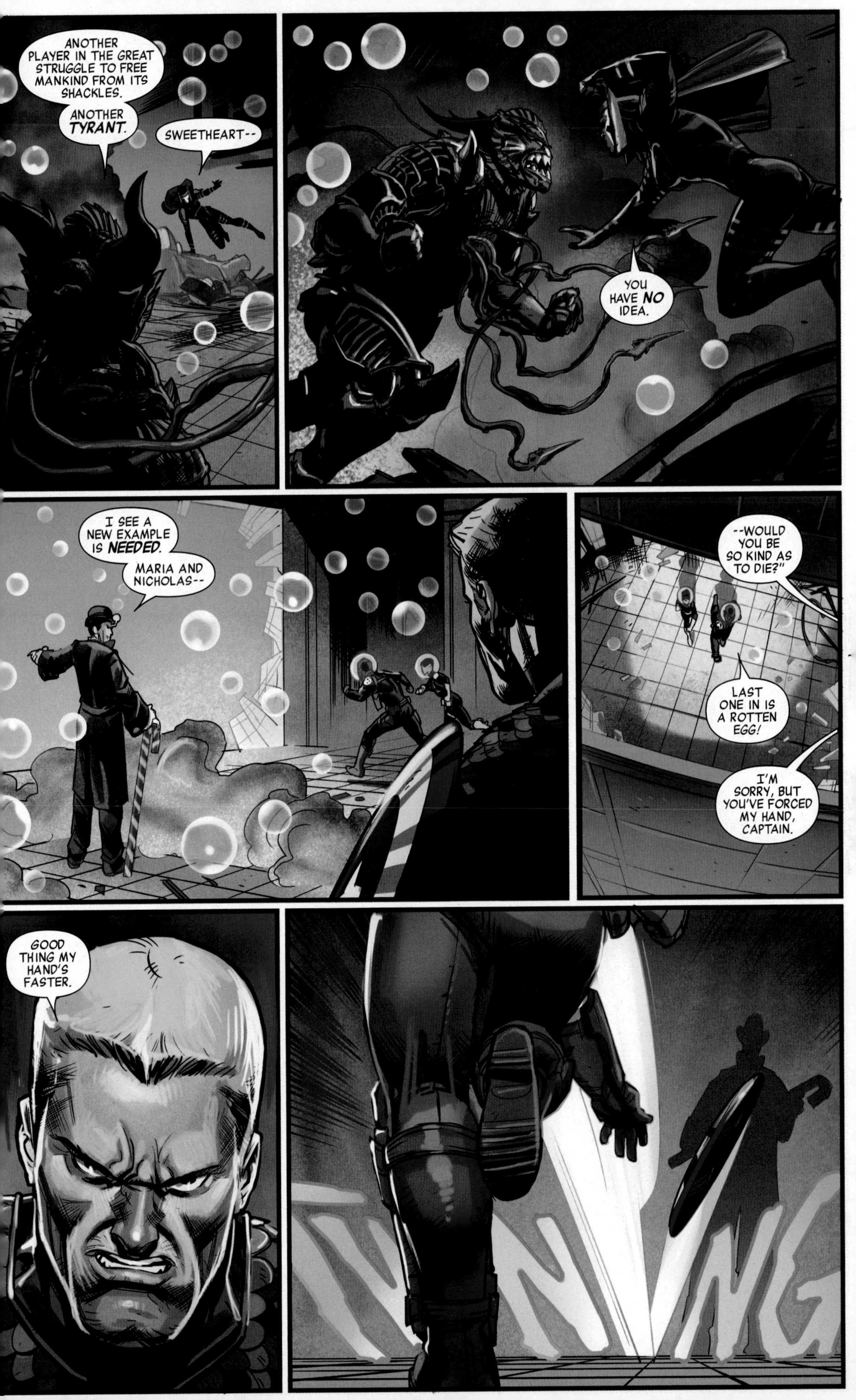
ANOTHER PLAYER IN THE GREAT STRUGGLE TO FREE MANKIND FROM ITS SHACKLES.
ANOTHER TYRANT.
SWEETHEART--
YOU HAVE NO IDEA.
I SEE A NEW EXAMPLE IS NEEDED.
MARIA AND NICHOLAS--
--WOULD YOU BE SO KIND AS TO DIE?"
LAST ONE IN IS A ROTTEN EGG!
I'M SORRY, BUT YOU'VE FORCED MY HAND, CAPTAIN.
GOOD THING MY HAND'S FASTER.

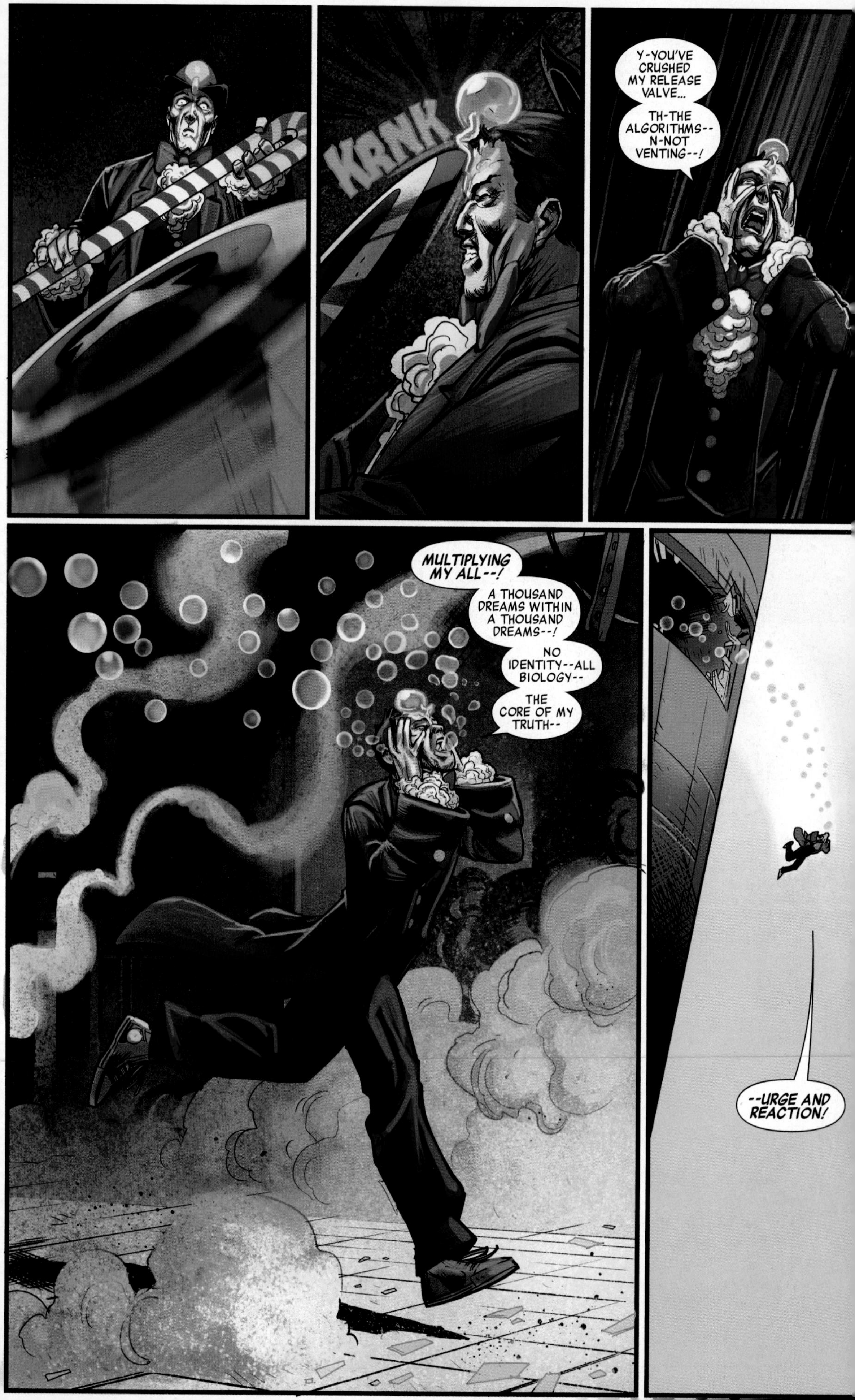
KRNK
Y-YOU'VE CRUSHED MY RELEASE VALVE...
TH-THE ALGORITHMS-- N-NOT VENTING--!
MULTIPLYING MY ALL--!
A THOUSAND DREAMS WITHIN A THOUSAND DREAMS--!
NO IDENTITY--ALL BIOLOGY--
THE CORE OF MY TRUTH--
--URGE AND REACTION!

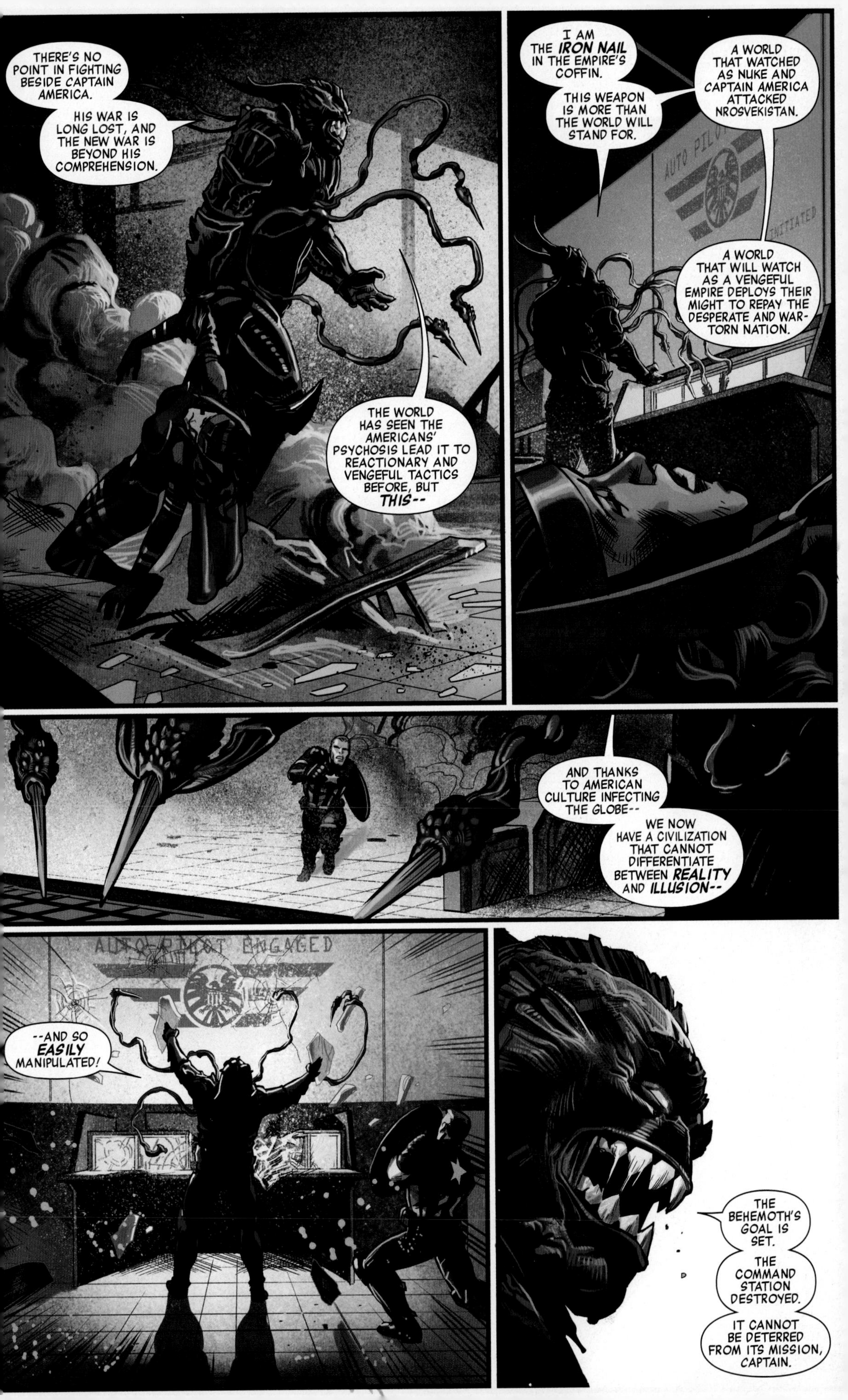
THERE'S NO POINT IN FIGHTING BESIDE CAPTAIN AMERICA.
HIS WAR IS LONG LOST, AND THE NEW WAR IS BEYOND HIS COMPREHENSION.
THE WORLD HAS SEEN THE AMERICANS' PSYCHOSIS LEAD IT TO REACTIONARY AND VENGEFUL TACTICS BEFORE, BUT THIS--
I AM THE IRON NAIL IN THE EMPIRE'S COFFIN.
THIS WEAPON IS MORE THAN THE WORLD WILL STAND FOR.
A WORLD THAT WATCHED AS NUKE AND CAPTAIN AMERICA ATTACKED NROSVEKISTAN.
A WORLD THAT WILL WATCH AS A VENGEFUL EMPIRE DEPLOYS THEIR MIGHT TO REPAY THE DESPERATE AND WAR-TORN NATION.
AND THANKS TO AMERICAN CULTURE INFECTING THE GLOBE--
WE NOW HAVE A CIVILIZATION THAT CANNOT DIFFERENTIATE BETWEEN REALITY AND ILLUSION--
AUTO-PILOT ENGAGED
--AND SO EASILY MANIPULATED!
THE BEHEMOTH'S GOAL IS SET.
THE COMMAND STATION DESTROYED.
IT CANNOT BE DETERRED FROM ITS MISSION, CAPTAIN.

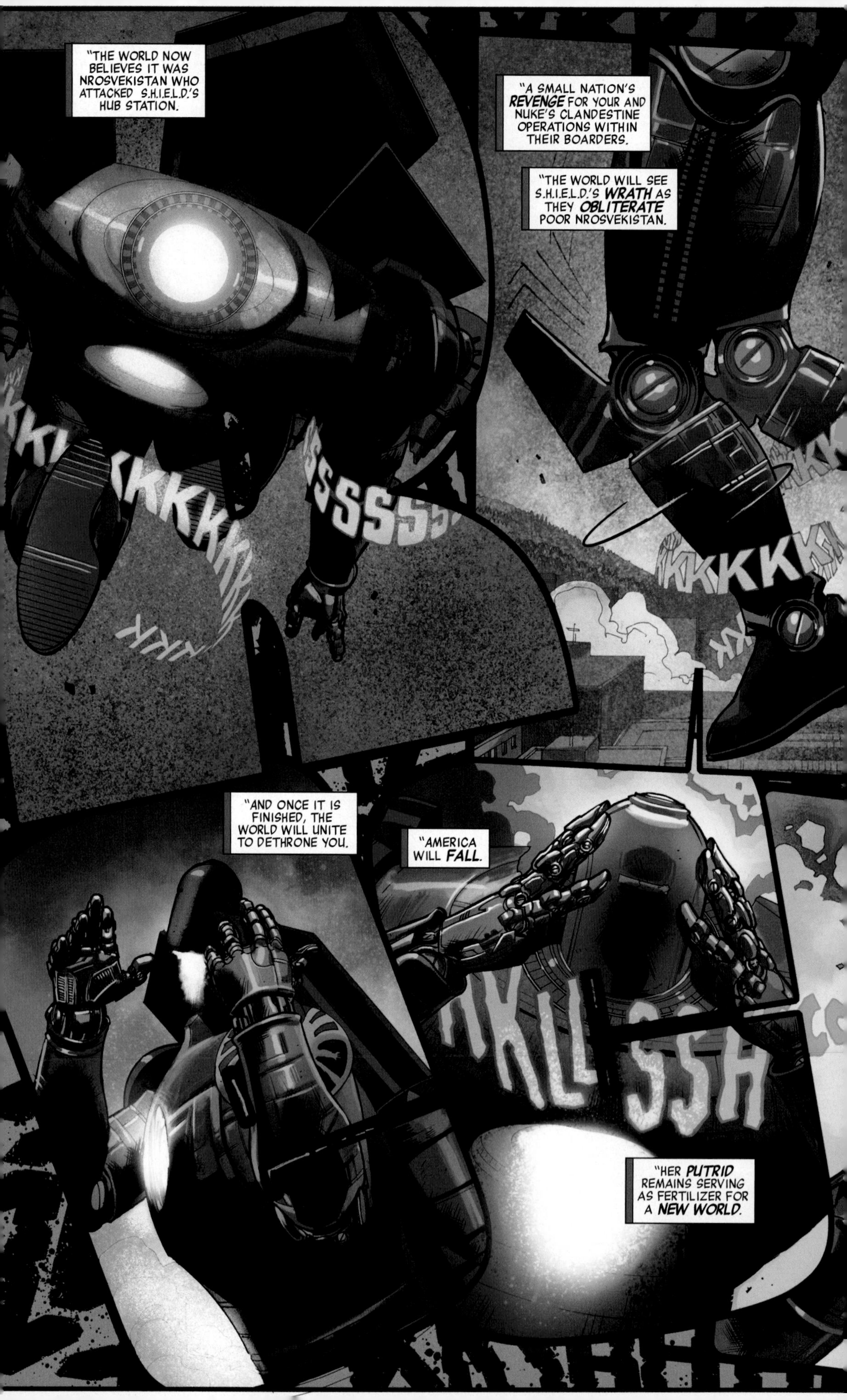
"THE WORLD NOW BELIEVES IT WAS NROSVEKISTAN WHO ATTACKED S.H.I.E.L.D.'S HUB STATION.
"A SMALL NATION'S REVENGE FOR YOUR AND NUKE'S CLANDESTINE OPERATIONS WITHIN THEIR BOARDERS.
"THE WORLD WILL SEE S.H.I.E.L.D.'S WRATH AS THEY OBLITERATE POOR NROSVEKISTAN.
KKKKK
SSSSS
"AND ONCE IT IS FINISHED, THE WORLD WILL UNITE TO DETHRONE YOU.
"AMERICA WILL FALL.
SSH
"HER PUTRID REMAINS SERVING AS FERTILIZER FOR A NEW WORLD.

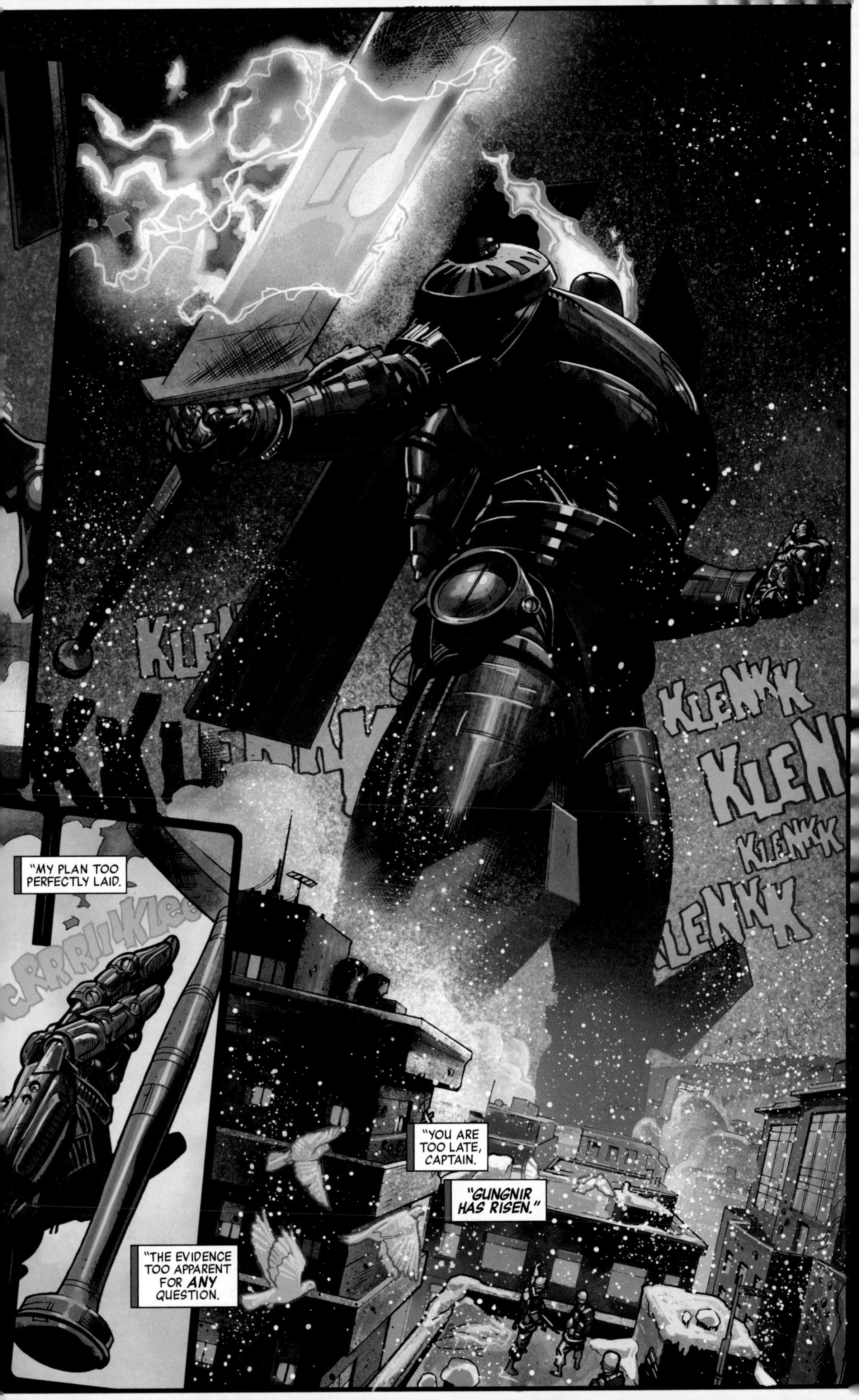
KLENKK
KKLENKK
KLENKK
KLENK
KLENKK
KLENKK
"MY PLAN TOO PERFECTLY LAID.
KRRRIIIKLEE
"THE EVIDENCE TOO APPARENT FOR ANY QUESTION.
"YOU ARE TOO LATE, CAPTAIN.
"GUNGNIR HAS RISEN."

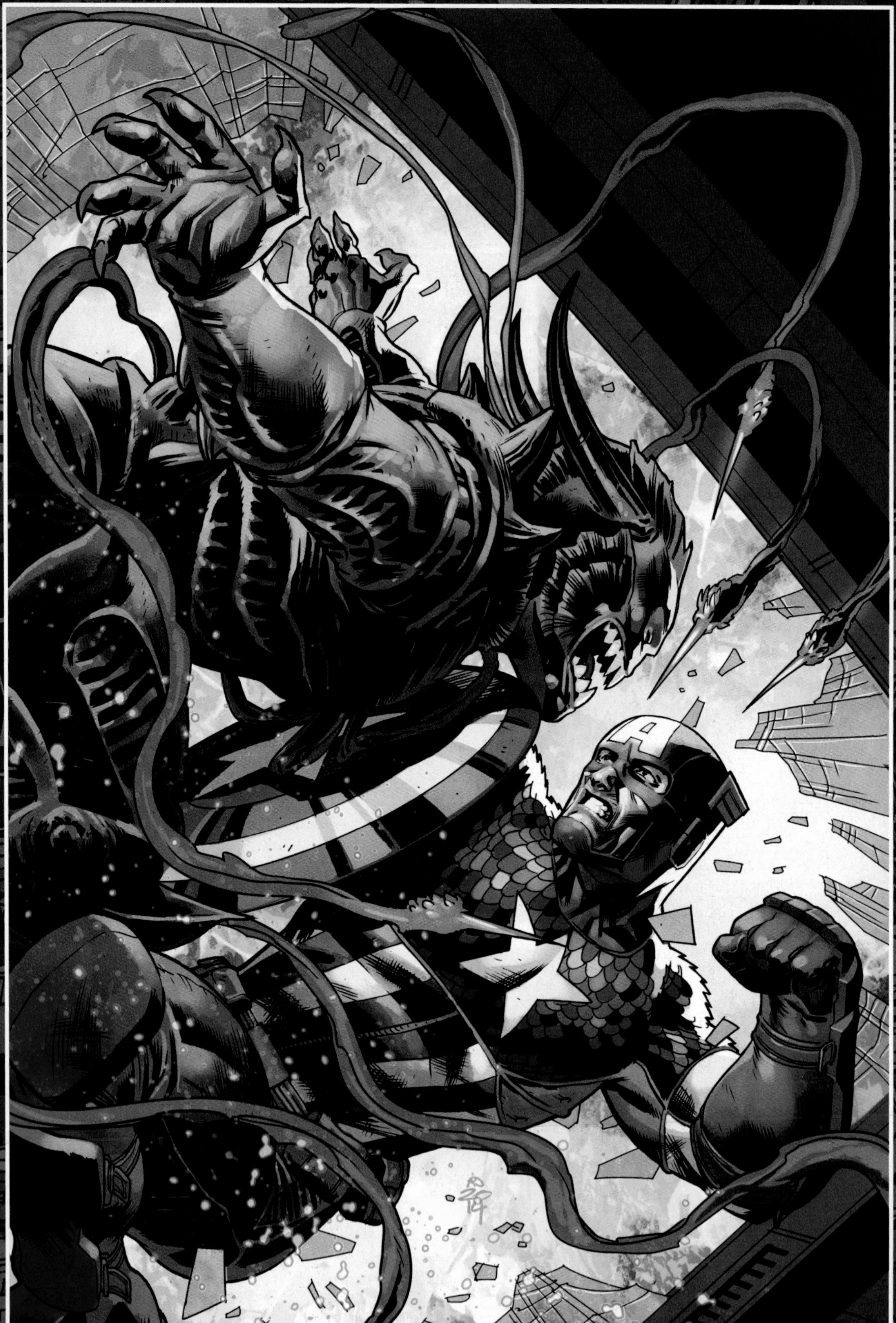

TWENTY-ONE

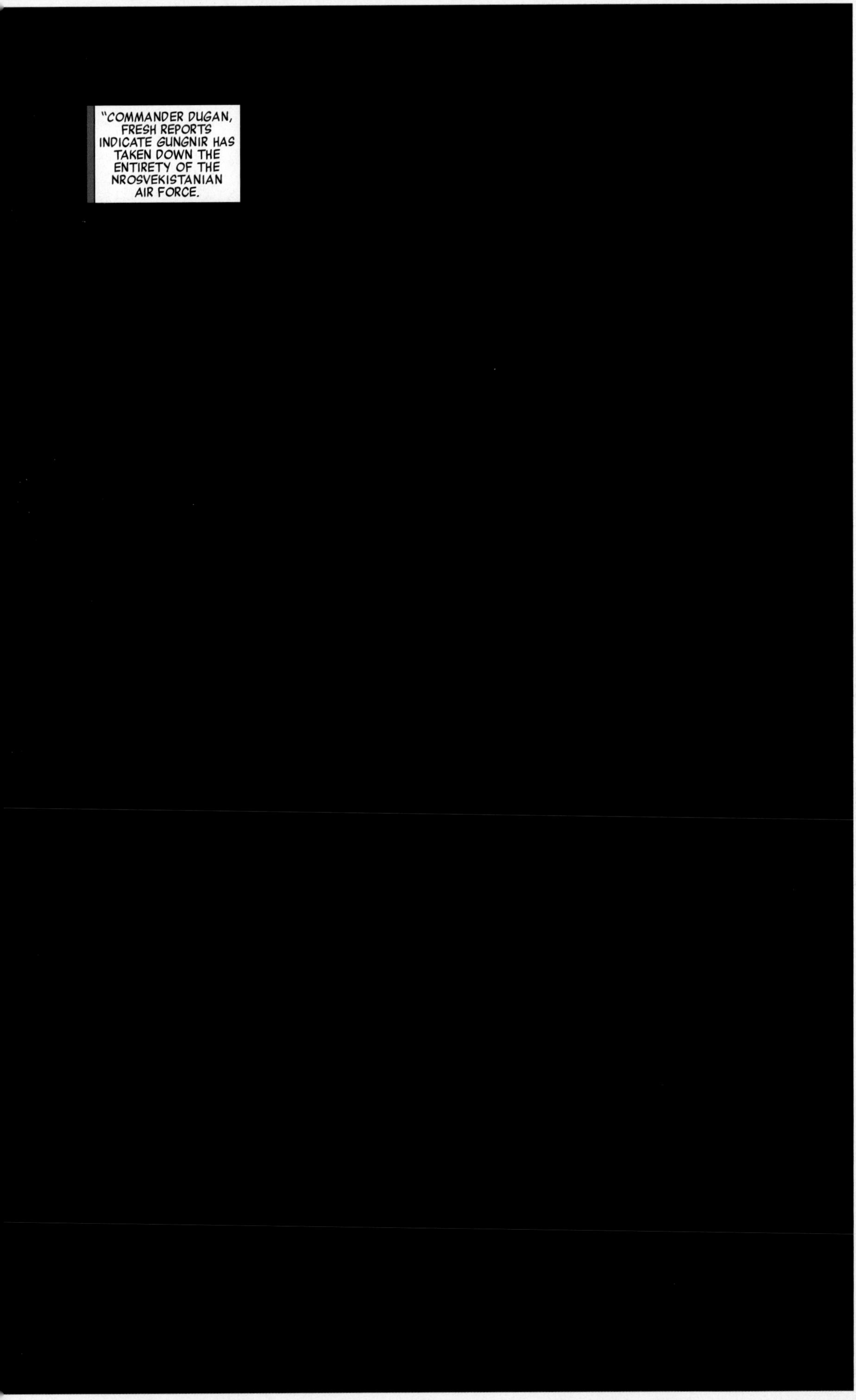
"COMMANDER DUGAN, FRESH REPORTS INDICATE GUNGNIR HAS TAKEN DOWN THE ENTIRETY OF THE NROSVEKISTANIAN AIR FORCE.

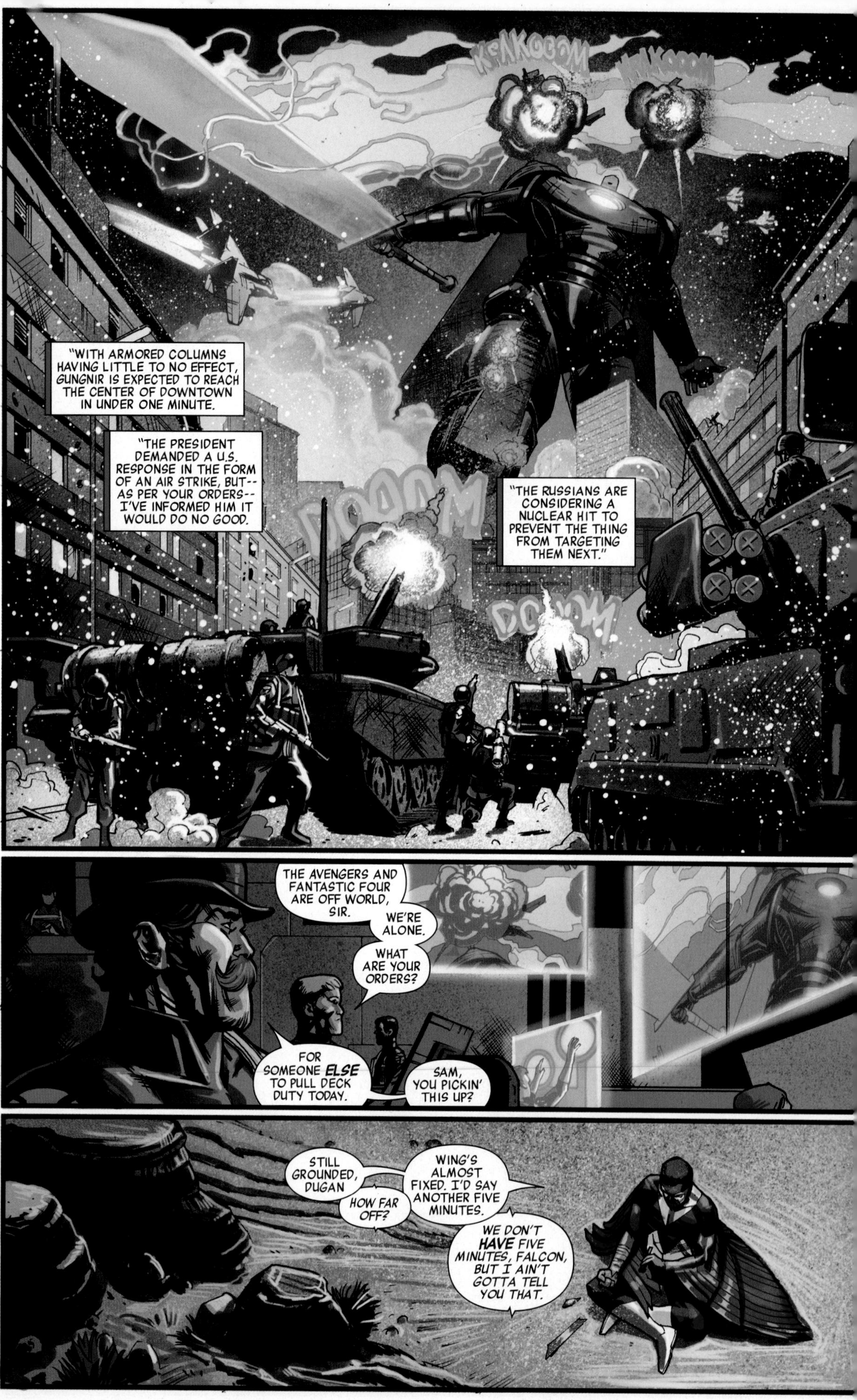
KRAKOOOM
KRAKOOOM
"WITH ARMORED COLUMNS HAVING LITTLE TO NO EFFECT, GUNGNIR IS EXPECTED TO REACH THE CENTER OF DOWNTOWN IN UNDER ONE MINUTE.
"THE PRESIDENT DEMANDED A U.S. RESPONSE IN THE FORM OF AN AIR STRIKE, BUT-- AS PER YOUR ORDERS-- I'VE INFORMED HIM IT WOULD DO NO GOOD.
DOOOM
"THE RUSSIANS ARE CONSIDERING A NUCLEAR HIT TO PREVENT THE THING FROM TARGETING THEM NEXT."
DOOOM
THE AVENGERS AND FANTASTIC FOUR ARE OFF WORLD, SIR.
WE'RE ALONE.
WHAT ARE YOUR ORDERS?
FOR SOMEONE ELSE TO PULL DECK DUTY TODAY.
SAM, YOU PICKIN' THIS UP?
STILL GROUNDED, DUGAN
HOW FAR OFF?
WING'S ALMOST FIXED. I'D SAY ANOTHER FIVE MINUTES.
WE DON'T HAVE FIVE MINUTES, FALCON, BUT I AIN'T GOTTA TELL YOU THAT.

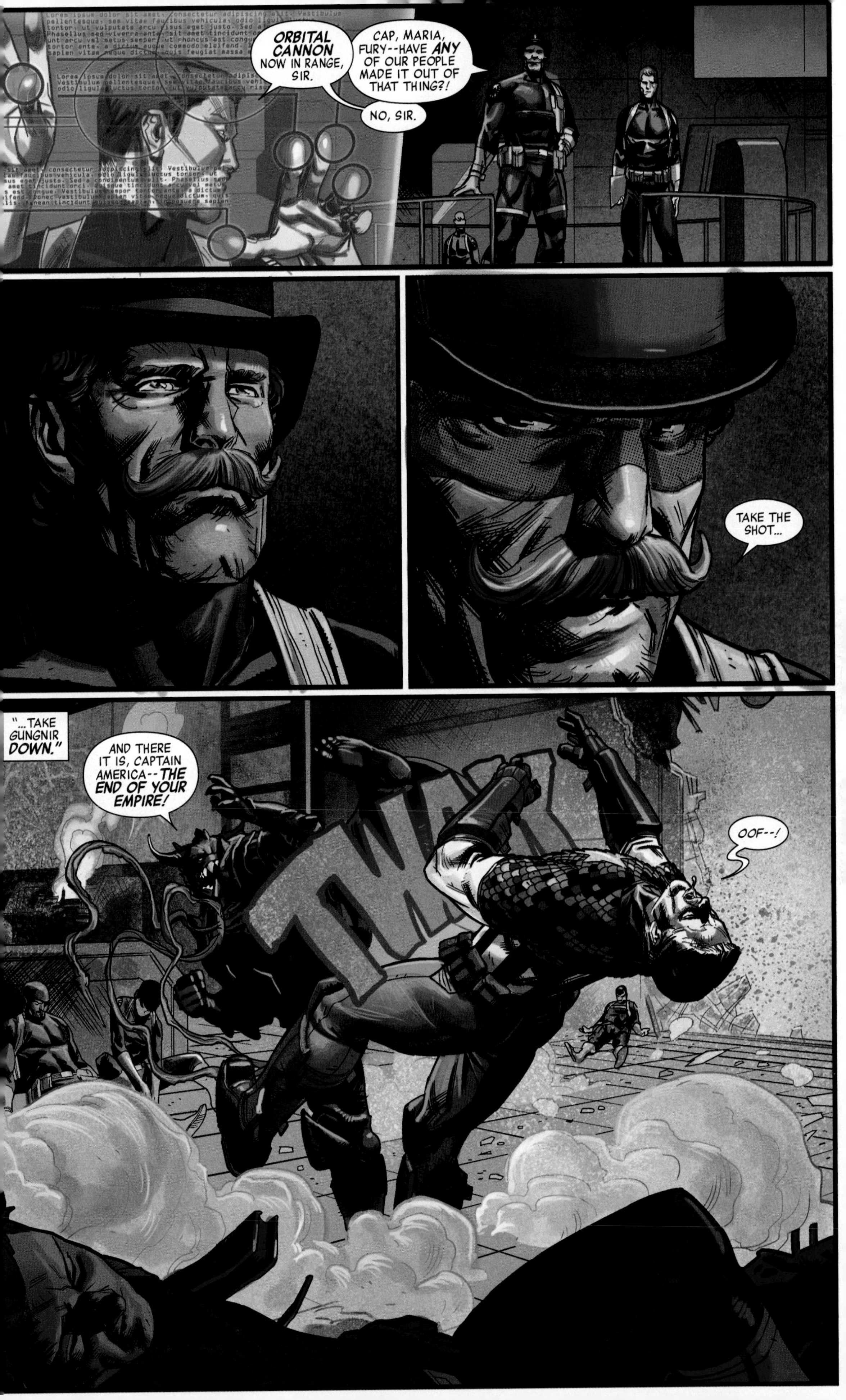
ORBITAL CANNON NOW IN RANGE, SIR.
CAP, MARIA, FURY--HAVE ANY OF OUR PEOPLE MADE IT OUT OF THAT THING?!
NO, SIR.
TAKE THE SHOT...
"...TAKE GUNGNIR DOWN."
AND THERE IT IS, CAPTAIN AMERICA--THE END OF YOUR EMPIRE!
OOF--!

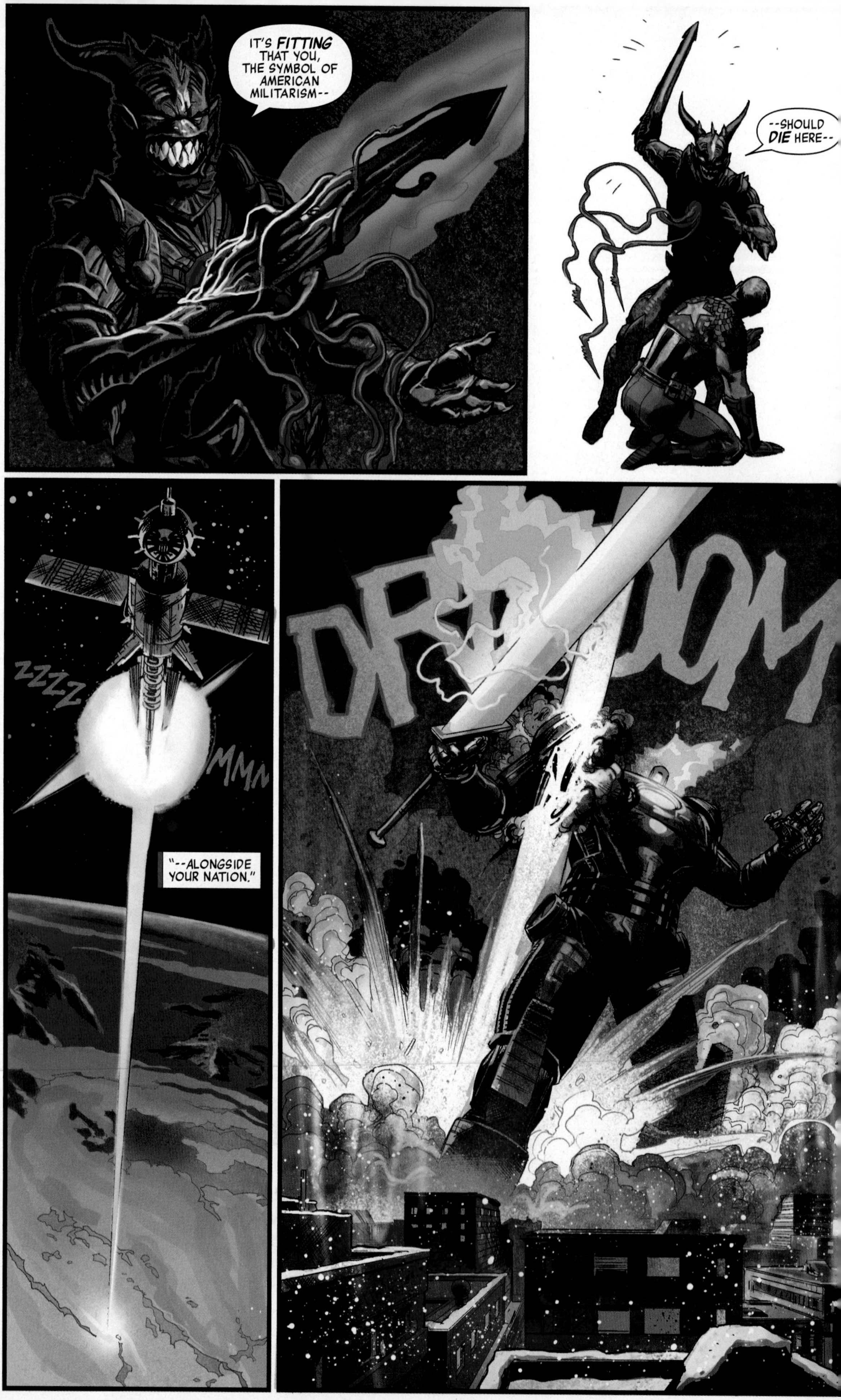
IT'S FITTING THAT YOU, THE SYMBOL OF AMERICAN MILITARISM--
--SHOULD DIE HERE--
ZZZZMMMN
"--ALONGSIDE YOUR NATION."
DRROOM

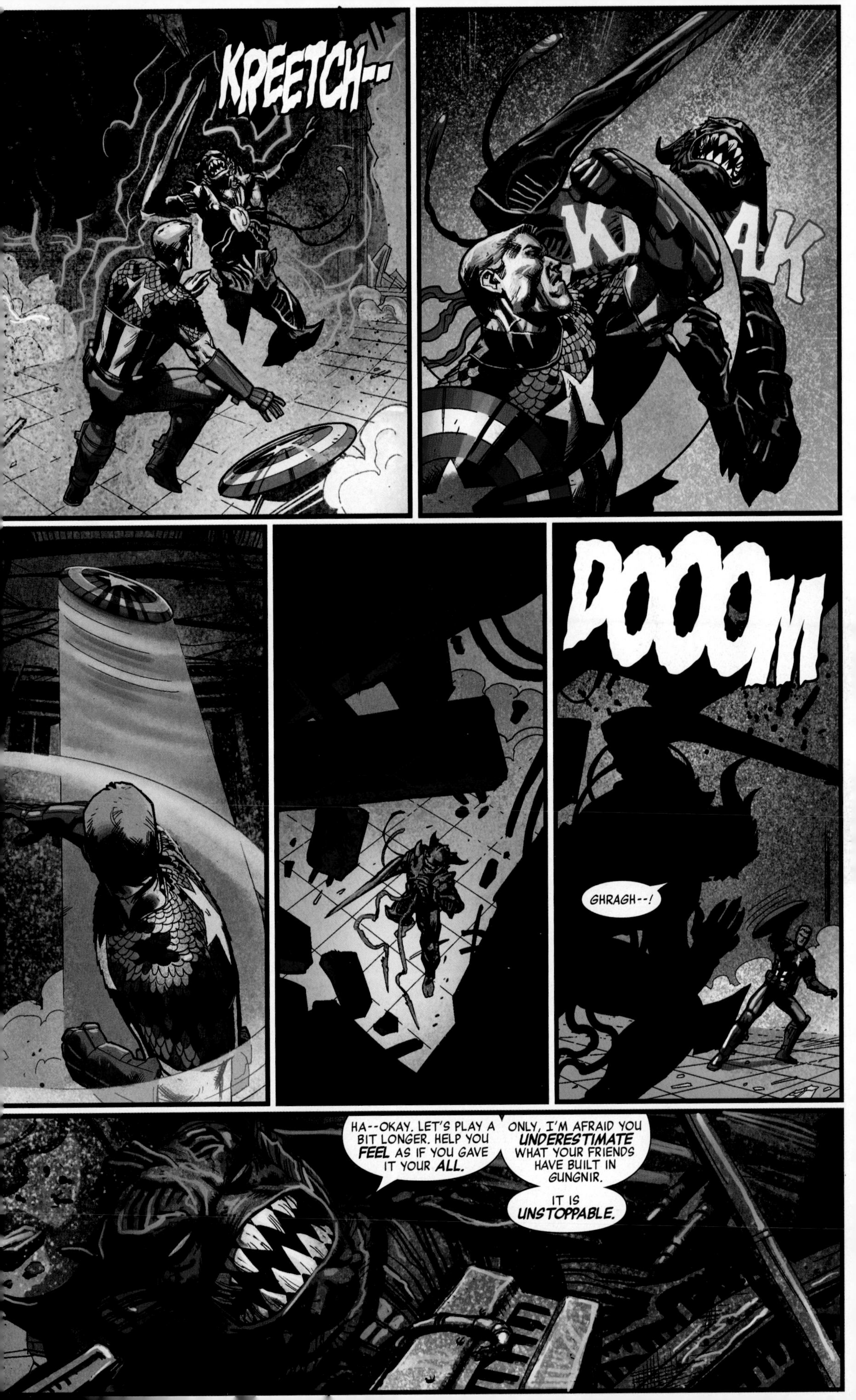
KREETCH--
KRAK
DOOOM
GHRAGH--!
HA--OKAY. LET'S PLAY A BIT LONGER. HELP YOU FEEL AS IF YOU GAVE IT YOUR ALL.
ONLY, I'M AFRAID YOU UNDERESTIMATE WHAT YOUR FRIENDS HAVE BUILT IN GUNGNIR.
IT IS UNSTOPPABLE.

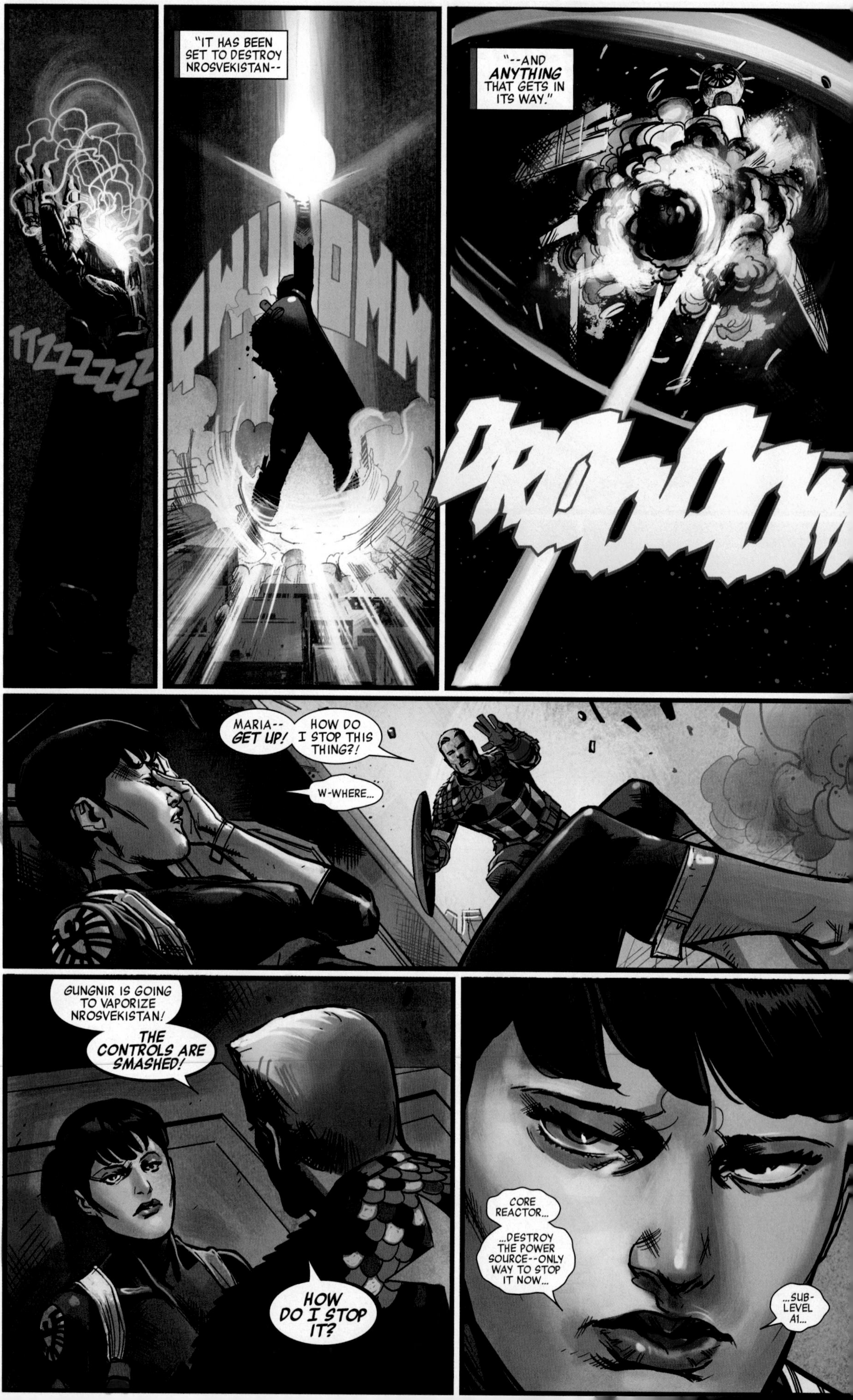
TTZZZZZZZ
"IT HAS BEEN SET TO DESTROY NROSVEKISTAN--
PWHOMM
"--AND ANYTHING THAT GETS IN ITS WAY."
DROOOOM
MARIA-- GET UP!
HOW DO I STOP THIS THING?!
W-WHERE...
GUNGNIR IS GOING TO VAPORIZE NROSVEKISTAN!
THE CONTROLS ARE SMASHED!
HOW DO I STOP IT?
CORE REACTOR...
...DESTROY THE POWER SOURCE--ONLY WAY TO STOP IT NOW...
...SUB-LEVEL A1...

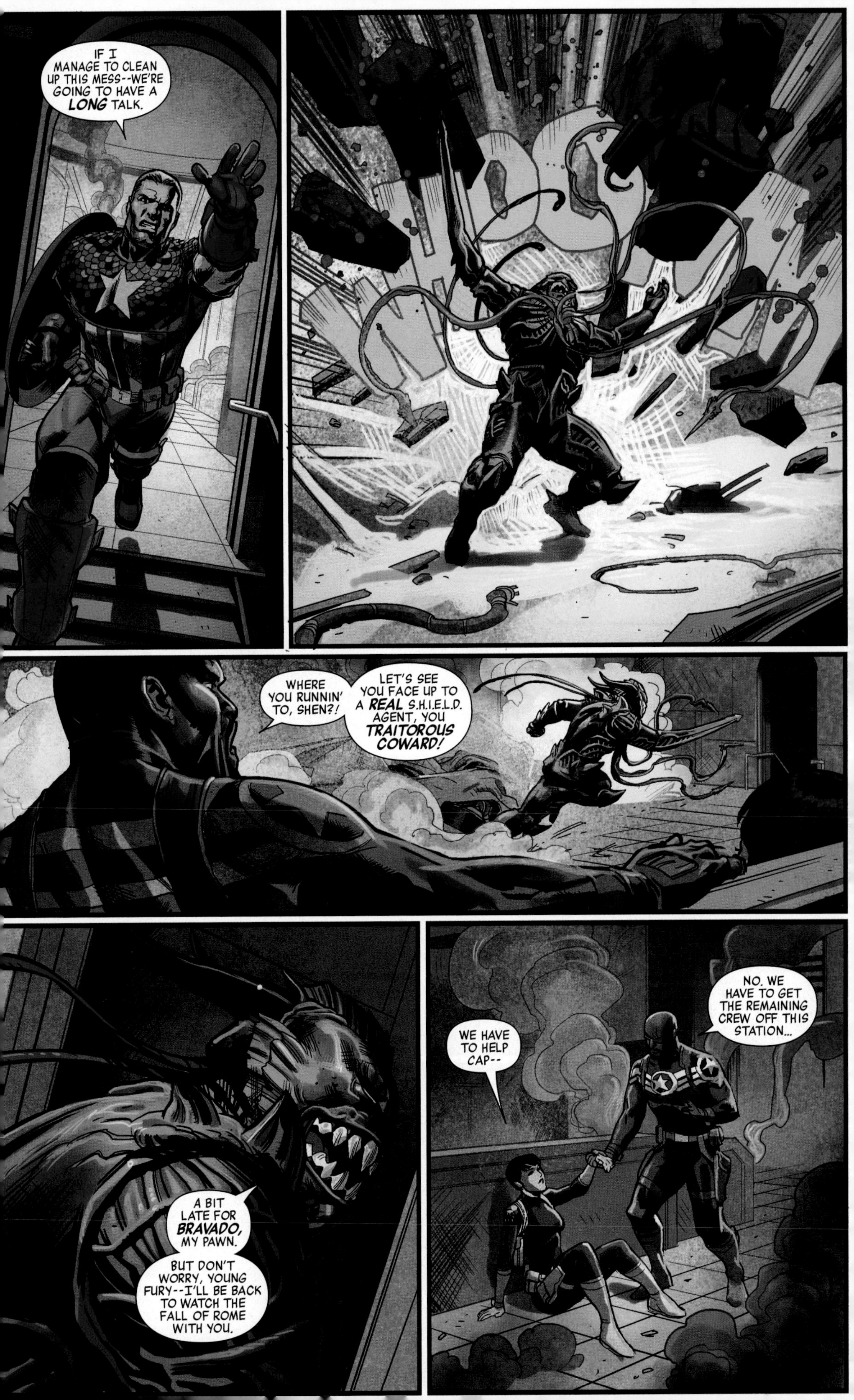

IF I MANAGE TO CLEAN UP THIS MESS--WE'RE GOING TO HAVE A **LONG** TALK.
WHERE YOU RUNNIN' TO, SHEN?!
LET'S SEE YOU FACE UP TO A **REAL** S.H.I.E.L.D. AGENT, YOU **TRAITOROUS COWARD!**
A BIT LATE FOR **BRAVADO,** MY PAWN.
BUT DON'T WORRY, YOUNG FURY--I'LL BE BACK TO WATCH THE FALL OF ROME WITH YOU.
WE HAVE TO HELP CAP--
NO. WE HAVE TO GET THE REMAINING CREW OFF THIS STATION...

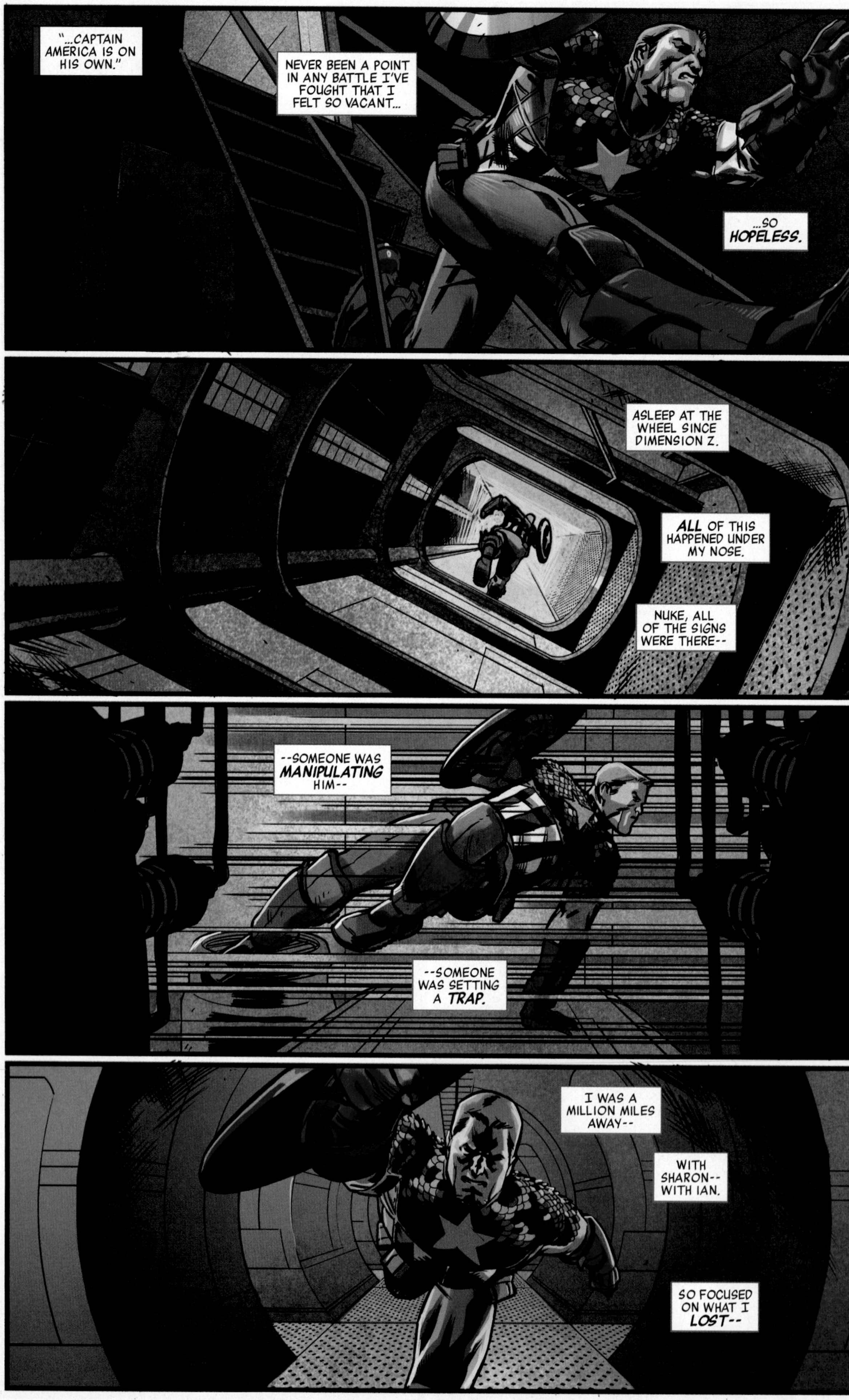
"...CAPTAIN AMERICA IS ON HIS OWN."
NEVER BEEN A POINT IN ANY BATTLE I'VE FOUGHT THAT I FELT SO VACANT...
...SO HOPELESS.
ASLEEP AT THE WHEEL SINCE DIMENSION Z.
ALL OF THIS HAPPENED UNDER MY NOSE.
NUKE, ALL OF THE SIGNS WERE THERE--
--SOMEONE WAS MANIPULATING HIM--
--SOMEONE WAS SETTING A TRAP.
I WAS A MILLION MILES AWAY--
WITH SHARON--WITH IAN.
SO FOCUSED ON WHAT I LOST--

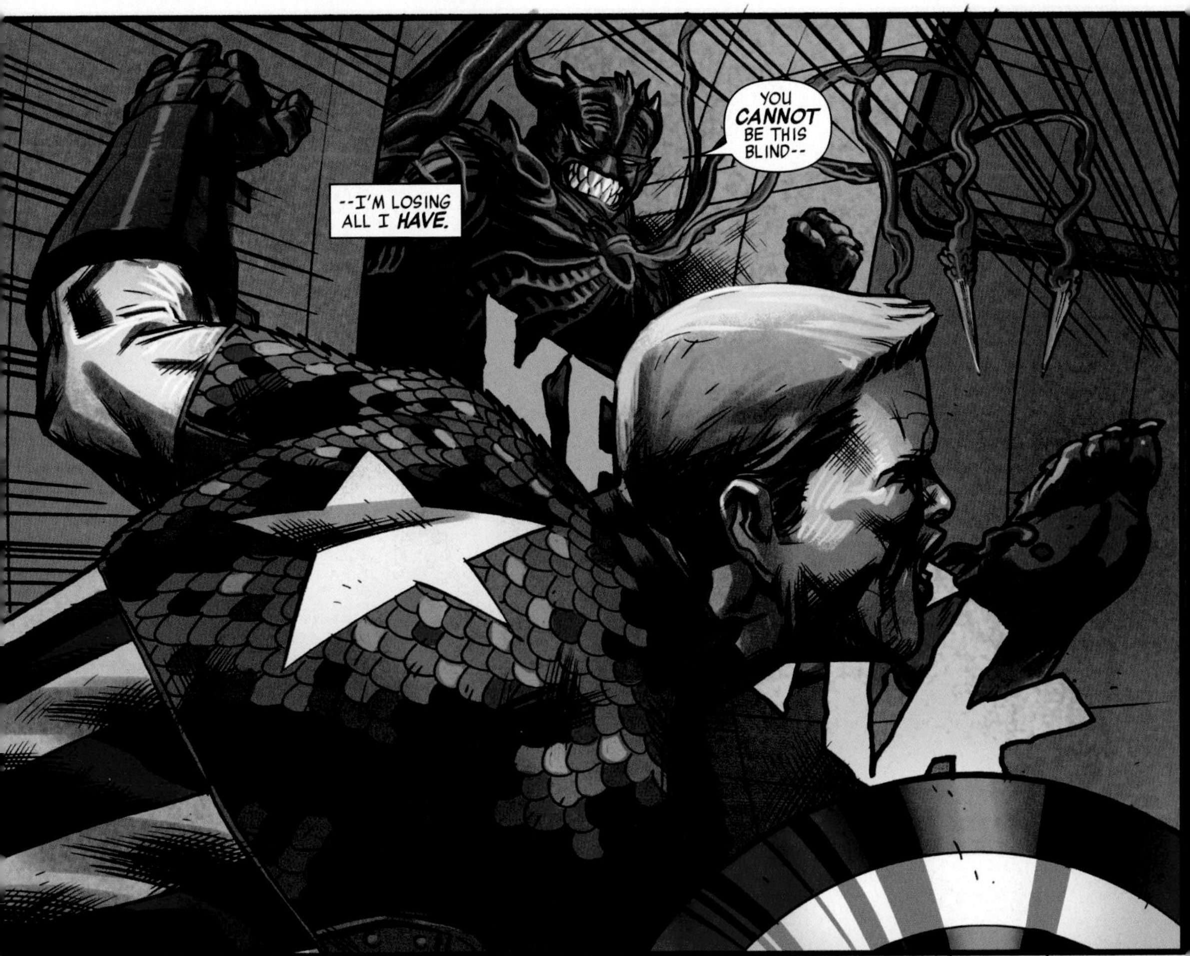
--I'M LOSING ALL I **HAVE.**
YOU **CANNOT** BE THIS BLIND--

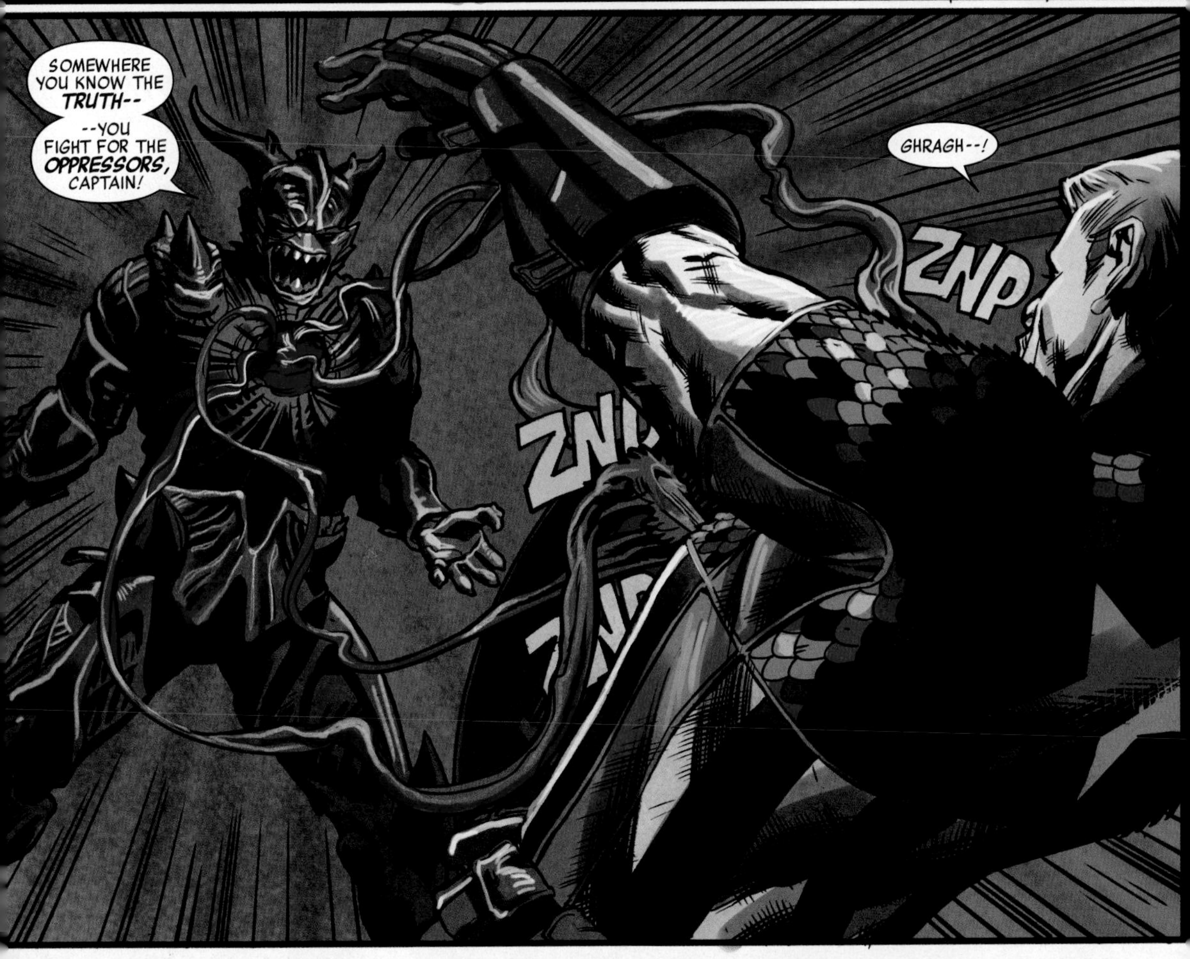
SOMEWHERE YOU KNOW THE **TRUTH--**
--YOU FIGHT FOR THE **OPPRESSORS,** CAPTAIN!
GHRAGH--!
ZNP
ZNP

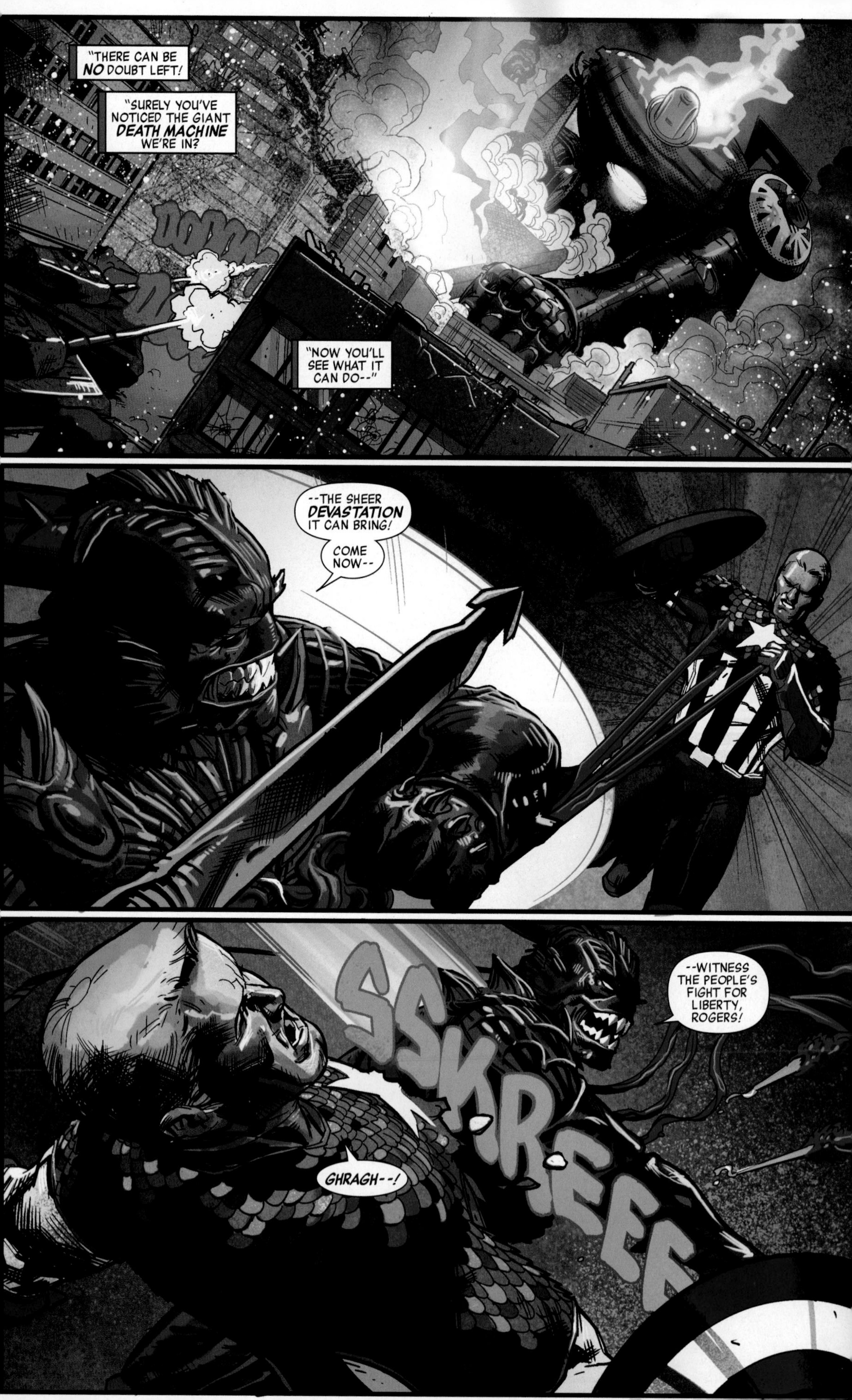
"THERE CAN BE NO DOUBT LEFT!
"SURELY YOU'VE NOTICED THE GIANT DEATH MACHINE WE'RE IN?
"NOW YOU'LL SEE WHAT IT CAN DO--"
--THE SHEER DEVASTATION IT CAN BRING!
COME NOW--
--WITNESS THE PEOPLE'S FIGHT FOR LIBERTY, ROGERS!
SSKREEE
GHRAGH--!

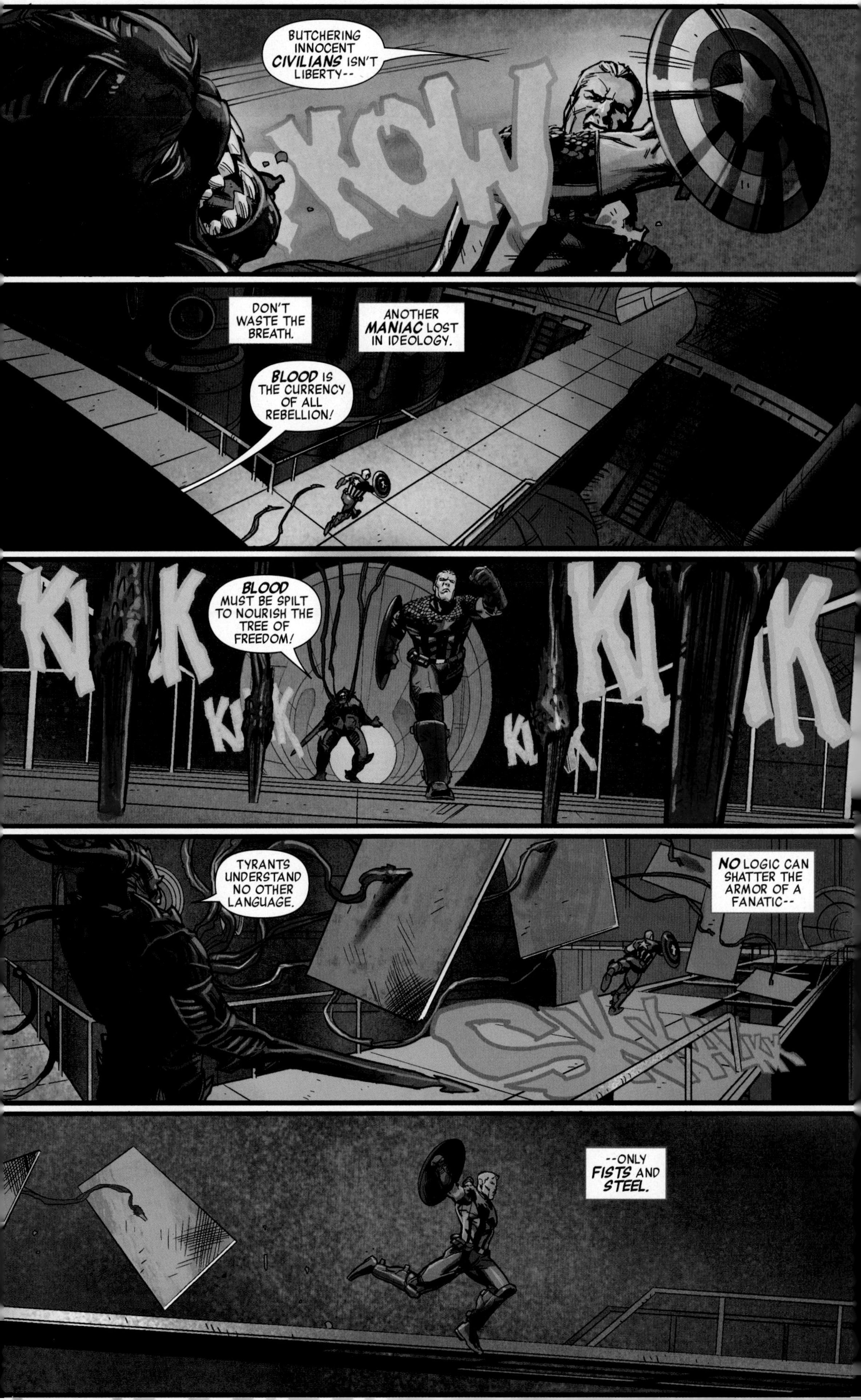
BUTCHERING INNOCENT CIVILIANS ISN'T LIBERTY--
KOW
DON'T WASTE THE BREATH.
ANOTHER MANIAC LOST IN IDEOLOGY.
BLOOD IS THE CURRENCY OF ALL REBELLION!
BLOOD MUST BE SPILT TO NOURISH THE TREE OF FREEDOM!
TYRANTS UNDERSTAND NO OTHER LANGUAGE.
NO LOGIC CAN SHATTER THE ARMOR OF A FANATIC--
--ONLY FISTS AND STEEL.

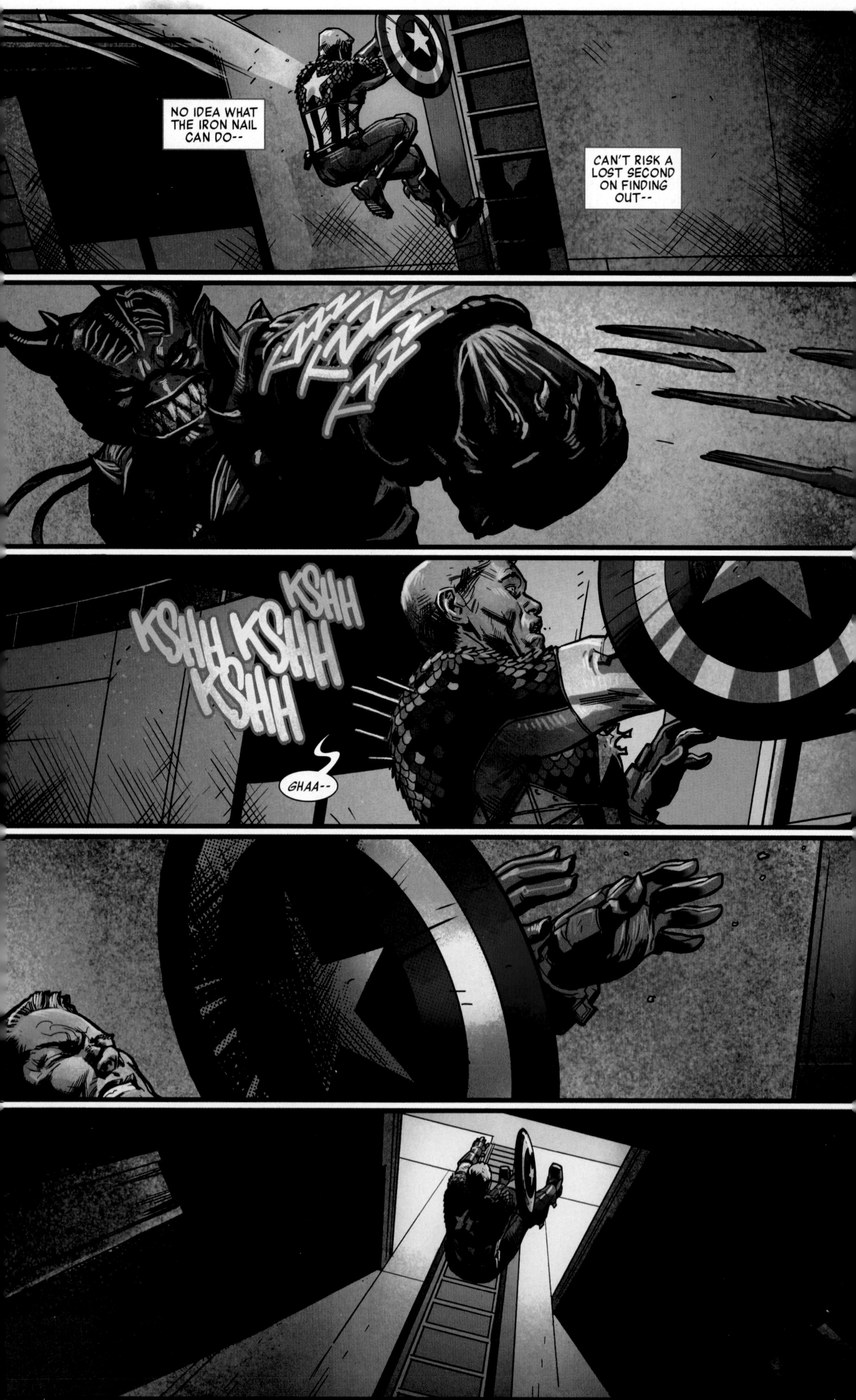
NO IDEA WHAT THE IRON NAIL CAN DO--
CAN'T RISK A LOST SECOND ON FINDING OUT--
KSHH KSHH KSHH KSHH
GHAA--

THUDD

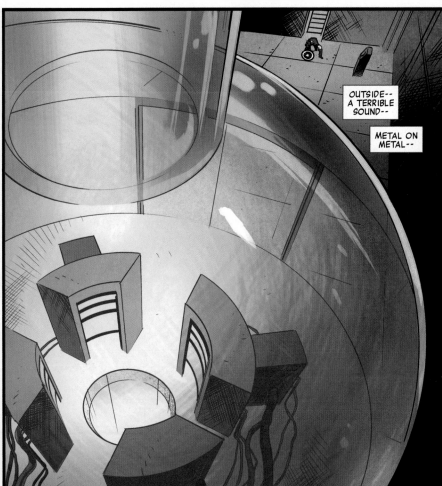

OUTSIDE-- A TERRIBLE SOUND--

METAL ON METAL--

CANNONS, TANKS--

ARMAMENT IMPACTING AGAINST STEEL--

A *FINAL* BEVY--

A *DESPERATE* ARMY RAINING DOWN ALL THEY HAVE TO SAVE THEIR PEOPLE.

TO SAVE THEIR COUNTRY FROM WHAT MINE BUILT.

ONE SHOT AT THIS--

DESTROY THE REACTOR.

FACE THE FIRE THAT FOLLOWS--

IT DOESN'T MATTER--ONLY *ONE* THING MATTERS--

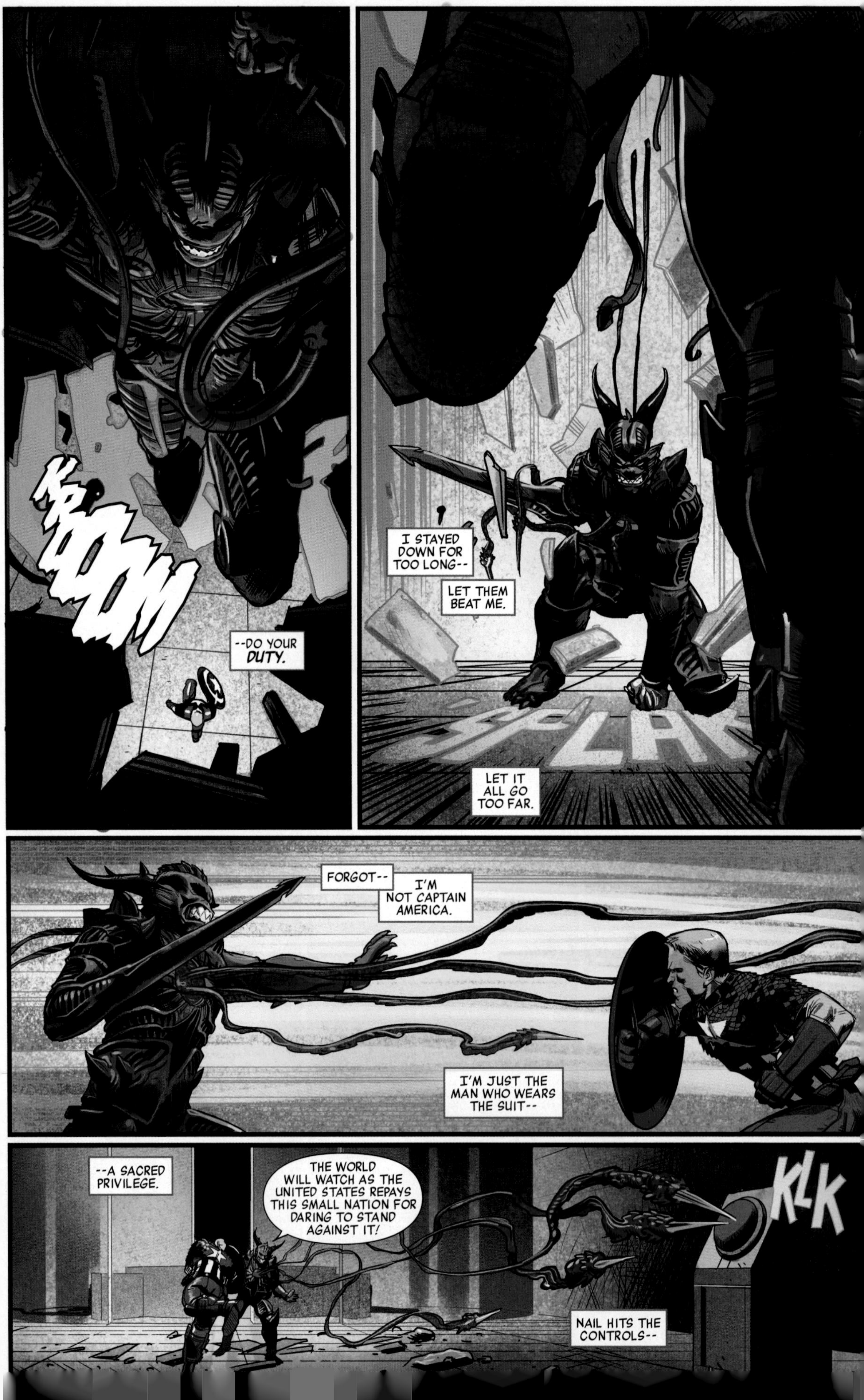

KRAKOOM
--DO YOUR DUTY.
I STAYED DOWN FOR TOO LONG--
LET THEM BEAT ME.
SPLAK
LET IT ALL GO TOO FAR.
FORGOT--
I'M NOT CAPTAIN AMERICA.
I'M JUST THE MAN WHO WEARS THE SUIT--
--A SACRED PRIVILEGE.
THE WORLD WILL WATCH AS THE UNITED STATES REPAYS THIS SMALL NATION FOR DARING TO STAND AGAINST IT!
KLK
NAIL HITS THE CONTROLS--

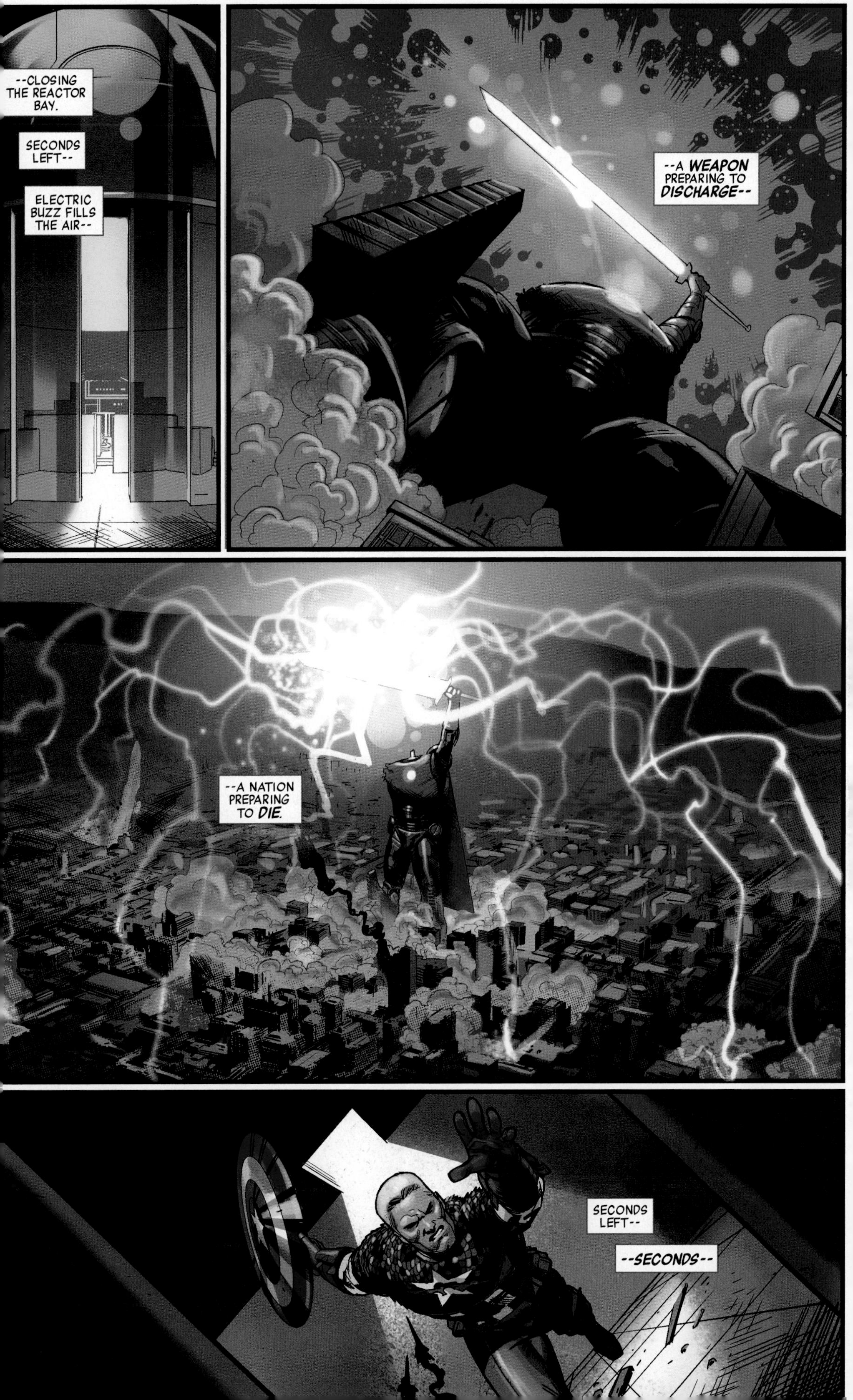
--CLOSING THE REACTOR BAY.
SECONDS LEFT--
ELECTRIC BUZZ FILLS THE AIR--
--A WEAPON PREPARING TO DISCHARGE--
--A NATION PREPARING TO DIE.
SECONDS LEFT--
--SECONDS--

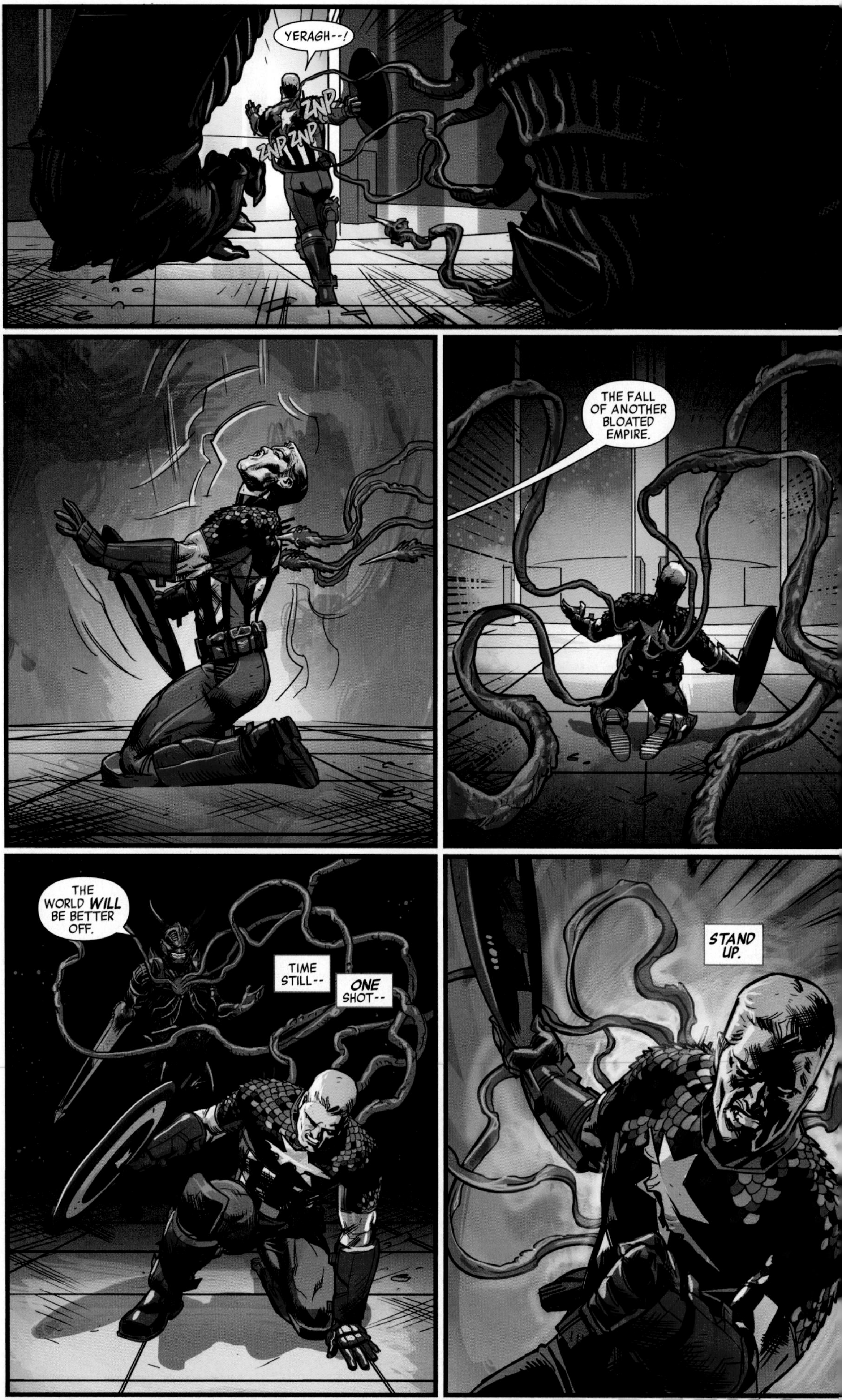
YERAGH--!
ZNP
ZNP ZNP
THE FALL OF ANOTHER BLOATED EMPIRE.
THE WORLD WILL BE BETTER OFF.
TIME STILL--
ONE SHOT--
STAND UP.

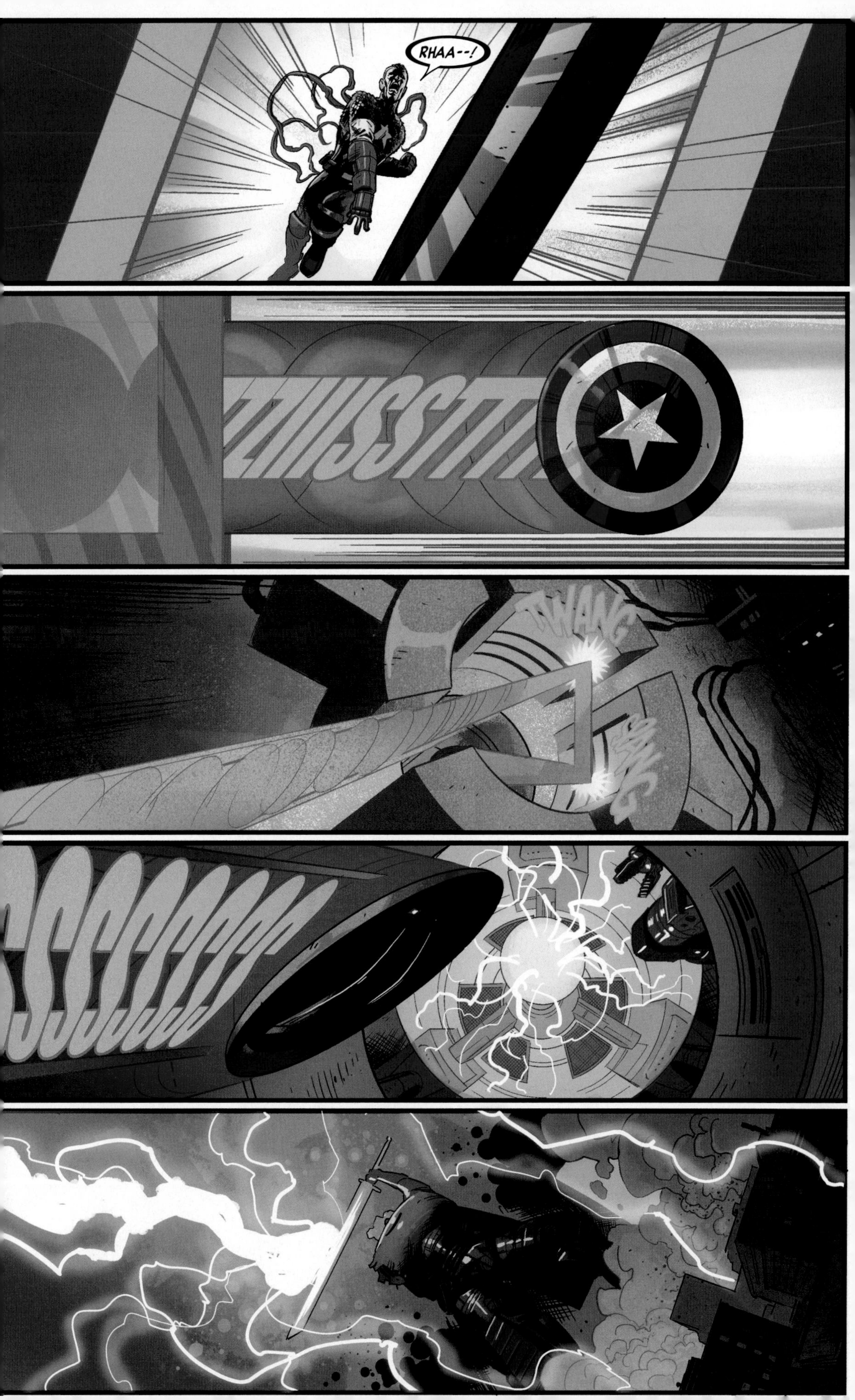
RHAA--!
TWANG

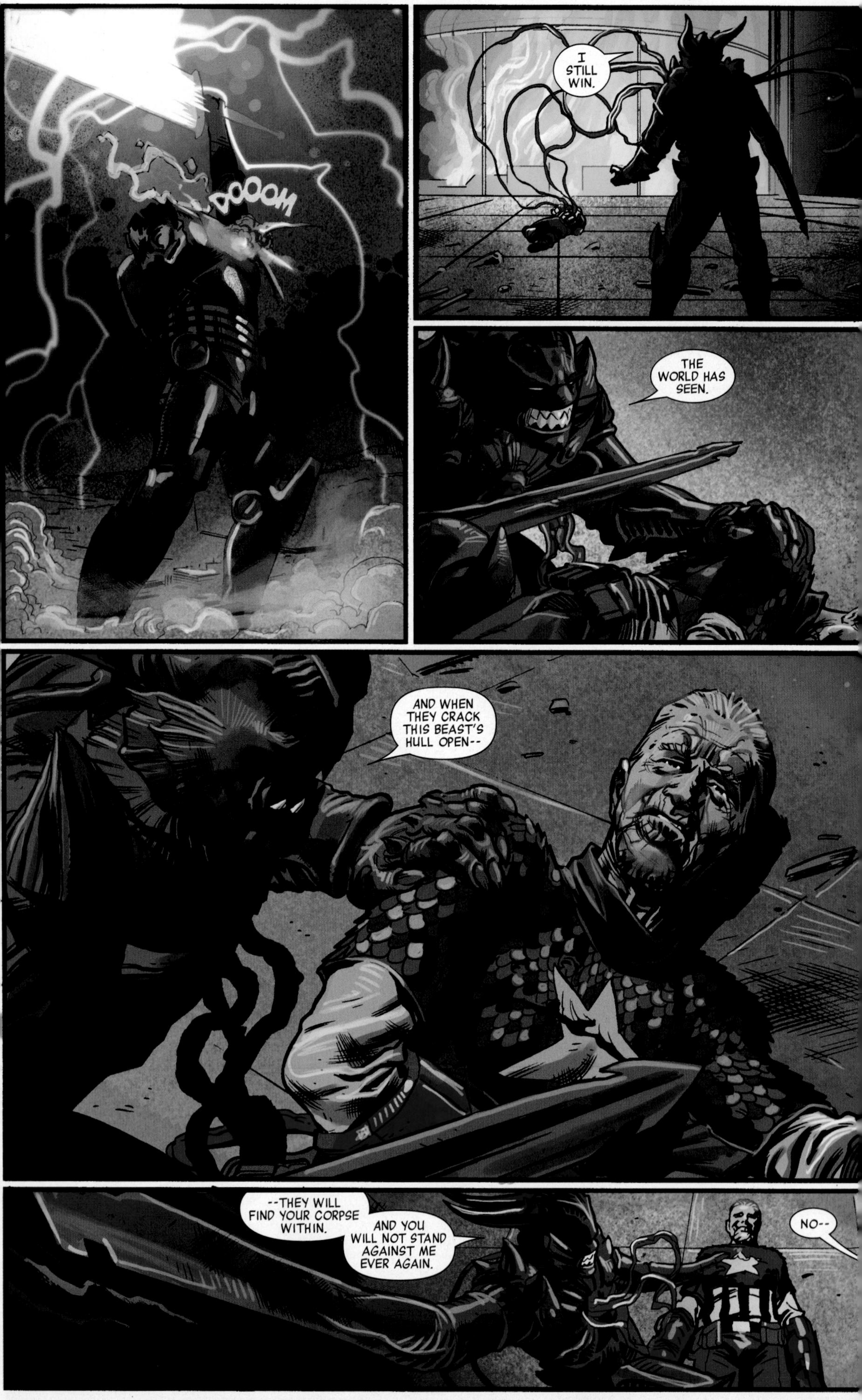
DOOOM
I STILL WIN.
THE WORLD HAS SEEN.
AND WHEN THEY CRACK THIS BEAST'S HULL OPEN--
--THEY WILL FIND YOUR CORPSE WITHIN.
AND YOU WILL NOT STAND AGAINST ME EVER AGAIN.
NO--

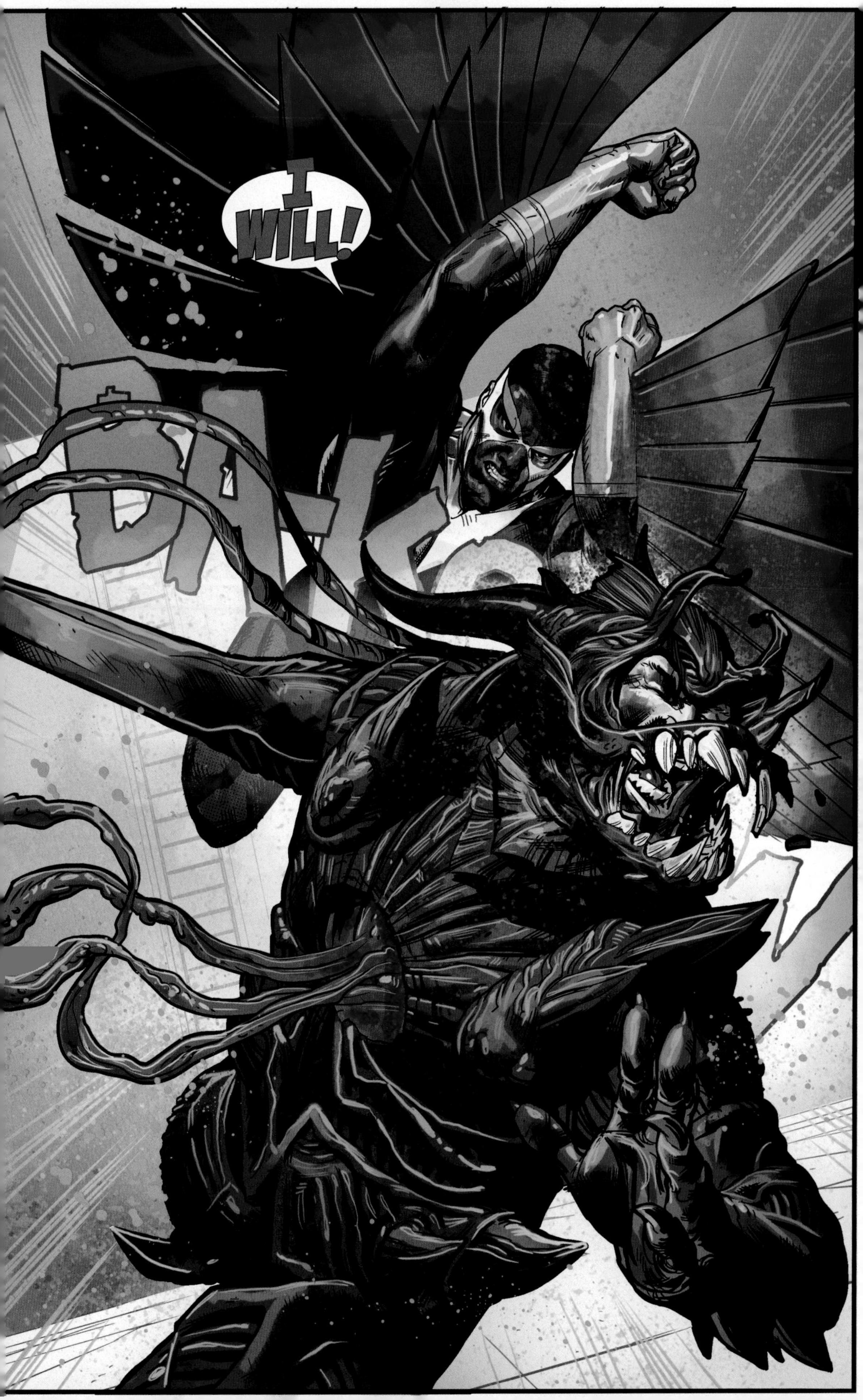
I WILL!

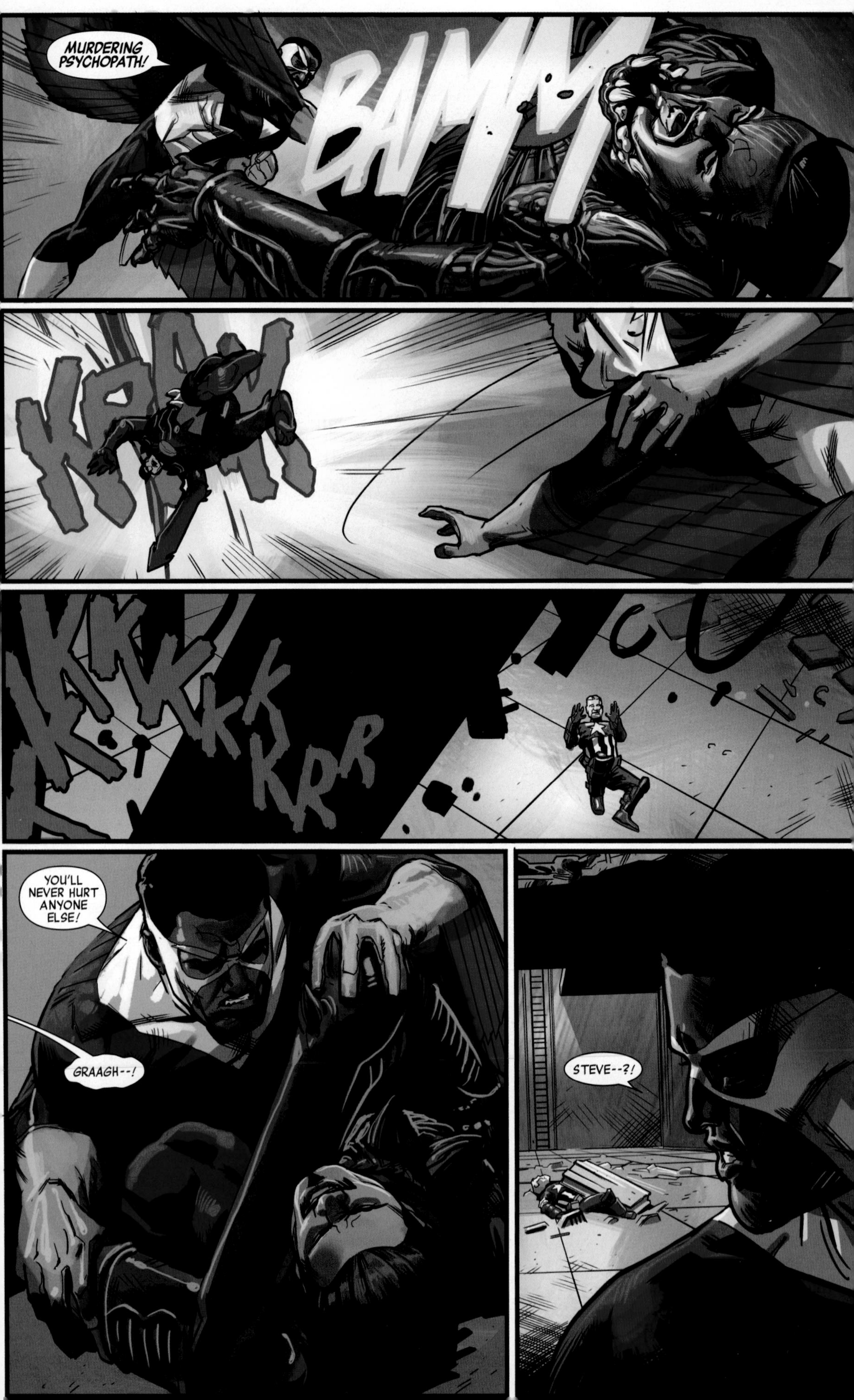
MURDERING PSYCHOPATH!
BAMM
KRAM
KKKKK
KRR
YOU'LL NEVER HURT ANYONE ELSE!
GRAAGH--!
STEVE--?!

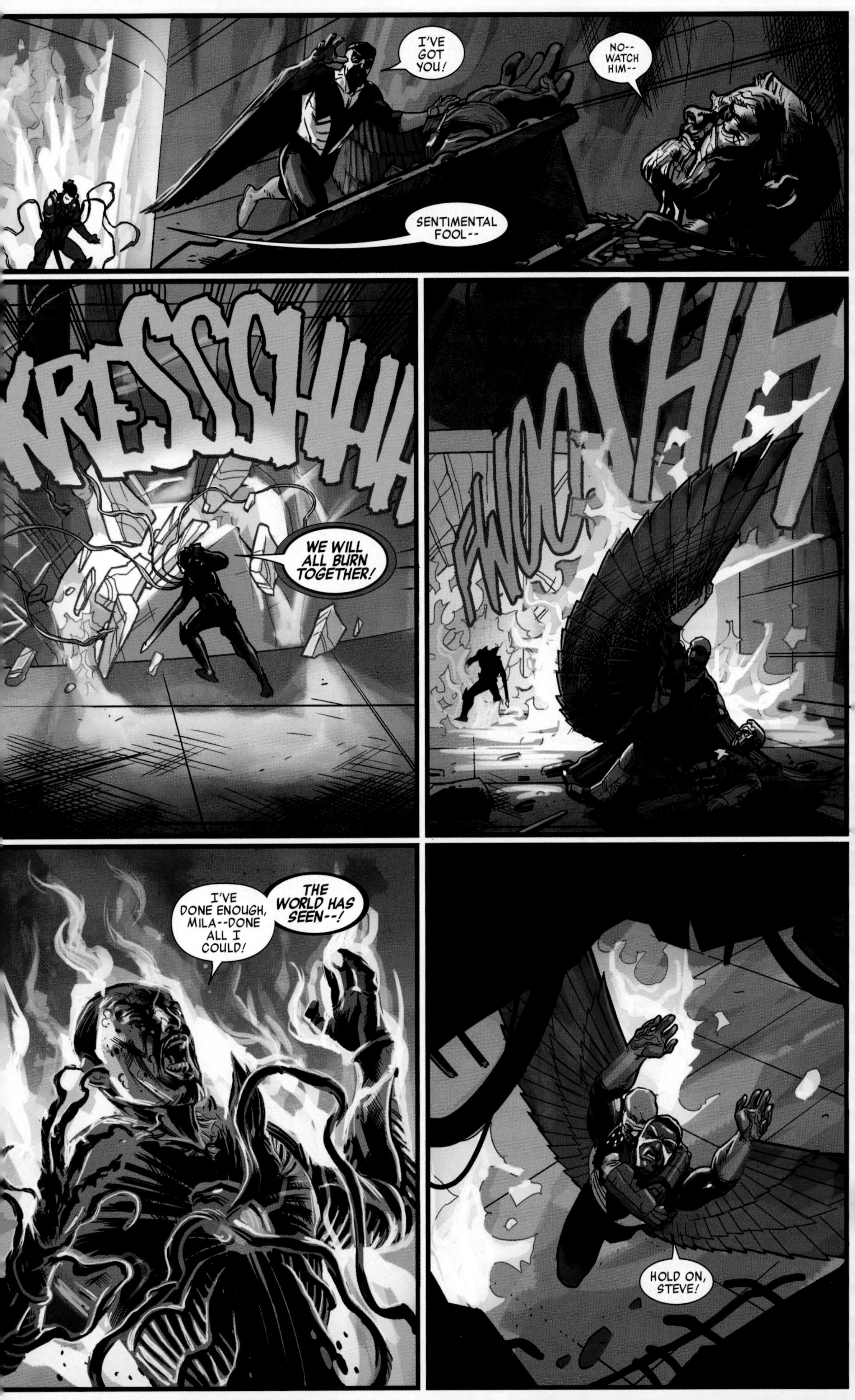
I'VE GOT YOU!
NO-- WATCH HIM--
SENTIMENTAL FOOL--
KRESSSCHHH
WE WILL ALL BURN TOGETHER!
FWOOSHH
I'VE DONE ENOUGH, MILA--DONE ALL I COULD!
THE WORLD HAS SEEN--!
HOLD ON, STEVE!

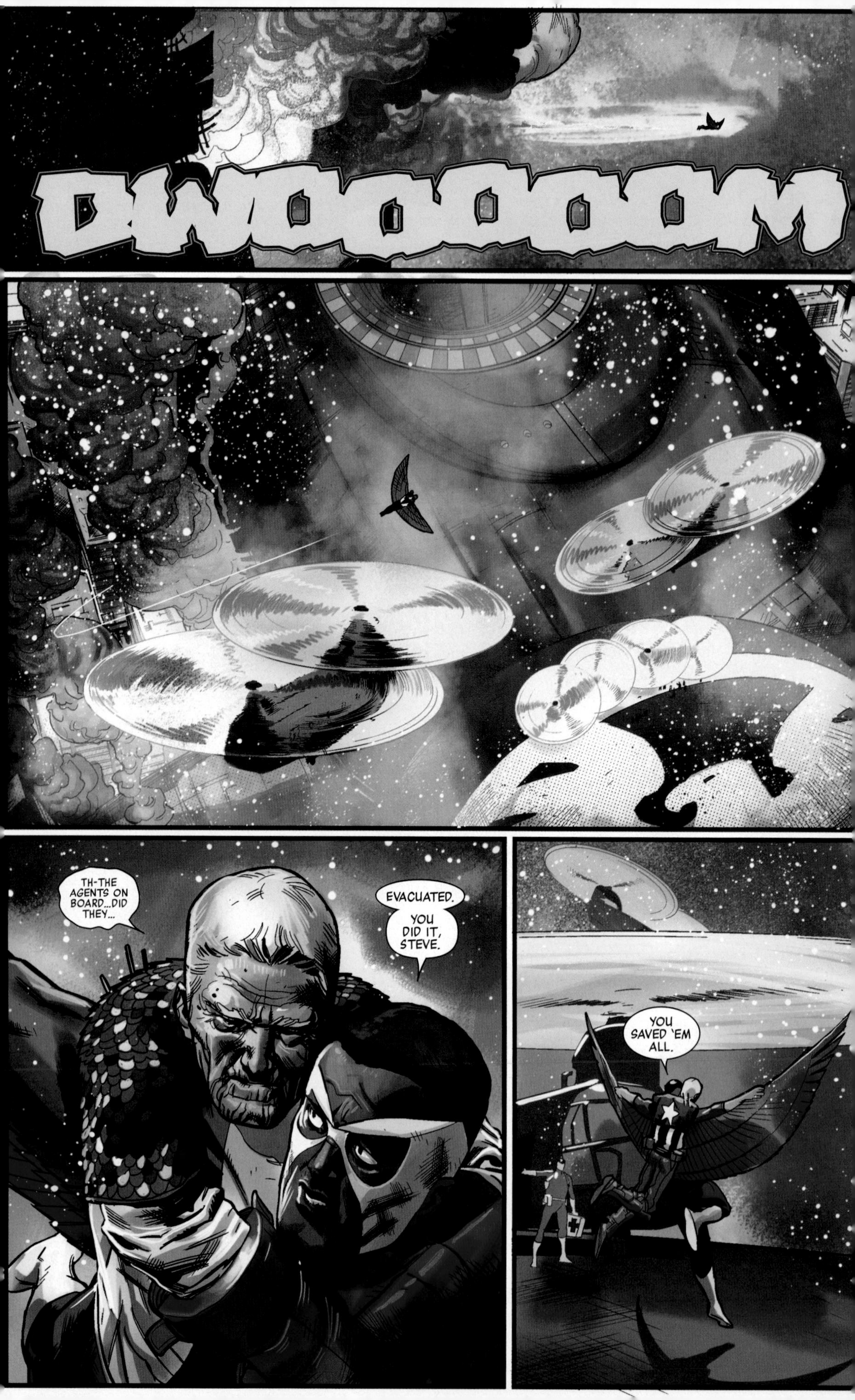
DWOOOOOM
TH-THE AGENTS ON BOARD...DID THEY...
EVACUATED.
YOU DID IT, STEVE.
YOU SAVED 'EM ALL.

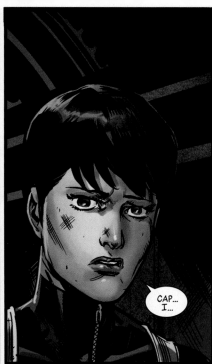

CAP... I...

NOT NOW, MARIA.

"NOT NOW."

"The law of sacrifice is uniform throughout the world. To be effective it demands the sacrifice of the bravest and the most spotless."
--Mahatma Gandhi

SUPER-SOLDIER NO MORE

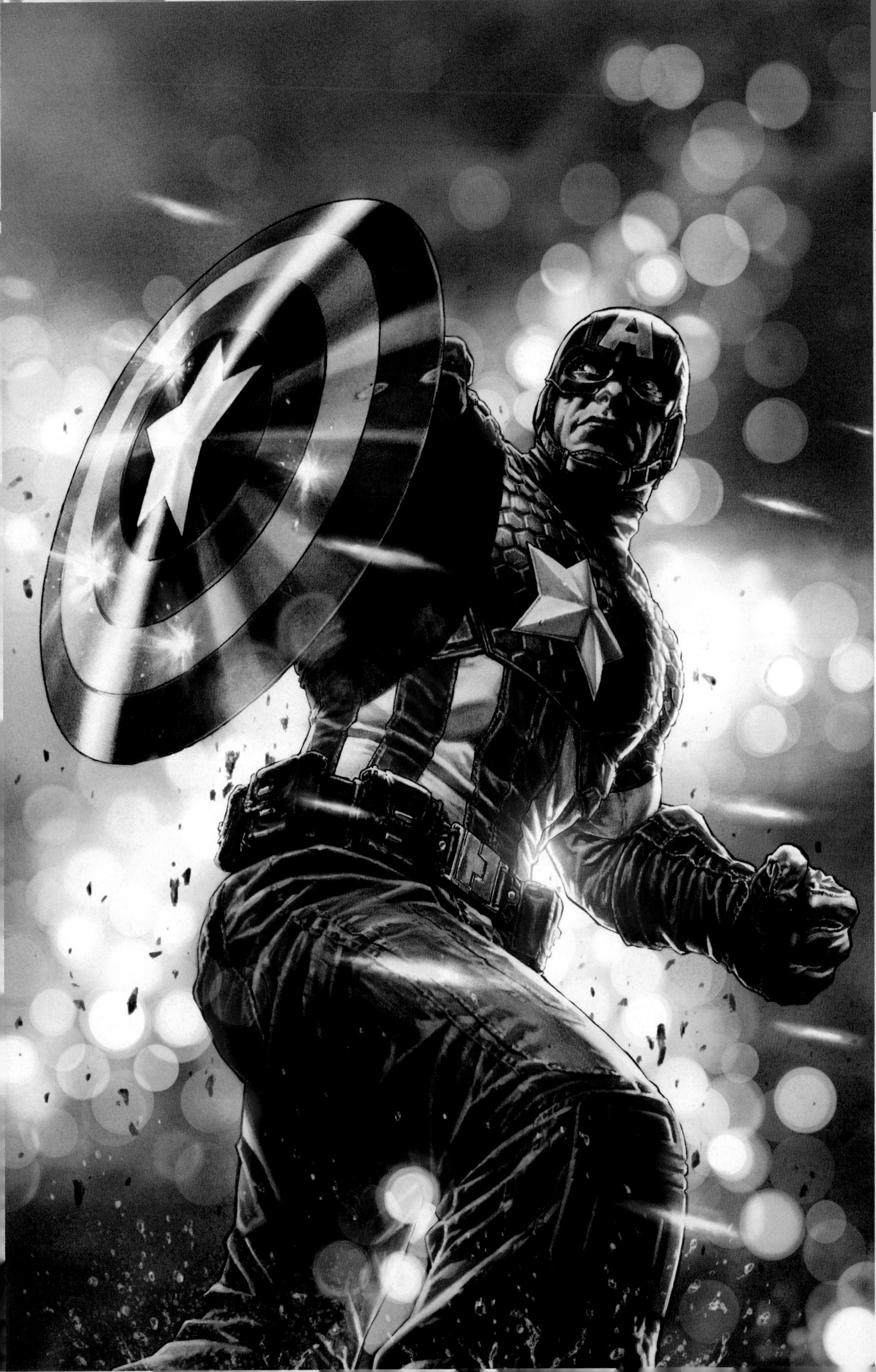

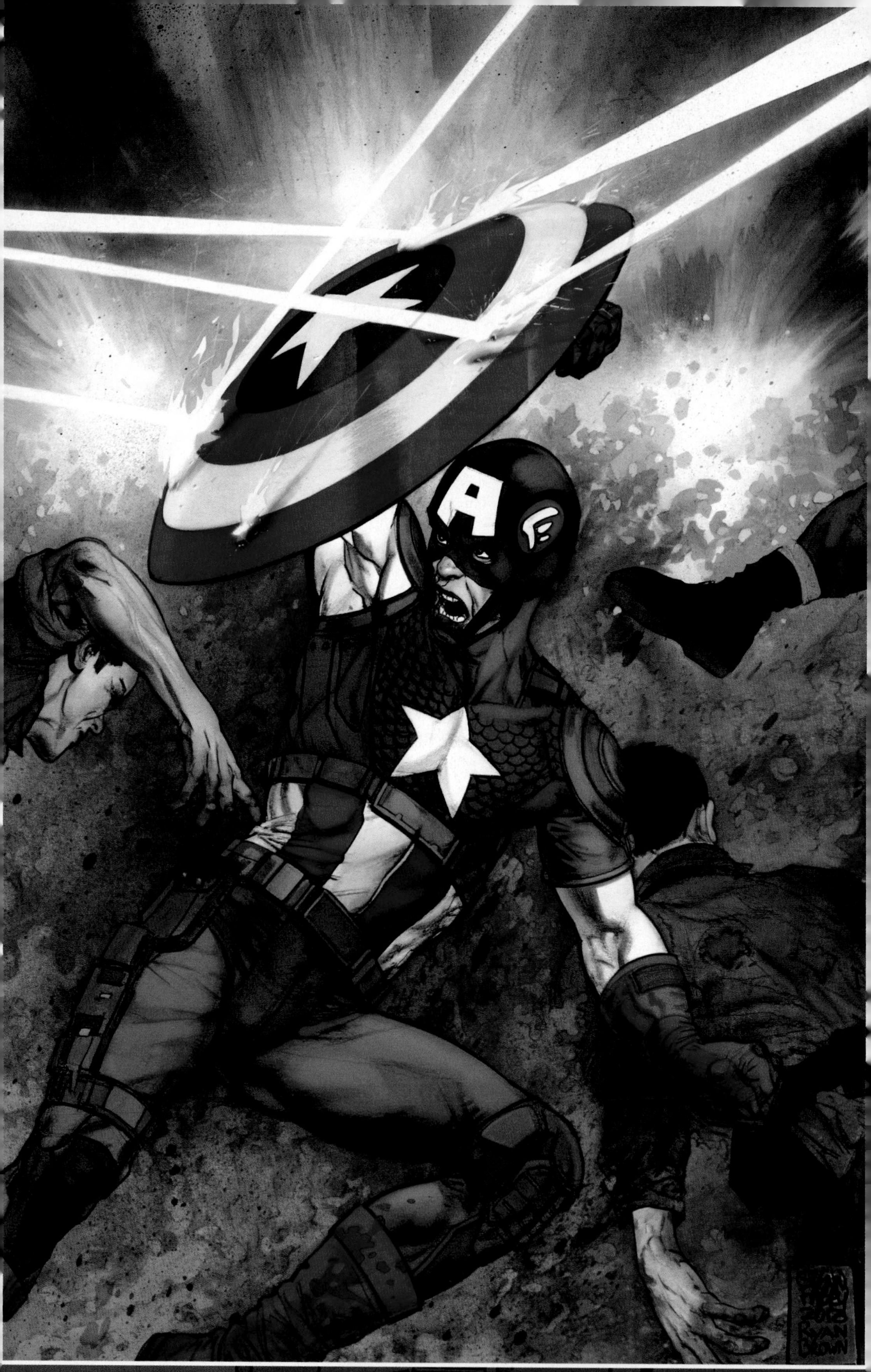
RYAN BROWN

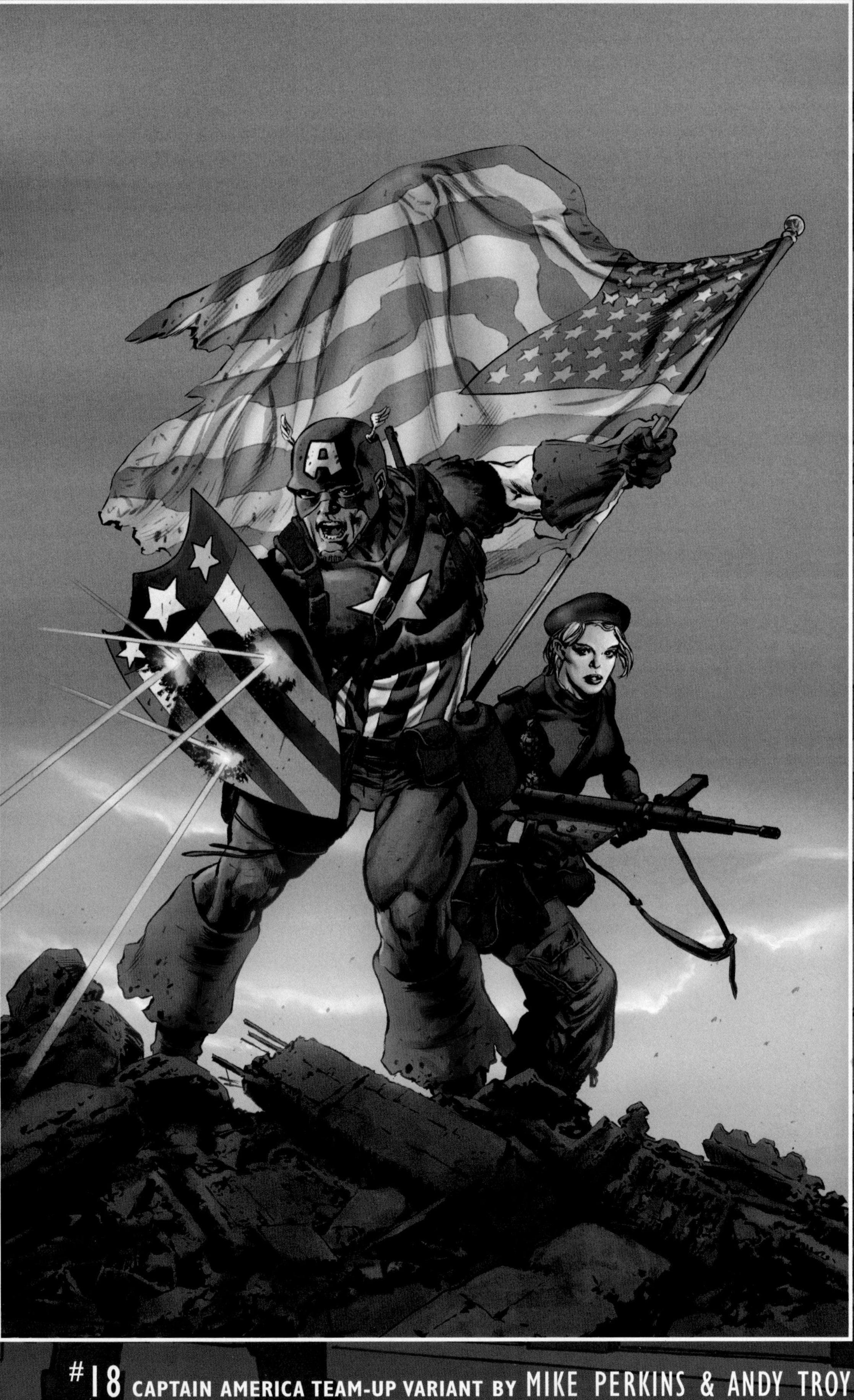

#18 CAPTAIN AMERICA TEAM-UP VARIANT BY MIKE PERKINS & ANDY TROY

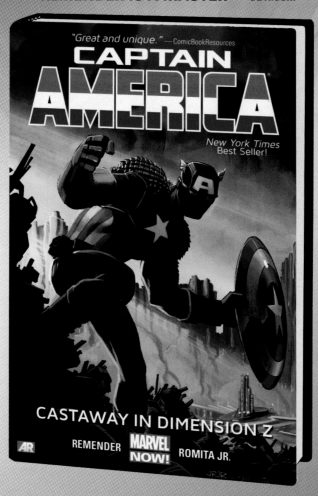